Maritime Cooperation in East Asia

Series Editors

Seokwoo Lee (*Inha University Law School*)
Keyuan Zou (*University of Central Lancashire*)

VOLUME 6

The titles published in this series are listed at *brill.com/mcea*

Regulation on Navigation of Foreign Vessels

Asia-Pacific State Practice

Edited by

Ted L. McDorman
Keyuan Zou
Seokwoo Lee

BRILL
NIJHOFF

LEIDEN | BOSTON

The Library of Congress Cataloging-in-Publication Data

Names: McDorman, Ted L., editor. | Zou, Keyuan, editor. | Lee, Seokwoo editor.
Title: Regulation on navigation of foreign vessels : Asia-Pacific state practice / edited by Ted L. McDorman, Keyuan Zou, Seokwoo Lee.
Description: Leiden ; Boston : Brill/Nijhoff, 2019. | Series: Maritime cooperation in East Asia, ISSN 2405-934X ; VOLUME 6 | Includes bibliographical references and index.
Identifiers: LCCN 2019005942 (print) | LCCN 2019006349 (ebook) | ISBN 9789004396272 (ebook) | ISBN 9789004396265 (hardback : alk. paper)
Subjects: LCSH: Law of the sea--Pacific Area. | Law of the sea--Southeast Asia. | Law of the sea--East Asia. | Navigable waters--Law and legislation--Pacific Area. | Navigable waters--Law and legislation--Southeast Asia. | Navigable waters--Law and legislation--East Asia. | Territorial waters. | Maritime boundaries. | Maritime law.
Classification: LCC KZA1146.P16 (ebook) | LCC KZA1146.P16 R44 2019 (print) | DDC 343.09/66--dc23
LC record available at http://lccn.loc.gov/2019005942

Typeface for the Latin, Greek, and Cyrillic scripts: "Brill". See and download: brill.com/brill-typeface.

ISSN 2405-934X
ISBN 978-90-04-39626-5 (hardback)
ISBN 978-90-04-39627-2 (e-book)

This book is printed on acid-free paper and produced in a sustainable manner.

Contents

Acknowledgments

This volume comprises papers (with updates and revisions) selected from the 4th Asia-Pacific Ocean Law Institutions Alliance (APOLIA) Conference. The APOLIA was initiated in 2012 between Professor Keyuan Zou at Lancashire Law School and Professor Seokwoo Lee of Inha University Law School during their discussion of the creation of a new academic organization that would focus its attention on ocean law and policy issues in the Asia-Pacific. It was set up in 2013 during its first official meeting held in Incheon, Korea with delegates from Australia, Canada, China, Indonesia, and South Korea. The organization is a hybrid organization accommodating both institutional and individual participation and associations. The APOLIA provides the forum for education, joint research, and organizational cooperation among its member institutions/individuals concerning challenges to tertiary education in the Asia-Pacific. It promotes the following three main areas: (a) education; (b) high quality research; and (c) capacity building for internationalization.

The 4th APOLIA Conference on 'Regulation on Navigation of Foreign Vessels in Asia-Pacific' was held in Zhoushan Islands, Zhejiang Province, China in June 2016. The Editors express their sincere appreciation to the Zhejiang University Centre for Ocean Law and Governance for funding and organizing the event. Appreciation also goes to Zhejiang University Ocean College and Guanghua Law School for their financial, organizational and logistic support. Our thanks also go to Anastasia Telesetsky who kindly reviewed some chapters of this volume.

We also express our sincere appreciation to Brill, the publisher, particularly Ms. Marie Sheldon and Ms. Johanna Lee for their constant support for the publication of the Book Series on *Maritime Cooperation in East Asia* including this book.

Illustrations

Figures

Tables

Notes on Contributors

Jay L. Batongbacal
is a lawyer from the Philippines with degrees of Master in Marine Management and Doctor in the Science of Law, both from Dalhousie University. He is presently an Associate Professor of the University of the Philippines College of Law and Director of the U.P. Institute for Maritime Affairs & Law of the Sea.

Leonardo Bernard
was a Research Fellow with the Centre for International Law (CIL), National University of Singapore (NUS), where he focused on international law and maritime boundaries disputes. Leo has researched and written extensively on the maritime disputes in the South China Sea and on the application of historic rights under international law. His paper on "The Effect of Fisheries on Maritime Boundary Delimitation" was awarded the Law of the Sea Institute (LOSI) Research Competition Award for Early Career Researchers in 2012. He has been invited to present his research on the South China Sea and maritime boundary disputes not only in Singapore, but also in the USA, Australia, Japan, Malaysia, Indonesia, South Korea and China. Leo was also involved in the editing of the books *Beyond Territorial Disputes in the South China Sea: Legal Framework for the Joint Development of Hydrocarbon Resources* and *The South China Sea Disputes and the Law of the Sea*, both are part of the CIL International Law book series. He is currently a Ph.D. candidate at the Australian National Centre for Ocean Resources and Security (ANCORS) at the University of Wollongong, Australia.

Warwick Gullett
is Professor and former Dean of Law in the School of Law and the Australian National Centre for Ocean Resources and Security (ANCORS) at the University of Wollongong. His research interests focus on the international law of the sea including legal protection of the marine environment, regulation of marine infrastructure developments, maritime enforcement and jurisdictional issues. He is the author of *Fisheries Law in Australia* (2008) and has co-edited three books including *Asia-Pacific and the Implementation of the Law of the Sea: Regional Legislative and Policy Approaches to the Law of the Sea Convention* (2016). He is Current Legal Developments Editor for the *Asia-Pacific Journal of Ocean Law and Policy*. Professor Gullett's work has been cited by the International Tribunal for the Law of the Sea and Australian environmental courts. He has supervised 10 Ph.D. students to completion.

Hadyu Ikrami
was, until recently, a Research Associate with the Centre for International Law (CIL) of the National University of Singapore, where he focused on ASEAN law and policy and law of the sea. He has published on a wide range of topics, including maritime security cooperation, illegal fishing, Indonesia's maritime governance, transitional justice, and terrorism. Hadyu has an LL.M. from Harvard Law School, an LL.B. from the University of Indonesia, and is admitted to the Indonesian Bar. He is currently an Analyst with Bower Group Asia, a government affairs and public policy consulting firm in Jakarta.

Young Kil Park
a Senior Researcher at Korea Maritime Institute (KMI), is currently a visiting scholar at University of Rhode Island and Naval War College. He served as Heads for Polar Policy Research Center and Maritime Territory Research Center at the KMI. His academic interests cover the law of the sea and Arctic governance. His recent publications include "The complex legal status of the Current Fishing Pattern Zone in the East China Sea", in *Marine Policy* Vol. 81 (2017) (co-authored) and "Korea's Response against IUU Fishing by Korean Vessels", in *Korean Yearbook of International Law* Vol. 3, ILA Korea Branch (2016).

Chie Kojima
is Professor of International Law at the Faculty of Law, Musashino University, Tokyo. She holds bachelor's, master's and Ph.D. degrees in law from Chuo University, and an LL.M. and J.S.D. from Yale University. She previously served as an Assistant Professor of Maritime Law and Policy at the World Maritime University in Malmö, a Senior Research Fellow at Max Planck Institute for Comparative Public Law and International Law in Heidelberg, and a law clerk at the International Court of Justice in The Hague. She is a member of the Editorial Boards of *Ocean Development and International Law* and *Asia-Pacific Journal of Ocean Law and Policy*.

Seokwoo Lee
is Professor of International Law, Inha University Law School, Korea (2003-present). He was Chairman of the Foundation for the Development of International Law in Asia (DILA) (2012–2017). He is Co-Editor-in-Chief of *Asia-Pacific Journal of Ocean Law and Policy* (APJOLP) and *Asian Yearbook of International Law* (Asian YBIL), Executive Editor of *The Korean Journal of International and Comparative Law* (KJICL), Co-Series Editor of the book series entitled Maritime Cooperation in East Asia, and Associate Editor of *Brill Research Perspectives in the Law of the Sea*, all published by Brill. He has

authored more than 90 publications in English in addition to his more than 80 publications in Korean. His representative recent book publication in English is: *The Making of International Law in Korea: From Colony to Asian Power* (co-authored, Brill/Nijhoff (2016)). He holds a D.Phil. (Oxford), LL.M.s (NYU, Minnesota, and Korea University), and LL.B. (Korea University).

Xinchang Liu
is currently Deputy Senior Manager, R&D Department, China Central Depository & Clearing Co. Shanghai Headquarters, China. She obtained a Ph.D. in International Law from Zhejiang University in 2017 and a B.A. in Law from East China University of Political Science and Law in 2012. She was a visiting scholar to University of Iowa during 2014–2015. Her publications appear in *Pacific Journal*, *Chinese Journal of International Law*, and *International Journal of Marine and Coastal Law*.

Ted L. McDorman
is a Professor at the Faculty of Law, University of Victoria, Victoria, British Columbia, Canada. He has written widely on ocean law and policy issues having published over 120 articles, chapters in books, etc. Since 2000, he has been editor-in-chief of *Ocean Development and International Law*. From 2002–2004 and again from 2011 to 2013, Professor McDorman was "academic-in-residence" in the Legal Affairs Branch of the Canadian Department of Foreign Affairs and International Trade (now Global Affairs Canada).

Tran Huu Duy Minh
is a Ph.D. candidate at the Utrecht University. Before starting his Ph.D. project, he was a lecturer at the International Law Faculty, Diplomatic Academy of Vietnam. His research interests include the law of the sea, the law of treaties, the settlement of international disputes, and public international law in general. He holds a B.A. and M.A. in International Relations from the Diplomatic Academy of Vietnam, and an LL.M. in Public International Law from the Utrecht University.

Lan-Anh T. Nguyen
is Deputy Director General of the Bien Dong Institute for Maritime Studies and Vice Dean of the International Law Faculty of the Diplomatic Academy of Vietnam. She is responsible for analyzing the legal aspects of the South China Sea disputes as well as other issues related to ocean law and policy. In this role, she offers legal analysis and advisory opinions to political, diplomatic, and security deliberations. Assoc. Prof. Nguyen often participates as a resource person and

leads Vietnamese delegation to track II and 1.5 conferences and workshops in order to engage other regional countries on maritime security and the ocean law and policy.

David M. Ong
is Research Professor of International and Environmental Law, Nottingham Trent University, UK, where he is co-Director of the Marine Ecological Resilience and Geological Resources (MERGeR) Centre, as well as being the Founding Director of the LL.M. Degree Course in Oil, Gas & Mining (OGM) Law. His main research interests are in the International Law of the Sea, International Environmental Law and International Development Finance Law. He has published in these areas in following selected journals: the *American Journal of International Law* (1999), *European Journal of International Law* (2001), *Tulane Environmental Law Journal* (2017) and the *Journal of International Economic Law* (2017).

Karen N. Scott
is a Professor of Law at the University of Canterbury in New Zealand, having previously taught at the University of Nottingham in the UK. She was the Head of the School of Law between 2015 and 2018, Vice-President of the Australian and New Zealand Society of International Law (ANZSIL) from 2011 – 2016 and the General Editor of the *New Zealand Yearbook of International Law* from 2009 to 2012. She researches and teaches in the areas of public international law, law of the sea and international environmental law. Karen has published over 70 edited books, journal articles and book chapters in these areas.

Zhen Sun
is a Research Officer at the WMU-Sasakawa Global Ocean Institute, World Maritime University in Malmö, Sweden. Prior to joining WMU, Zhen was a Research Fellow at the Centre for International Law, National University of Singapore between 2013 and 2018. She was a member of the Ocean Law and Policy team, in which she worked on a wide range of subjects in the law of the sea. Zhen received a Ph.D. from the University of Cambridge, a LL.M. (with distinction) from the University of Edinburgh, and a LL.M. from China University of Political Science and Law.

Anastasia Telesetsky
is a Professor of Law at the University of Idaho College of Law in the United States where she is a faculty member for the Natural Resources and Environmental Law program. She is also a member of the IUCN World Commission

on Environmental Law and the state practice editor for the *Asia Pacific Journal of Ocean Law and Policy*. She is a former recipient of a Fulbright Fellowship, Bosch Fellowship, and Axford Fellowship.

Keyuan Zou
is Harris Professor of International Law at the Lancashire Law School, and Director of the Institute for International & Comparative Law, University of Central Lancashire (UCLan), United Kingdom. Before joining UCLan, he worked at Dalhousie University (Canada), Peking University (China), University of Hannover (Germany) and National University of Singapore. He has published over 160 refereed English papers in over 30 international journals and various edited books. His single-authored books include *Law of the Sea in East Asia, China's Marine Legal System and the Law of the Sea, China's Legal Reform*, and *China-ASEAN Relations and International Law*. His recent edited volumes include *Sustainable Development and the Law of the Sea* (2016), and *Global Commons and the Law of the Sea* (2018). He is member of Editorial Boards of *International Journal of Marine and Coastal Law, Ocean Development and International Law, Journal of International Wildlife Law and Policy, Marine Policy, Copenhagen Journal of Asian Studies, Journal of Territorial and Maritime Studies, Chinese Journal of International Law*, and Advisory Boards of *Global Journal of Comparative Law, Asia-Pacific Journal of Ocean Law and Policy*, and *Korean Journal of International & Comparative Law*.

Introduction

CHAPTER 1

Regulation on Navigation of Foreign Vessels: Asia-Pacific State Practice

Ted L. McDorman, Keyuan Zou and Seokwoo Lee

1 Introduction

This edited book, "*Regulation on Navigation of Foreign Vessels: Asia-Pacific State Practice,*" is a collection of country papers focused on one of the more contentious and diverse subject areas of the international law of the sea – foreign vessel rights of navigation in national waters. It is volume six of the series Maritime Cooperation in East Asia and the third volume of the series that provides essays focused on national legislation and policies on specific international law of the sea issues. The first collection of this kind in the series was Seokwoo Lee and Warwick Gullett, eds., *Asia-Pacific and Implementation of the Law of the Sea: Regional Legislative and Policy Approaches to the Law of the Sea Convention* (2016). The second was Anastasia Telesetsky, Warwick Gullett and Seokwoo Lee, eds., *Marine Pollution Contingency Planning: State Practice in Asia-Pacific States* (2017).

Navigation has long been at the core of the international law of the sea. From the Grotius doctrine of freedom of seas to the 1982 United Nations Convention on the Law of the Sea (LOSC)[1] the navigational rights of vessels from all nations have been preserved. On the other hand, with the development of the law of the sea, the regime of maritime navigation has become more delicate and differentiated in the different maritime zones. This evolution is reflected in the LOSC where freedom of navigation is preserved on the high seas, and it is also preserved in the exclusive economic zone (EEZ) as long as it is not incompatible with other provisions concerning the EEZ. As the territorial sea is part of the coastal state's territory, foreign vessels enjoy the right of innocent passage. According to the LOSC, innocent passage and/or transit passage applies to straits used for international navigation.[2]

While there is general stability regarding the legal regime for maritime navigation in the law of the sea, controversies remain in the implementation of

1 U.N. Convention on the Law of the Sea, 1833 *U.N.T.S.* 397.

2 See *ibid.*, Part 3.

 | DOI:10.1163/9789004396272_002

the regime and divergences in state practice, particularly in the Asia-Pacific region. For example, China and the United States hold different views and positions respecting the freedom of navigation in the South China Sea.[3] The domestic laws of Asia-Pacific coastal states are not always consistent with the LOSC respecting, e.g., the implementation of the right of innocent passage. This is well reflected in the relevant chapters of this volume. This book is designed to provide a systematic overview and summary of the practices of Asia-Pacific states concerning navigational rights of foreign vessels in the context of the law of the sea.

II Structure and Contents

In addition to this introductory chapter, the volume contains four parts in accordance with the geography of the Asia Pacific region: Northeast Asia; Southeast Asia; North America; and Australasia. Part 1 examines how the three major Northeast Asian countries – China, Japan and Korea – regulate foreign vessels with respect to navigation.

In Chapter 2, Keyuan Zou and Xinchang Liu focus their attention on China and note that China's regulations regarding the navigation of foreign vessels generally conform with the existing rules of the international law of the sea. The chapter begins with an examination of the basic rights and obligations of foreign vessels under Chinese law and then proceeds to explain how China deals with port control; foreign vessel registration; and how it manages the impact of foreign vessels in its waters in relation to dangerous waste, the prevention of marine pollution, maritime accidents, along with regulations concerning internal waters. The authors then focus on the important questions in regard to innocent passage, hot pursuit and archipelagic sea lane passage. They note that when China ratified the LOSC in 1996, it declared that the provisions of the LOSC relevant to innocent passage would not prejudice the rights of a coastal state to require a foreign state to obtain permission or give prior notice to the coastal state for the passage of its warships through the territorial sea of a coastal state. In regard to archipelagic sea lane passage, the authors observe that, while in theory China's position is consistent with the LOSC, in practice, China is involved in numerous disputes with other states in regard to the Paracel Islands and the features in the South China Sea. In the last two sections of the chapter, attention is given to China's regulations concerning the

3 For details, see Zou Keyuan, "Navigation in the South China Sea: Why Still an Issue?," *International Journal of Marine and Coastal Law*, Vol. 32, 2017: 243–267.

EEZ and China's vessel routeing system adopted by the International Maritime Organization (IMO). In conclusion, the chapter notes that while the domestic regulation of foreign vessels in China is comprehensive, there are areas where more regulation is necessary given the requirements of international law and changing circumstances.

Chie Kojima follows in Chapter 3 with an examination of "Japan's Practice Regarding the Regulation on Navigation of Foreign Vessels." She explains that the freedom of navigation has been a central concern for Japanese ocean policy due to the importance of shipping to the Japanese economy. Her analysis begins looking at how Japan has regulated foreign vessels in Japanese ports looking specifically at foreign warships, foreign commercial vessels, and identifying ships from particular countries that are prohibited. In regard to innocent passage within Japan's territorial sea, the chapter sets out the relevant statutory framework pointing out that, in principle, foreign warships are able to exercise the right of innocent passage in the territorial sea of Japan with certain limitations – most notably, the prohibition on foreign warships that carry nuclear weapons which is based on Japan's domestic policy, "Three Non-Nuclear Principles," of not possessing nuclear weapons, not producing them and not permitting their entry into the country. She also notes the prohibition of "suspicious vessels" (*fushin-sen*) from innocent passage. The term "suspicious vessels" is not formally delineated in Japanese law, but is often referenced in government documents and in the media. She goes on to explain Japan's approach to the navigation of foreign vessels in straits and Japan's EEZ examining the relevant Japanese statutes that address these issues. She points out that foreign vessels generally enjoy the freedom of navigation in the Japanese EEZ, but that there are circumstances where the Japanese Coast Guard can intervene, such as when foreign vessels engage in fishing in the EEZ; cause marine pollution; or carry radioactive material. Lastly, Professor Kojima touches on Japan's routeing arrangements in its national waters. In its conclusion, the chapter notes that Japan has been consistent in maintaining freedom of navigation as a high priority in both its domestic and foreign policies.

The final chapter in Part 1, contributed by Seokwoo Lee and Young Kil Park, examines Korea's regulation on the navigation of foreign vessels. The authors note that since Korea's ratification of the LOSC in 1996, it has made significant efforts to implement the Convention through domestic legislation. They examine how Korea regulates foreign vessels within its territorial sea and note that the relevant statute, the Territorial Sea and Contiguous Zone Act, was passed on 6 December 1995, which was prior to Korea's ratification of the LOSC. The Korean government recently revised this Act to provide that any matters that are unregulated by the Act as they relate to Korea's territorial sea or its contiguous zone are to be governed in accordance with treaties and customary international law. With respect to the navigation of foreign vessels in straits, they point out that Korea has the Korea Strait and the Jeju Strait. While both Japan and Korea have limited their territorial sea to 3 nautical miles, for the Jeju Strait, the Korean government has not addressed the territorial sea area. The authors observe that if the Jeju Strait is deemed to be a "normal" international strait, transit passage would apply which would significantly limit the scope of regulation and jurisdiction that could be exercised by Korea as the littoral state. They note that Korea would also bear the burden of permitting the right of flight over the area by foreign aircraft. In relation to the navigation of foreign vessels in Korea's EEZ, the authors outline the legislative framework which includes the Exclusive Economic Zone Act and the Maritime Security Act. They look specifically at the issues of fishing in the West/Yellow Sea, marine scientific research, the passage of North Korean vessels, the Proliferation Security Initiative (PSI), and UN Security Council sanctions against North Korea and its impact on Korea's treatment of North Korean vessels. They note that North Korean vessels have passed through South Korean territorial waters and EEZ on the basis of the 2004 South-North Maritime Agreement. However, since the sinking of the *Cheonan* in 2010, the passage of North Korean vessels in the waters of South Korea has been prohibited. They add that international control over the navigation of North Korean vessels has been further strengthened through the PSI and UN Security Council resolutions.

Part 2 of the book looks at the countries in Southeast Asia and how they regulate the navigation of foreign vessels in national waters. In Chapter 5, Hadyu Ikrami and Leonardo Bernard focus on Indonesia, the world's largest archipelagic state possessing important trade routes between China and India, most notably, the Straits of Malacca and Sunda. Respecting how Indonesia deals with the passage of foreign vessels, the authors focus their attention on innocent passage, archipelagic sea lanes passage, and transit passage through straits used for international navigation. They note that pursuant to Indonesian law, all vessels have the right of innocent passage through the territorial sea and archipelagic waters of Indonesia to navigate between the high seas, between different parts of the Indonesian EEZ, or between the high seas and the Indonesian EEZ. They explain that in Indonesian law that passage is considered innocent if it does not pose a threat to the peace, order, or security of Indonesia, and if it is in accordance with international law. With respect to foreign vessels' activities in Indonesian waters, they examine how Indonesia deals with fisheries, port control, investigation into incidents, foreign vessels and aircraft protected by sovereign immunity, and submarine cables, electricity generation, and marine scientific research. They describe the IMO-approved routeing arrangements that exist in Indonesian waters. The chapter explains that Indonesia has pursued cooperation with Malaysia and Singapore in managing the straits they share and has also stepped up its enforcement measures against IUU fishing by seizing or sinking foreign vessels that engaged in such fishing.

In Chapter 6, "Navigation of Foreign Vessels in Malaysian Waters: Between Compliance with International Law and National Regulation of Discretion," Professor David Ong examines how Malaysia regulates foreign vessel navigation. His analysis is focused on assessing whether Malaysia is in compliance with international obligations to ensure innocent passage and freedom of navigation within waters under its jurisdiction, and the extent to which discretion exists on this issue with Malaysian domestic law. He notes that the geographical position of Malaysia is unique given that it is:

> arguably a hydrographically divided country, with peninsular Malaysia being separated by the southern part of the South China Sea from the two Malaysian (federal) states of Sabah and Sarawak on Borneo Island.

In his discussion of Malaysia's approach to the freedom of navigation, he notes that one of the contentious issues is the Malaysian domestic legal requirements for prior authorization for the passage of nuclear-powered ships within its territorial sea and the prior consent for military exercises or manoeuvres within its EEZ. He follows with an examination of the Malaysian inferred straight baselines system and the implications for innocent passage within Malaysia's internal waters and territorial sea. He comments that Malaysia's state practice in this regard seems to be at variance with the LOSC and observes that almost all East Asian littoral states have implemented straight baselines. He then moves to a discussion of the Malaysian Exclusive Economic Zone Act and its implications on navigational freedoms given the authority of Malaysian authorities to regulate vessels in the EEZ. Professor Ong addresses the issue of state responsibility in the event of excessive Malaysian regulation of navigational freedoms. While he observes that Malaysia has shown a propensity to address its non-compliance with applicable international norms in a manner to ensure that it stays within the limits of the law, however, significant questions remain over the status of Malaysian domestic law provisions that are incompatible with Malaysia's international legal obligations particularly under the LOSC.

Next, Jay Batongbacal in Chapter 7 examines "Archipelagic States and Maritime Navigation: Perspectives and Practice in the Philippines". After providing the background to the treatment of archipelagoes within the LOSC context, the author explains the approach taken by Indonesia and the Philippines – the two largest mid-ocean archipelagic states – in the negotiations leading up to the conclusion and ratification of the LOSC. He notes that there are two passage regimes that exist in archipelagic waters enclosed by straight archipelagic baselines drawn in accordance with the technical requirements of LOSC Part 4. The first regime is that of innocent passage enjoyed by ships of all states through archipelagic waters. The second regime is that of archipelagic sea lanes passage found in LOSC Article 53, which is comprised of two elements: archipelagic sea lanes, and the right of archipelagic sea lanes passage. He observes that the Philippine position with respect to foreign vessels travelling through the archipelago has been to accept only the regime of innocent passage. He points out that the Philippines has pursued efforts to reduce maritime traffic in its archipelagic waters to only a few identifiable routes and that both legislation has been enacted with the intent to directly regulate the manner of exercise of passage rights through its waters, such as limiting them to only designated sea lanes.

In Chapter 8, Zhen Sun focuses on Singapore which borders the Straits of Malacca and Singapore, a strait used for international navigation as defined in the LOSC. She points out that Singapore is separated from Malaysia by the Strait of Johor within a couple of nautical miles from Indonesia and by the Singapore Strait with the widest point being less than 10 nautical miles. She identifies the marine areas that are under Singapore's jurisdiction, including internal waters, limited territorial sea and potential claim to an EEZ and then addresses the regulation of vessels within the waters under Singapore's sovereignty by explaining: the system of vessel registration, Singapore's port regulations and port state control, and Singapore's regulations relating to innocent passage and transit passage. She reports that Singapore has proclaimed its right to claim a territorial sea and an EEZ but has yet to adopt legislation on maritime zones. After briefly describing the trilateral cooperation that exists between Indonesia, Malaysia, and Singapore in regard to the straits, Dr. Sun looks at the IMO routeing measures in the Singapore Strait STRAITREP (the mandatory ship reporting system established in the Malacca and Singapore straits) and the rules of navigation, and the enforcement jurisdiction over foreign vessels.

Rounding out Part 2 is Chapter 9, wherein Lan-Anh T. Nguyen and Tran Huu Duy Minh examine "Vietnam's Regulations and Practice on Navigation of Foreign Vessels." They point out that Vietnam has more than 3200 kilometers of coastline along the South China Sea, which is one of the world's most active sea routes. Given this, Vietnam has strategic interests in maintaining freedom of navigation. They explain that the navigation of foreign vessels in Vietnamese maritime zones is governed by the Law of the Sea of Vietnam and the

Maritime Law of 2015, which superseded the old law of 2005. The specific rules and regulations that apply to foreign vessels, the right of navigation, and port control are described. This follows with a discussion of Vietnam's approach to innocent passage with the authors noting that the 2015 Law of the Sea of Vietnam affirms the right of innocent passage for all vessels and that the Law and its regulations are almost identical with the provisions for innocent passage in the LOSC with the exception that foreign vessels must not use or threat to use force against the sovereignty, independence and territorial integrity of other states while exercising innocent passage. They go on to explain in detail the legislation dealing with the innocent passage of foreign military vessels and foreign nuclear-powered vessels. Finally, the chapter examines how Vietnam treats foreign vessels operating within its EEZ with an emphasis on safety zones for artificial installations and structures; military activities; and navigation in the Gulf of Tonkin.

Part 3 examines how the North American states of Canada and the United States manage foreign vessels in their respective national waters. In Chapter 10, Professor Ted L. McDorman notes that Canada is surrounded by the Atlantic, the Pacific, and the Arctic and that there is significant foreign vessel commercial traffic traveling to and from Canadian ports and through its EEZ on the Atlantic and Pacific sides, but that in the Arctic there is little foreign commercial traffic within Canadian waters. After providing an overview of the relevant Canadian domestic legislation pertaining to the navigation of foreign vessels, Professor McDorman explains the contours of four international legal disputes that have arisen as a result of Canada's regulation of foreign commercial vessels in its waters which involve: the Northwest Passage (Arctic Coast); the Head Harbour Passage (Atlantic Coast); the Strait of Juan de Fuca (Pacific Coast); and Canada's Arctic Waters.

Professor Anastasia Telesetsky's Chapter 11, "United States Practice Regarding Innocent Passage and Navigational Transit", begins with a summary of the U.S. legal practice regarding the treatment of foreign vessels engaged in innocent passage within U.S. territorial waters. She notes that historically, the United States has long recognized the freedom of the seas and that in the 21st Century, the United States understands that the freedom of navigation encompasses both the rights of innocent passage with U.S. territorial seas and transit rights within EEZs. The United States generally allows for innocent passage of all ships within its territorial sea subject to the exceptions that are consistent with customary international law. Professor Telesetsky also examines navigational transit rights for foreign vessels in the U.S. EEZ, noting that the United States permits foreign vessels to operate within its EEZ and does not require any notification from vessels that are transiting in compliance with navigational freedoms provided in the LOSC. The author describes the U.S. Freedom of Navigation Program, established during the Carter administration where "the U.S. began to regularly deploy naval ships and air force patrols to assert the right of innocent passage and right to transit across the globe." She comments that the motivation has been to ensure that maritime nations do not acquiesce to excessive claims and thereby relinquish their rights. After observing how some other states have a perspective contrary to the U.S. Freedom of Navigation policies, Professor Telesetsky posits that the United States must be clearer about its understanding of the extent of a given excessive maritime claim by another country.

Finally, Part 4 concerns Australasia and how Australia and New Zealand regulate the navigation of foreign vessels. Warwick Gullett notes that Australia's approach to foreign vessel navigation is impacted by its location, size and the characteristics of its maritime jurisdiction. Australia is reliant on seaborne trade and vulnerable to ship groundings and collisions, as well as customs, quarantine and immigration threats. As a result, Australia's strategic interests are that international shipping is to be safe and efficient and that all efforts are to be made to minimise threats. He notes that while Australia does not have any specific regulations on innocent passage in the territorial sea or freedom of navigation in its EEZ, it has introduced a number of measures that restrict navigation in certain areas. The regulatory structure and strategic priorities for navigation in Australia are described with it noted that the Australian Maritime Safety Authority (AMSA) is the federal government entity responsible for ensuring safe navigation in Australian waters. Professor Warwick's analysis examines various topics including protection areas for submarine cables and offshore petroleum and greenhouse gas facilities; security areas; vessel security and information requirements; fishing; Australia's EEZ adjacent to Antarctica; historic bays in South Australia; compulsory pilotage in the Great Barrier Reef and Torres Strait; shipping management; and ballast water.

In the final chapter, Professor Karen N. Scott explains that New Zealand is highly dependent on shipping for international trade and is subject to certain risks with increased foreign vessel traffic such as oil spills, equipment failures, crew injuries, fires, collisions, groundings and, more recently, welfare issues. Given these circumstances, she notes that the priorities for New Zealand's regulation of foreign vessels include measures for the protection of the environment; measures designed to protect the commercial exploitation of living and, more recently, non-living resources; and measures to protect seafarers working in New Zealand waters. She explains that the regulation of foreign vessels in the waters of New Zealand are an interplay of international standards and domestic law. She includes a description of the information requirements relating to foreign vessels arriving at New Zealand ports or entering New Zealand waters, observing that over the last decade vessels globally have been required to provide increasing amounts of information to coastal and port states en route to a port or even when crossing a coastal state's maritime zones. Professor Scott focuses attention on regulating the passage of foreign vessels in New Zealand's internal waters in particular respecting nuclear powered ships and the passage of foreign vessels in the territorial sea and EEZ.

III Conclusion

State practice in the Asia-Pacific region is uniform on the one hand and diverse on the other. All the coastal states examined in this book except for the United States are parties to the LOSC and have domestic legislation that implements the Convention. Though the United States is not yet a party to the Convention, it asserts that it complies in general with the LOSC as it reflects customary international law. This is most particularly the case concerning navigation. Divergence in Asian-Pacific state practice exists. For example, in terms of legislation, all three Northeast Asian countries share the Continental (Civil) Law tradition,[4] while the four countries in North America and Australasia share the Common Law tradition.[5] In Southeast Asia, the legislative picture is more colourful with a mixing of legal traditions. Such legal cultures and traditions inevitably have the impact on the legislation concerning oceans and ocean activities. There are also different practices and national policies that influence the legislative implementation of the LOSC. The difference tends to occur regarding the implementation of the right of innocent passage for warships through the territorial sea and in the implementation of the LOSC regime for international straits.

Maritime disputes respecting territory and boundaries also generate obstacles to normal or routine navigation at sea. As is well known, there are such disputes in the East China Sea, South China Sea, and Sea of Japan (East Sea). The situation in the South China Sea is particularly complicated. The safety of navigation relies on regional cooperation among the coastal states and also on the settlement of maritime disputes.

4 It is noted that Hong Kong Special Administrative Region of China continues its Common Law Tradition even after the handover in 1997.

5 It is noted that there is also Continental (Civil) Law tradition in Canada due to the province of Quebec.

As a final note, it is recognized the coverage of this book in terms of state practice in the Asia-Pacific region is not comprehensive. Missing are chapters from the Latin American countries along the Pacific coast and the Pacific island countries. We hope that this can be remedied by future endeavors.

PART 1

Northeast Asia

CHAPTER 2

Regulation on Navigation of Foreign Vessels: China's Practice

Keyuan Zou and Xinchang Liu

I Introduction

China has a legislative framework of basic rights and obligations for foreign vessels that includes regulations on port control, foreign vessel registration, protection of waterways, prevention of marine pollution, maritime accidents and other related subjects. China's regulations on navigation of foreign vessels include both general rules governing foreign vessels, such as guidelines and principles, and detailed specific rules concerning foreign vessels in different maritime zones. The first part of this chapter will focus on the regulations applicable to foreign vessels. The second and third parts will discuss innocent passage and archipelagic sea-lane passage respectively, with the fourth part dealing with straits used for international navigation. The last two parts of this chapter will focus on China's regulations concerning the exclusive economic zone (EEZ) and China's routeing systems.

II Regulations concerning Foreign Vessels

1 *Rights and Obligations of Foreign Vessels*

China has enacted a series of laws and regulations governing the navigation of foreign vessels based on general international law, including the United Nations Convention on the Law of the Sea (LOSC),[1] such as the 1992 Law on the Territorial Sea and the Contiguous Zone,[2] the 1998 Law on the Exclusive Economic Zone and the Continental Shelf,[3] the 1982 Maritime Traffic Safety Law,[4] the Regulations Governing Supervision and Control of Foreign Vessels,[5]

1 U.N. Convention on the Law of the Sea, 1833 *U.N.T.S.* 397.
2 Law on the Territorial Sea and the Contiguous Zone, 25 February 1992.
3 Law on the Exclusive Economic Zone and the Continental Shelf, 26 June 1998.
4 Maritime Traffic Safety Law, 2 September 1983.
5 Regulations Governing Supervision and Control of Foreign Vessels, 1979.

 | DOI:10.1163/9789004396272_003

and the Rules for the Control of Non-Military Vessels of Foreign Origin Passing Through the Qiongzhou Strait.[6] These laws and regulations set out the basic rights and obligations of foreign vessels in different jurisdictional waters. For example, Article 8 of the Regulations Governing Supervision and Control of Foreign Vessels provides that the Harbour Superintendency Administration is fully authorized to detain a foreign vessel, or to order a vessel to stop, to change route or to return to the port under any of the following circumstances: (1) where the vessel is unseaworthy; (2) there has been a violation of Chinese laws and regulations; (3) the vessel was involved in a marine accident; (4) there was non-payment of expenses for which the vessel is liable; or (5) "other cases prohibiting the vessel from sailing".[7] Article 9 provides that: "vessels navigating in Chinese port areas and coastal waters shall not be engaged in activities endangering the national safety, rights and interests of the People's Republic of China and shall comply with regulations governing straits, waterways, routes and areas closed to navigation."[8]

2 *Port Control*

Respecting port control, the Regulations Governing Supervision and Control of Foreign Vessels contain detailed provisions, such as Article 5 that provides that:

> Upon arrival at the port, vessels shall immediately submit the Entry Report and other relevant forms for check-up; besides, vessels shall submit ship's papers and relevant documents for examination and be subject to inspections. Prior to leaving, vessels shall submit the Departure Report and other relevant forms for clearance examination and may only leave the port after port clearance has been obtained.

Article 6 stipulates that:

> arms and ammunition on board are to be sealed up by the Harbour Superintendency Administration. Radio-telegraph transmitter, radiotelephone transmitter, signal rockets, flare signals and signal guns shall only be used in case of emergency, and a report shall be made to the Harbour Superintendency Administration immediately afterwards.

6 Rules for the Control of Non-Military Vessels of Foreign Origin Passing through the Qiongzhou Strait, 8 June 1964.
7 Regulations Governing Supervision and Control of Foreign Vessels, *supra* note 5, Article 8.
8 *Ibid.*, Article 9.

"Shooting, swimming, fishing, setting off of firecrackers or fireworks and other actions calculated to endanger the order and security of the port" are prohibited by Article 7. Also of note is Article 22: "In order to ensure the safety of the port and vessels, when ordered to shift berth or to sail ahead of or behind the schedule, vessels shall observe such orders as given by the Harbour Superintendency Administration."

3 *Foreign Vessel Registration*

The Regulations of the People's Republic of China Governing the Registration of Ships[9] is China's most important regulation on vessel registration. Article 2 provides that:

> [t]he following ships shall be registered in accordance with the provisions of these Regulations: (1) Ships owned by citizens of the People's Republic of China whose residences or principal places of business are located within the territory thereof; (2) Ships owned by enterprises with legal person status established under the laws of the People's Republic of China and whose principal places of business are located within the territory thereof, provided that foreign investment is involved, the proportion of registered capital contributed by Chinese investors shall not be less than 50 per cent; (3) Service ships of the Government of the people's Republic of China and ships owned by institutions with legal person status; (4) Other ships whose registration is deemed necessary by the competent authority of harbour superintendency of the People's Republic of China. Military ships, fishery ships and sports craft shall be registered in compliance with the provisions of the relevant laws and regulations.

Article 4 provides that: "A ship shall not have dual nationality. A ship registered abroad whose former registration of nationality has not been suspended or deleted shall not be granted the Chinese nationality." Thus, Chinese vessel registration is not open to foreign owned or operated vessels. With very few exceptions only vessels owned by Chinese legal entities or nationals, or bareboat chartered to them, can be registered in China and fly the Chinese flag.[10]

---

9 Regulations of the People's Republic of China Governing the Registration of Ships, 2 June 1994 (Amended).

10 <www.nortonrosefulbright.com/knowledge/publications/133555/china-flag-vessels-an-overview>.

4 *Shipping of Dangerous Wastes*

China ratified the Basel Convention on the Control of Transboundary Movements of Hazardous Wastes and Their Disposal[11] on 17 December 1991, and has promulgated rules on this issue. According to Article 39 of the Marine Environmental Protection Law,[12] it is prohibited to transship dangerous wastes through the internal waters or territorial seas of China. Moreover, prior written permission must be obtained from the administrative department in charge of environment protection under the State Council for the shipping of any dangerous wastes through the other sea areas under the jurisdiction of China. In case of the movement of any dangerous wastes through the sea areas under the jurisdiction of China in violation of the provisions above, Article 79 of the Marine Environmental Protection Law directs that the State administrative department in charge is to order the vessel illegally shipping the dangerous wastes to withdraw from the relevant sea areas and impose a fine of no less than 50,000 yuan but no more than 500,000 yuan.

In November 2010 China issued the Administrative Provisions on the Prevention and Control of Marine Environmental Pollution by Vessels and Their Operations which came into force on 1 February 2011.[13] It contains seven chapters governing vessel-source pollution, carriage of hazardous polluting goods, dismantling of vessels, and other vessel-related operations.

5 *Protection of Waterways*

The 1983 Maritime Traffic Safety Law directs that all personnel on vessels are to observe the relevant rules and regulations concerning maritime traffic safety to ensure the safety of the vessels in navigation, berthing and operations.[14] Related to this non-military vessels of foreign nationality may not enter the internal waters and harbours in China without the approval of the competent authorities.[15] However, in circumstances such as critical illness of personnel, engine breakdown or vessel distress including seeking shelter from weather, a vessel may enter China's internal waters or harbours as long as it reports to the competent authority and follows the authority's directions. Foreign military vessels may not enter the territorial waters of China without the approval of the Government.[16] Vessels of foreign nationality entering and

---

11 Basel Convention on the Control of Transboundary Movements of Hazardous Wastes and Their Disposal, 1673 *U.N.T.S.* 57.

12 Marine Environmental Protection Law (amended), 1999, Article 39.

13 See <en.pkulaw.cn/Display.aspx?lib=law&Cgid=141265>.

14 Maritime Traffic Safety Law, *supra* note 4, Article 9.

15 *Ibid.*, Article 11.

16 *Ibid.*

leaving a harbour of China, navigating or shifting berths in the harbour area, or approaching or leaving mooring points or loading spots outside the harbour must have onboard a pilot designated by the competent authority.[17]

6 *Prevention of Marine Pollution*

Article 5 of the Marine Environmental Protection Law provides that the State administrative department in charge of maritime affairs is responsible for monitoring any marine environment pollution caused by non-military vessels in the waters of China. The Department is responsible for the investigation and cleanup of pollution accidents. In the event of a pollution accident caused by a foreign vessel navigating, berthing or operating in waters under the jurisdiction of China, there should be an inspection on board the vessel in question. Where a pollution accident caused by a vessel results in fishery damages, the competent fishery administrative department shall be invited to take part in the investigation.[18]

In 2015, China amended the Provisions of the People's Republic of China on the Administration of Emergency Preparedness for and Emergency Response to Vessel-Induced Pollution to the Marine Environment.[19] These Provisions apply not just to vessels operating within the sea areas of China but also to preparedness for an emergency response to vessel-induced pollution accidents that take place outside the sea areas of China which have caused or may cause pollution to Chinese sea areas.

7 *Maritime Accidents*

Specific regulations governing maritime accidents include the Regulations of the People's Republic of China on the Investigation and Handling of Maritime Traffic Accidents (1990),[20] the Ship Safety Inspection Rules of the People's Republic of China (2009),[21] and the Regulations of the People's Republic of China Governing Survey of Ships and Offshore Installations (1993).[22]

---

17 *Ibid.*, Article 13.

18 Marie Environmental Protection Law, *supra* note 12, Article 5.

19 Provisions of the People's Republic of China on the Administration of Emergency Preparedness for and Emergency Response to Vessel-Induced Pollution to the Marine Environment, 12 May 2015.

20 Regulations of the People's Republic of China on the Investigation and Handling of Maritime Traffic Accidents, 3 March 1990.

21 Ship Safety Inspection Rules of the People's Republic of China, 30 November 2009.

22 Regulations of the People's Republic of China Governing Survey of Ships and Offshore Installations, 14 February 1993.

The Regulations of the People's Republic of China on the Investigation and Handling of Maritime Traffic Accidents provides that the harbour superintendency agency is to be responsible for implementing the Regulations.[23] The maritime traffic accidents referred to in these Regulations, according to Article 4, mean the following accidents that may happen to vessels and installations: (1) collision, strike or damage by waves; (2) hitting hidden rocks or running aground; (3) fire or explosion; (4) sinking; (5) damage or loss of machinery parts or important tools during a voyage which affects the vessel's seaworthiness; (6) other maritime traffic accidents which cause losses in property and human lives.

The competent authority for the management of foreign vessels is the China Maritime Bureau (formerly known as Harbour Superintendency Administration) of the Ministry of Communications. It was restructured in 1999 to include the Bureau of Vessels Inspection. Twenty local maritime branches have been set up directly subordinated to the Ministry of Communications. The Maritime Bureau is entrusted with the following functions: (1) supervision of the implementation of marine traffic regulations for foreign ships; (2) issuing authorizations to foreign ships that seek to enter or depart from Chinese ports; (3) appointment and arrangement of pilotage for foreign vessels which are permitted to enter or leave Chinese ports; (4) supervision of the technical status of foreign ships, and maintenance of traffic order and safety; and (5) investigation and handling of issues arising from marine incidents.[24]

There are three laws and regulations that govern the navigation of foreign vessels in internal waters. These laws cover (1) harbour waters; (2) certain strategic waterways,[25] and (3) the Qiongzhou Strait.[26]

The general regulation governing China's waterways is the Regulation of China on the Administration of Navigable Waterways.[27] There are two regulations concerning the passage of merchant vessels through internal strategic waterways: the Lao Tieh Shan Channel and the inner water area of the

23 Regulations of the People's Republic of China on the Investigation and Handling of Maritime Traffic Accidents, 1990, Article 2.

24 See: Zou Keyuan, "Curbing marine environmental degradation: China's new legislation," *International Journal of Marine and Coastal Law*, 2001, 16, p. 355.

25 A strategic waterway is a narrow body of water on an important transportation route or sea lane.

26 See: Zou Keyuan, "Navigation of foreign vessels within China's jurisdictional waters," *Maritime Policy & Management*, 2002, 29, pp. 351–374.

27 Regulation of the People's Republic of China on the Administration of Navigable Waterways, 27 December 2008.

Encounter Rock in the Bohai Sea (or Bay).[28] In 2000, China adopted two new rules respecting the Chengshan Jiao Promontory, which stands at the mouth of the Bohai Sea. Vessels on their way to Tianjin, Yantai, Qinhuangdao and Dalian usually have to go through this channel. It is the busiest sea route in China and has more maritime accidents than any other sea area in China. What was adopted was a ship routeing system that consists of a traffic separation scheme, an inshore traffic zone and a precautionary area,[29] and a mandatory ship reporting system that applies to fishing vessels that are more than 24 meters, cargo ships weighing 300 tons or more and passenger ships.[30] These two systems were approved by the International Maritime Organization (IMO) and implemented by China in 2000.[31]

III Innocent Passage

The Declaration on China's Territorial Sea promulgated by China on 4 September 1958 stated: "no foreign vessels for military use and no foreign aircraft may enter China's territorial sea and the air space above it without the permission of the Government of the People's Republic of China."[32] The scope of the Declaration is specifically limited to vessels for military use. In practice, China recognizes the right of innocent passage for merchant ships, provided that they are in compliance with relevant Chinese laws and regulations. The intention behind the 1958 Declaration was to deter U.S. warships, which were supporting the Nationalist Chinese in Taiwan, from approaching the coast of mainland China.[33]

The spirit and content of the Declaration on innocent passage were endorsed in later Chinese laws and regulations. Article 11 of the Maritime Traffic Safety Law of the People's Republic of China, already noted, provides that "Military vessels of foreign nationality may not enter the territorial waters of the People's Republic of China without the approval of the Government of the

28 See: Zou Keyuan, "Navigation of foreign vessels," *supra* note 26.

29 *Ibid.*

30 *Ibid.*

31 *Ibid.*

32 Declaration of the Government of the People's Republic of China on China's Territorial Sea, 4 September 1958.

33 See: Zou Keyuan, "Innocent passage for warships: The Chinese doctrine and practice," *Ocean Development & International Law*, 1998, 29, pp. 195–223.

People's Republic of China."[34] In the Law of the People's Republic of China on the Territorial Sea and the Contiguous Zone, Article 6 provides that:

> Foreign ships for non-military purposes shall enjoy the right of innocent passage through the territorial sea of the People's Republic of China in accordance with the law. Foreign ships for military purposes shall be subject to approval by the Government of the People's Republic of China for entering the territorial sea of the People's Republic of China.[35]

Article 7 further states that: "Foreign submarines and other underwater vehicles, when passing through the territorial sea of the People's Republic of China, shall navigate on the surface and show their flag." Article 8 states that China:

> has the right to take all necessary measures to prevent and stop non-innocent passage through its territorial sea. Cases of foreign ships violating the laws or regulations of the People's Republic of China shall be handled by the relevant organs of the People's Republic of China in accordance with the law.

Pursuant to Article 9 China:

> may, for maintaining the safety of navigation or for other special needs, request foreign ships passing through the territorial sea of the People's Republic of China to use the designated sea lanes or to navigate according to the prescribed traffic separation schemes. The specific regulations to this effect shall be promulgated by the Government of the People's Republic of China or its competent authorities concerned.

Article 10 directs that: "In the case of violation of the laws or regulations of the People's Republic of China by a foreign ship for military purposes or a foreign government ship for non-commercial purposes when passing through the territorial sea of the People's Republic of China, the competent authorities of the People's Republic of China shall have the right to order it to leave the territorial sea immediately and the flag State shall bear international responsibility for any loss or damage thus caused."

When China ratified the LOSC in 1996, it made the following statement concerning innocent passage.

34 Maritime Traffic Safety Law, *supra* note 4, Article 11.

35 Law on the Territorial Sea, *supra* note 2, Article 6.

> The provisions of the United Nations Convention on the Law of the Sea concerning innocent passage through the territorial sea shall not prejudice the right of a coastal State to request, in accordance with its laws and regulations, a foreign State to obtain advance approval from or give prior notification to the coastal State for the passage of its warships through the territorial sea of the coastal State.[36]

It is to be noted that there exist different views on the practices on innocent passage for warships in the world community.[37]

IV Hot Pursuit

The right of hot pursuit is provided in Article 111 of the LOSC. China's domestic law on the right of hot pursuit is consistent with the above Article. Article 14 of Law on the Territorial Sea stipulates that:

> The competent authorities concerned of the People's Republic of China may, when they have good reasons to believe that a foreign ship has violated the laws or regulations of the People's Republic of China, exercise the right of hot pursuit against the foreign ship. Such pursuit shall be commenced when the foreign ship or one of its boats or other craft engaged in activities by using the ship pursued as a mother ship is within the internal waters, the territorial sea or the contiguous zone of the People's Republic of China. If the foreign ship is within the contiguous zone of the People's Republic of China, the pursuit may be undertaken only when there has been a violation of the rights as provided for in the relevant laws or regulations listed in Article 13 of this Law. The pursuit, if not interrupted, may be continued outside the territorial sea or the contiguous zone until the ship pursued enters the territorial sea of its own country or of a third State. The right of hot pursuit provided for in this Article shall be exercised by ships or aircraft of the People's Republic of China for military purposes, or by ships or aircraft on government service authorized by the Government of the People's Republic of China.

Also, Article 12 of Law on the Exclusive Economic Zone and the Continental Shelf provides that China "has the right to take necessary measures against

36 See: Zou Keyuan, "Innocent passage for warships," *supra* note 33, pp. 195–223.
37 *Ibid.*

violations of its laws and regulations in its exclusive economic zone and on its continental shelf and to investigate for legal responsibility according to law, and may exercise the right of hot pursuit."

There are some problems with the above legislation concerning hot pursuit. First, the specific reference of "the competent authorities" in Article 111 of the LOSC should be defined on a case-by-case basis. Different states have different authorities that regulate the navigation of foreign vessels. In China, law enforcement at sea is complicated as more than one department regulates navigation at sea. Thus, it is necessary to define clearly what is meant by "the competent authorities."

Second, as to the commencement of hot pursuit, a necessary requirement of lawful hot pursuit is not provided for in this legislation, that is – "The pursuit may only be commenced after a visual or auditory signal to stop has been given at a distance which enables it to be seen or heard by the foreign ship."[38] The acknowledgement in advance, known as the signal to stop, is of considerable significance since the pursuit is considered to have lawfully started only at the moment when a signal to stop is clearly given to the suspected vessel.[39]

Third, there is a lack of wording on continued pursuit after a hot pursuit is undertaken by the pursuing ship or aircraft.[40] Pursuit must be uninterrupted as continuity of pursuit is the jurisdictional link that keeps the coastal state claim against the pursued vessel alive. Hot pursuit may continue onto the high seas only so long as it is not interrupted. This requirement ensures that enforcement actions are not taken against the wrong vessel in violation of an innocent vessel's right to navigate freely on the high seas.[41]

Fourth, China's jurisdiction within the contiguous zone includes "security" matters which are not included in the scope of when hot pursuit can be exercised,[42] as China's Law on Territorial Sea and Contiguous Zone stipulates that China "has the right to exercise control in the contiguous zone to prevent and impose penalties for activities infringing the laws or regulations concerning security, the customs, finance, sanitation or entry and exit control within its land territory, internal waters or territorial sea."[43] This may give China a

38 See: Yu Mincai, "The Implementation of the Right of Hot Pursuit and China's Maritime Law Enforcement," *China Oceans Law Review*, 2005, 1, p. 403.

39 Nicholas M. Poulantzas, *The Right of Hot Pursuit in International Law*, 2002, p. 204.

40 Yu Mincai, "Hot Pursuit and China's Maritime Law Enforcement," *supra* note 38, p. 403.

41 Craig H. Allen, "Doctrine of Hot Pursuit: A Functional Interpretation Adaptable to Emerging Maritime Law Enforcement Technologies and Practices," *Ocean Development and International Law*, 1989, 20, p. 319.

42 Yu Mincai, "Hot Pursuit and China's Maritime Law Enforcement," *supra* note 38, p. 404.

43 Law on Territorial Sea, *supra* note 2, Article 13.

greater opportunity to exercise hot pursuit, which was not the original intent of the wording in the LOSC.

China's laws on the right of hot pursuit are too general, and may create difficulties for marine law enforcement seeking to utilize hot pursuit.[44]

V Archipelagic Sea Lane Passage

China has no legislation governing archipelagic se lane passage. China has encircled the Xisha Islands (Paracel Islands) with straight baselines. The United States has protested that China is not allowed to establish archipelagic straight baselines around the Paracel Islands according to the definition of archipelagos and archipelagic State in the LOSC.[45]

VI Straits Used for International Navigation

Pursuant to the LOSC straits used for international navigation are regulated by the transit passage regime provisions in Part III. Article 37 notes two criteria for determining whether a waterway is defined as the strait used for international navigation, the waterway must be "used for international navigation between one part of the high seas or an exclusive economic zone and another part of the high seas or an exclusive economic zone." These criteria can be regarded as applying a geographic standard and a functional standard.[46] However, Article 45 provides that:

> The regime of innocent passage, in accordance with Part II, Section 3, shall apply in straits used for international navigation: (a) excluded from the application of the regime of transit passage under Article 38, paragraph 1; or (b) between a part of the high seas or an exclusive economic zone and the territorial sea of a foreign State.

There are two different rules of passages for straits used for international navigation established in the LOSC, one applies to transit passage, the other to innocent passage.

---

44 *Ibid.*

45 Zou Keyuan, "Navigation of foreign vessels," *supra* note 26, p. 367.

46 Zou Keyuan, "Redefining the Legal Status of the Taiwan Strait," *International Journal of Marine and Coastal Law*, 2000, 15, pp. 251–252.

There are three main straits within China's jurisdictional waters, the Taiwan Strait, the Bohai Strait, and the Qiongzhou Strait. For the Qiongzhou Strait, there are specific regulations including the Rules for the Control of Non-Military Vessels of Foreign Origin Passing through the Qiongzhou Strait,[47] and the Provisions on Administration of Ferry Transport in the Qiongzhou Straits (2005).[48] The Qiongzhou Strait is situated between the Hainan Island and the Leizhou Peninsula. It is about 50 miles long and extends between 9.8–19 miles wide. The 1958 Declaration on the Territorial Sea expressly declared that the Qiongzhou Strait was China's "internal strait." As a Chinese authority explained the Qiongzhou Strait:

> is an important sea route linking the mainland with the Hainan Island and a convenient navigation route between our country and Southeast Asian countries. It has an extremely important meaning for our economy and national defense. Historically, it has always been subject to our sovereign jurisdiction and has constituted an inalienable, composite part of our territory. Since liberation our country has always administered it as an internal strait. The present Declaration is merely to reaffirm once more a historical fact.[49]

Whether the Qiongzhou Strait was an internal strait of China was unclear before the 1958 Declaration. It may be assumed that Qiongzhou Strait's status as an internal strait was to a large extent a result of China's use of straight baselines to enclose the coastal sea areas as its internal waters, although at that time the exact delineation was not publicly known.[50] In the 1958 Declaration on the Territorial Sea, the Bohai Strait was also considered as China's internal strait.

The above two waterways are not "straits used for international navigation," as defined in the LOSC since these straits are neither "between one part of the high seas or an exclusive economic zone and another part of the high seas or an exclusive economic zone" nor are they "between a part of the high seas or an exclusive economic zone and the territorial sea of a foreign State."

---

47 Rules for the Control of Non-Military Vessels of Foreign Origin Passing through the Qiongzhou Strait, 8 June 1964.

48 Provisions on Administration of Ferry Transport in the Qiongzhou Straits, 24 January 2005.

49 Fu Zhu, 1959, "Concerning of Our Country's Territorial Sea (Beijing)," reprinted in J.A. Cohen and H. Chiu, *People's China and International Law* (Princeton, New Jersey: Princeton University Press, 1974), p. 486.

50 Zou Keyuan, "Navigation of foreign vessels," *supra* note 26, pp. 351–374.

The Taiwan Strait is located between Taiwan and mainland China, with its widest breadth of 116 nautical miles connecting the East China Sea and the South China Sea.

As set out in the LOSC, "the legal status of the waters beyond the territorial seas of States bordering straits" is EEZ or high seas. At one time, China declared that the waters in Taiwan Strait were high seas.[51] However, since the adoption of the LOSC in 1982, the legal status of the Taiwan Strait has been changed. Under China's domestic legislation, China's EEZ area covers the whole strait such that there are internal waters, a territorial sea, and an EEZ in the Taiwan Strait with each zone subject to legal governance under relevant Chinese laws and regulations. That is to say, the water area in the Taiwan Strait, which is not part of China's internal waters or of territorial sea, has become part of China's EEZ. Due to the change of the legal status of the Taiwan Strait, the navigation of foreign vessels is no longer subject to the freedom of high seas but rather to the legal regime for the EEZ, although under the LOSC there is no substantive difference in terms of navigation between legal regime for the high seas and that for the EEZ.[52] China publicized part of its straight baseline system in May 1996 at the time of China's ratification of the LOSC. The publicized baselines include along the mainland coast of the Taiwan Strait. If there is a navigational route inside the publicized baselines, then the PRC has the full control over the passage of foreign vessels.[53]

The Taiwan Strait is complicated by cross-Strait relations. Both sides of the Strait have laws and regulation. The lack of a clear demarcation line of jurisdiction has resulted in overlapping areas which can cause problems for the navigation of foreign vessels in the Taiwan Strait. Both sides have agreed on certain matters regarding the Strait. The Provisions Governing the Administration of the Direct Shipping between the Two Sides of the Taiwan Strait issued under Decree No.6 of the Ministry of Communications of the PRC in 1996,[54] in which shipping between the two sides is defined as "domestic transportation under special administration" is an example.

In 2002, the Ministry of Communication published the Notice of the Ministry of Communications on Strengthening the Administration of Tramp Ship

51 See Declaration on China's Territorial Sea, 1958.

52 See: Zou Keyuan, "Navigation of foreign vessels," *supra* note 26, p. 365.

53 Zou Keyuan, "Redefining the Legal Status of the Taiwan Strait," *supra* note 46, p. 252.

54 Provisions Governing the Administration of the Direct Shipping between the Two Sides of the Taiwan Strait issued under Decree No.6 of the Ministry of Communications of the PRC, 1996.

Transport across the Taiwan Strait.[55] The Notice provides that in accordance with the Measures for the Administration of Shipping Across the Taiwan Strait promulgated by the Ministry of Communications in August 1996 and the Regulations of the People's Republic of China on International Shipping promulgated by the State Council in December 2001, no enterprise or ship may, without the approval of the communications authority under the State Council operate water transport directly from China's mainland to Taiwan area or vice versa, or through a third place.

The Port of Hong Kong has always had a key role in the economic development of the Hong Kong SAR (Special Administrative Region) and the surrounding region. It is one of the busiest container ports in the world.[56] The administrative department of the port is the Marine Department of the Hong Kong SAR. Its principal functions are to ensure the safe operation of the port and all Hong Kong waters as well as to operate the Hong Kong Shipping Register and safeguard the quality of the Hong Kong registered ships.

The Marine Department has established a comprehensive legal system to govern navigation. The focus of the legislation is on regulation of merchant shipping and navigation within the port area of Hong Kong. As Hong Kong is an integrated part of People's Republic of China, the general legislation of China, including the Law on the Territorial Sea and Contiguous Zone and Law of the Exclusive Economic Zone and Continental Shelf, applies in the Hong Kong area.

VII Navigation in the EEZ

1 *Regulation on Vessel-Source Pollution within the EEZ*

The most important and comprehensive legislation concerning China's maritime environment protection is the Marine Environment Protection Law, discussed above, which regulates issues of pollution resulting from foreign vessels. Article 62(1) provides: "No vessels and their related operations shall, in the sea areas under the jurisdiction of the People's Republic of China, discharge pollutants, wastes, ballast water, vessel garbage and other harmful substances into the sea in violation of the provisions of this law."[57] On 2 September 2009, the State Council passed the Regulations on the Prevention and Control

55 Notice of the Ministry of Communications on Strengthening the Administration of Tramp Ship Transport across the Taiwan Strait, date issued, 26 November 2002.

56 <www.mardep.gov.hk/en/aboutus/home.html>.

57 Marine Environment Protection Law, *supra* note 12, Article 62(1).

of Vessel-induced Pollution to the Marine Environment, further defining and detailing the jurisdiction related to matters of pollution from foreign vessels.

Article 91(3) of the Marine Environmental Protection Law provides: "Those who causes serious consequences of heavy losses of public and private property or human injuries and deaths of persons by major marine environment pollution accident, shall be investigated and imposed upon criminal responsibility by law."[58] As for specific penalties, Article 338 of the Criminal Law of the People's Republic of China provides a related reference.[59]

China's legislation regulating foreign vessel related marine pollution does not differentiate between the different maritime zones rather providing a set of general rules that govern all of China's maritime zones.

2 *Military Vessels*

The LOSC does not explicitly deal with whether foreign vessels can engage in military activities within a coastal state's EEZ. China has some general requirements in its Law on the Exclusive Economic Zone and the Continental Shelf. Article 11 provides:

> All states shall, on the premise that they comply with international law and the laws and regulations of the People's Republic of China, enjoy the freedom of navigation in and flight over its exclusive economic zone, the freedom to lay submarine cables and pipelines and the convenience of other lawful uses of the sea related to the freedoms mentioned above in the exclusive economic zone and on the continental shelf of the People's Republic of China.[60]

Based on recent practices, China expects foreign vessels present within China's EEZ to comply with China's domestic law.

For example, in March 2009, the *USNS Impeccable* (T-AGOS 23) engaged in military activities in China's EEZ and five PRC vessels stopped the *Impeccable*. The U.S. government protested that the PRC's action was reckless, unprofessional, and unlawful. China responded that the *Impeccable's* presence in China's EEZ was in violation of Chinese domestic law and international law.[61] China's interception of the *USNS Impeccable* does not mean that China

58 *Ibid.*, Article 91(3).

59 Criminal Law of the People's Republic of China, 1979, Article 338.

60 Law on the Exclusive Economic Zone and the Continental Shelf, *supra* note 3, Article 11.

61 See: On 10 March 2009, Chinese Foreign Ministry spokesman Ma Zhaoxu said that the LOSC and the Law on the Exclusive Economic Zone and the Continental Shelf of the People's Republic of China, the Provisions of the People's Republic of China on Administration of

absolutely excludes military vessels from navigating in China's EEZ; rather that China requires foreign military vessels when passing through China's EEZ to obey China's domestic law, respect China's security interest, and not undertake activities that may threaten China's national security.[62]

Regarding military surveying activities, Article 9 of China's EEZ Law provides: "All international organizations, foreign organizations or individuals that wish to conduct marine scientific research in the exclusive economic zone or on the continental shelf of the People's Republic of China shall be subject to approval of the competent authorities of the People's Republic of China and shall comply with the laws and regulations of the People's Republic of China." From this it can be concluded that the rights of military vessels are limited when conducting such activities, even if they are in the pretext of marine scientific research. China does not recognize an absolute freedom to military vessels operating in its EEZ.

Article 12 of the same Law provides:

> The People's Republic of China may, in the exercise of its sovereign rights to explore its exclusive economic zone and to exploit, conserve and manage the living resources there, take such necessary measures as visit, inspection, arrest, detention and judicial proceedings in order to ensure that the laws and regulations of the People's Republic of China are complied with. The People's Republic of China has the right to take necessary measures against violations of its laws and regulations in its exclusive economic zone and on its continental shelf and to investigate for legal responsibility according to law, and may exercise the right of hot pursuit.

This article gives a further legal basis for the interception of the *Impeccable*.

Impeccable-like military demonstrations have increased in the South China Sea. The conflicts between the United States and China are rooted in different understandings of the freedom of the seas. For the United States, the freedom of the seas is an absolute concept. For China, it is a conditional concept such that when freedom of navigation is in conflict with state sovereignty or national security, it should give way.

Foreign-related Marine Scientific Research all provide related regulations on activities of foreign vessels within the EEZ. The Chinese government consistently practices according to these laws. The USNS *Impeccable* operated within China's EEZ without permission, which violated international law and China's domestic law. Available at <mil.news.sina.com.cn/2009-03-16/1540545587.html>.

62 For more, see Zou Ligang, "A Discussion on China's Power to Govern Foreign Countries' Military in the Exclusive Economic Zone," *China Legal Science*, 2012, No. 6.

3 *Fishing Vessels*

The Law on the Exclusive Economic Zone provides general rules on enforcement actions against foreign fishing vessels within China's EEZ. China does not have an integrated set of regulations on marine resources, instead, it has several laws and administrative rules regulating these issues, such as the Fisheries Law,[63] the Measures for the Management of Marine Nature Reserves,[64] and the Regulations of Pelagic Fishery.[65] The Ministry of Agriculture has adopted measures such as the Interim Measures on Management of Foreigners, Foreign Ships' Activity within Waters of People's Republic of China,[66] and the Provisions on the Administration of Fishery Administrative Cruising within the Exclusive Economic Zone.[67]

The Interim Measures on Management of Foreigners, Foreign Ships' Fishing Activity within the Waters of the People's Republic of China gives detailed direction (Articles 5–7), rules regarding foreign fishery vessels navigating in China's EEZ, and includes penalties for illegal navigation (Articles 11–20). For China, the right of navigation and state sovereignty over natural resources within its maritime area are not separate issues, and a foreign vessels' right of navigation may be compromised by state sovereignty over natural resources, such as the management and conservation measures of fish resources. The laws mentioned above are among those that apply to foreign fishing vessels' right of navigation.

4 *Marine Scientific Research Vessels*

As stated above, Article 9 of Law on the Exclusive Economic Zone and the Continental Shelf provides that:

> All international organizations, foreign organizations or individuals that wish to conduct marine scientific research in the exclusive economic zone or on the continental shelf of the People's Republic of China shall be subject to approval of the competent authorities of the People's Republic of China and shall comply with the laws and regulations of the People's Republic of China.

63 Fisheries Law of the People's Republic of China, 28 December 2013.
64 Measures for the Management of Marine Nature Reserves, 2007.
65 Regulations of Pelagic Fishery, 2003.
66 Interim Measures on Management of Foreigners, Foreign Ships' Activity within Waters of People's Republic of China, 1999.
67 Provisions on the Administration of Fishery Administrative Cruising within the Exclusive Economic Zone, 14 November 2005.

As for surveying and mapping, there is the Surveying and Mapping Law of the People's Republic of China,[68] Article 7 stipulates that:

> A foreign organization or individual that conducts surveying and mapping in the territorial air, land and waters, as well as other sea areas under the jurisdiction of the People's Republic of China must be subject to the approval of the department of surveying and mapping administration under the State Council jointly with the department of surveying and mapping administration in the armed forces, and must abide by the relevant laws and regulations of the People's Republic of China. A foreign organization or individual that conducts surveying and mapping in the territorial air, land and waters of the People's Republic of China must take the form of an equity joint venture or contractual joint venture with the relevant departments or entities of the People's Republic of China, and may not involve any state secret or harm the state security.

The situation concerning marine scientific research is complicated as China has national security concerns. As indicated above, China has opposed the U.S. military vessels operating in China's EEZ in the name of marine scientific research. Although the LOSC does not explicitly provide for the regulation of foreign vessel's military activities in the EEZ nevertheless China has asserted the right to protect its security.

VIII IMO Approved Routeing Arrangements

As noted above, the Chengshan Jiao routeing system is the only routeing system in Chinese waters that has been adopted by the IMO.

In Chinese navigable waters, there are five key areas in which shipping density is high, sea routes are crossing, traffic is congested, and maritime accidents occur frequently. These are the Bohai Strait (Laotieshang Channel), the Chengshan Jiao waters, the Changjiangkou waters, the Zhujiangkou waters and the Qiongzhou Strait.[69] Ship routeing measures were introduced in the 1970s on an optional basis for the South-North Route between Changjiangkou waters and Bohai Sea. The arrangement of the South-North Route drew on the rich

68 Surveying and Mapping Law of the People's Republic of China, 29 August 2002.

69 See: H Ma, Z. Wu, and Z. Liu, "New Development of Ships Routeing in Chinese Navigable Waterways," *International Journal on Marine Navigation and Safety of Sea Transportation*, 2008, No. 2, pp. 127–130.

navigational experiences from other parts of the world, in particular the traffic separate scheme in the Dover Strait.[70]

Since 2002, there have been a number of domestic routeing systems developed and implemented, such as: the Changjiangkou routeing system (implemented in September 2002); the Changjiang Jiangsu routeing system (in July 2003); the Zhujiangkou routeing system (implemented in March 2004); the Changjiang Anhui routeing system (implemented in October 2005); the Changjiang Shanghai routeing system (implemented in March 2006); the Laotieshan Channel routeing system (implemented in June 2006); the Qiongzhou Strait routeing system (implemented in January 2007); and the Changjiang Sanxia routeing system (implemented in December 2005).[71]

In 2011, the Ministry of Communications published general plans for the national coastal shipping routeing system, and for coastal routes, setting the goal of establishing 26 routeing systems in China in 3 to 5 years, so as to achieve "waterborne highways". China is not only establishing new routeing systems, it also is adapting the existing systems to take into account development. For example, as the 2000 Chengshan Jiao ship routeing system no longer satisfied the requirements of shipping, China submitted two proposals to IMO for revising "Chengshan Jiao ship routeing system" and "Chengshan Jiao ship reporting system" in June 2014. The proposals were approved by IMO and the two systems went into force on 1 July 2015.

IX Conclusion

Although the laws and regulations described above are comprehensive and generally in conformity with the LOSC and/or other applicable international rules, they are far from adequate or perfect. Amongst other things, China needs to establish explicit and detailed rules ensuring foreign vessels' right of innocent passage in accordance with the LOSC.

As well, while China's EEZ-related legislations covers matters like vessel-source pollution within the EEZ and fishing vessel navigation, regulations on military vessel navigation and military activities are not clear or adequate. Finally, although China has established many ship roueting systems in various waters, there is a need to adapt to ever changing situations and requirements.

70 *Ibid.*

71 *Ibid.*

CHAPTER 3

Japan's Practice regarding the Regulation on Navigation of Foreign Vessels

Chie Kojima

1 Introduction

Freedom of navigation has always been at the center of Japanese ocean policy. The dramatic increase of imports and exports via shipping over the last half a century underlines the economic importance of this policy for Japan.[1] 99.6 percent of Japan's imports and exports rely on maritime transport, more than 50 percent of which is associated with the maritime trade with other Asia-Pacific States.[2] Japanese corporations own 2,561 commercial vessels involved in international shipping, accounting for 10 percent of the total ship tonnage of the world.[3]

Maritime security threats arising from political tensions among East Asian countries, including those related to territorial disputes, have created concerns within both the public and private sectors involved in maritime transport. Moreover, increasing maritime crimes such as illegal fishing, drug smuggling and illegal dumping also threaten the security of Japan. In 2015, the Japan Coast Guard (JCG)[4] investigated 9,444 cases and identified numerous vessels involved in maritime crimes.[5] The JCG conducted inspections of 4,865 foreign

1 The Japanese Shipowner's Association, Kaiun tōkei yōran 2015, *available at*: http://www.jsanet.or.jp/data/pdf/2015data40-8.pdf [Available only in Japanese].

2 The Japanese Shipowner's Association, Shipping Now 2016–2017, *available at*: http://www.jsanet.or.jp/data/shipping.html [Available only in Japanese], p. 13.

3 *Id.*

4 The JCG with about 12,000 coast guard officers has a need for reinforcing its capacity in law enforcement due to Japan's long coastline and vast EEZ area. In 2000, the JCG introduced Dial Number 118 for anyone who is in distress at sea, witnessed a ship in distress, witnessed crime scenes such as discharges of oil and illegal fishing, witnessed a suspicious vessel, or have information on smuggling of people or drugs.

5 The 9,444 cases are divided in to 4,730 cases for violations of maritime law; 2,562 cases for violations of fishery law; 8 cases for violations of immigration law; 52 cases for violations of arms/drug control law; 919 cases for violations of marine environmental law; 877 cases for violations of criminal law; and 296 cases for violations of other laws. Statistics on maritime crimes as involving the Japanese Coast Guard can be found *at*: http://www.kaiho.mlit.go.jp/doc/hakkou/toukei/toukei.html [Available only in Japanese].

DOI:10.1163/9789004396272_004

vessels: 4,819 vessels in Japan's internal waters, 35 vessels in the territorial sea, two vessels in the contiguous zone, and nine vessels in the exclusive economic zone (EEZ).[6] There are increasing cases of transnational crimes such as drug smuggling involving transactions with foreign ships on the high seas.[7]

This chapter provides an overview of Japanese regulation and State practice regarding the navigation of foreign vessels in the Japanese ports, territorial sea, straits and EEZ. It also highlights the important effect of maritime security on recent legislative developments in Japan.

II Regulation of Foreign Vessels

1 *Basic Rights and Obligations of Foreign Vessels in Japanese Ports*

(a) Foreign Warships

Bilateral agreements as well as specific consent gives a legal basis for foreign warships to enter Japanese ports. An example of an agreement is the 1960 Agreement under Article VI of the Treaty of Mutual Cooperation and Security between Japan and the United States regarding Facilities and Areas and the Status of United States Armed Forces in Japan.[8]

Foreign warships and other governmental vessels enjoy immunities in Japanese ports. However, if a crewmember of a foreign warship landed in Japanese territory commits a crime not related to their official duties, Japan can exercise its jurisdiction over the individual.[9]

(b) Foreign Commercial Vessels

Japan allows foreign commercial vessels to enter its ports but requires them to follow certain procedures such as providing prior notification of information necessary for the protection of Japan's national security. The notification requirement is set out in Article 15 of the Customs Act[10] and Article 4 of the Act

---

6 *Id.*

7 For example, in February 2016, yakuza members were arrested for smuggling about 100 kilograms of stimulant drugs received from a foreign ship on the high seas. *Asahi Shimbun*, "Police bust seaborne drug smuggling ring in Kagoshima" (12 February 2016).

8 Agreement under Article VI of the Treaty of Mutual Cooperation and Security between Japan and the United States, Regarding Facilities and Areas and the Status of United States Armed Forces in Japan, Jan. 19, 1960, *entered into force* Jun. 23, 1960, U.S.–Japan, 11 *U.S.T.* 1632.

9 See the case concerning the English Sailors in Kobe in the Osaka High Court, *Japan v. Smith and Stinner*, High Court of Osaka (Sixth Criminal Division), Nov. 5, 1952, [1952] *Int'l L. Rep.* 221 (No. 47).

10 Act No. 61 of 2 April 1954.

on Port Regulations.[11] Article 12, paragraph 5 of the Port and Harbor Act stipulates that a port authority will accept such notification from ships entering the port.[12] Bilateral agreements have been concluded that applies most-favored-nation treatment, such as Article XIX, paragraph 3 of the 1953 Japan – United States Friendship, Commerce and Navigation Treaty.[13] As a Contracting Party to the 1923 Convention and Statute of the International Regime of Maritime Ports,[14] Japan is bound by Article 2 of the Statute to provide equal treatment to vessels of other Contracting Parties and to provide freedom of access to ports, the use of the ports, and the full enjoyment of the benefits of navigation.

In practice, Japan does not exercise its criminal jurisdiction over foreign vessels in its ports except in cases where the crime disturbs the peace or the good order of the port, where a Japanese national is involved in the crime, where general passengers are involved in the crime, or where the assistance of the local authorities has been requested by a diplomatic agent or consular officer of the flag State.[15] Bilateral treaties confirm this practice, for example, Article 21, paragraph 2, of the 1963 Consular Convention between Japan and the United States[16] stipulates that

> [T]he administrative authorities of the receiving state should not [...] (a) concern themselves with any matter taking place on board a vessel except for the preservation of peace and order or in the interests of public health or safety, or (b) institute prosecutions in respect of crimes or offenses committed on board a vessel in the ports or in the waters of the receiving state unless they are of a serious character or involve the tranquility of the port or unless they are committed by or against persons other than members of the crew who are not nationals of the receiving state.[17]

11 Act No. 174 of 15 July 1948.

12 Act No. 218 of 31 May 1950.

13 Article XIX, paragraph 3 stipulates: "Vessels of either Party shall have liberty, on equal terms with vessels of the other Party and on equal terms with vessels of any third country, to come with their cargoes to all ports, places and waters of such other Party open to foreign commerce and navigation. Such vessels and cargoes shall in all respects be accorded national treatment and most-favored-nation treatment within the ports, places and waters of such other Party". Friendship Commerce and Navigation, Apr. 2, 1953, U.S.–Japan, 4 U.S.T. 2063, T.I.A.S. No. 2863.

14 Convention and Statute of the International Regime of Maritime Ports, 1923, 7 *L.N.T.S.* 73.

15 Japan Maritime Center ed., *Kaiyō-hō to senpaku no tsūkō (2nd edn)*, 2010, pp. 51–2.

16 Consular Convention between United States and Japan, Mar. 22, 1963, U.S.–Japan, 2 *I.L.M.* 746.

17 *Ibid.*, Article 21, paragraph 2, further stipulates that "[c]rimes or offenses against the laws of the receiving state regarding public health, customs or immigration committed on

With regard to civil proceedings, Article 34, paragraph 2, of the 1964 Consular Convention between Japan and the United Kingdom,[18] for example, similarly stipulates immunity from civil jurisdiction on certain matters in principle.

> The courts of the receiving State shall not entertain civil proceedings arising out of any dispute between the master and any member of the crew of a vessel of the sending State as to wages or contracts of service, except where they are satisfied that the competent consular officer of the sending State has been notified of the proceedings and has not raised objection.

(c) Prohibition of Ships from Specific Countries

On 25 August 2003, the Japanese authorities including coast guard, customs and immigration officers, inspected the *Mangyongbong-92*, a North Korean ferry which traveled irregularly from Wonsan in North Korea to Niigata in Japan. The inspection was the result of a local prefecture ordinance allowing the mayor to deny docking rights based on safety and environmental concerns.[19] No irregularities were found during the inspection but there were some problems with the vessel's safety equipment that had to be rectified, causing a delay. The next month the vessel was subject to two more inspections.[20]

As a consequence of this incident, Japan enacted a new law in 2004, the Act on Special Measures Concerning the Prohibition of Entry of Specified Ships into Ports,[21] which enables the government to ban the entry of ships from a designated country for certain periods of time in the interest of maintaining peace and security. As a result of this law North Korean vessels have been prohibited from entering Japanese ports.

---

board a vessel in the ports or waters of that state shall be deemed to be included in the crimes or offenses involving the tranquility of the port."

18 Consular Convention between Japan and the United Kingdom, May 4, 1964, *entered into force* October 10, 1965, U.K.–Japan, 1966 *Gr. Brit. T.S.* No. 1 (Cmnd. 2833).

19 The media reported that the ferry was allegedly involved in "illegal transportation of materials with military potential to North Korea, illegal cash remittances and espionage activities". See, *North Korean ferry may be banned from future port calls: Abe, The Japan Times*, (4 June 2003).

20 Ko Swan Sik, *Chronicle of Events and Incidents Relating to Asia with Relevance to International Law*, July 2002–June 2004, 11 Asian Yearbook of International Law 277 (2003–2004), p. 301.

21 Act No. 125 of 2004.

2 *Port State Control*

Japan started to exercise port state control (PSC) on visiting commercial vessels in 1983 in order to eliminate substandard ships. The system was strengthened as a result of the Tokyo Memorandum of Understanding adopted in 1993.[22] Following the *Nakhodka* oil spill in 1997, Japan have engaged PSC officers specialized in controlling foreign vessels. PSC officers conduct inspections in accordance with the conventions of the International Maritime Organization (IMO) to which Japan is a party, such as the 1973 International Convention for the Prevention of Pollution from Ships as modified by the Protocol of 1978 (MARPOL 73/78),[23] the 2004 International Convention for the Control and Management of Ships' Ballast Water and Sediments (BWM Convention),[24] the 1978 International Convention on Standards of Training, Certification and Watchkeeping for Seafarers (STCW Convention),[25] and the 2006 Maritime Labour Convention (MLC).[26] PSC officers may board all vessels except for governmental vessels and check certificates of insurance on board.[27] If PSC officers identify serious non-compliance with international standards by a foreign vessel, that vessel may be ordered not to navigate until effective measures are taken.[28]

III Innocent Passage in the Territorial Sea

1 *Legislation on Innocent Passage*

Japan designated a 12 nautical mile territorial sea in the Act on the Territorial Sea of 1977.[29] The 1977 Act was amended and renamed the Act on the Territorial Sea and Contiguous Zone in 1996 (1996 Territorial Sea Act).[30] The 1996 Territorial Sea does not define innocent passage. It is to be noted that Japan allows foreign vessels to exercise their right of innocent passage in areas which

---

22 Memorandum of Understanding on Port State Control in the Asia-Pacific Region, *available at*: http://www.tokyo-mou.org/doc/Memorandum%20rev15.pdf.

23 International Convention for the Prevention of Pollution from Ships, 1340 *U.N.T.S.* 61.

24 International Convention for the Control and Management of Ships' Ballast Water and Sediments, 30 *I.L.M.* 1455.

25 International Convention on Standards of Training, Certification and Watchkeeping for Seafarers (STCW Convention), 1361 *U.N.T.S.* 2, as amended.

26 Maritime Labour Convention, *U.N.T.S.*, registration 51299.

27 See www.mlit.go.jp/maritime/insurance_portal.htm. Japan requires all Japanese vessels engaged in international shipping to obtain P&I insurance (e.g., Act on Liability for Oil Pollution Damage, Act No. 95 of 27 December 1975, Art. 39-7).

28 See www.ogb.go.jp/unyu/2344/015502.

29 Act No. 30 of 2 May 1977.

30 Act No. 73 of 14 June 1996 (Territorial Sea Act).

became internal waters as a result of Japan adopting straight baselines in the 1996 Act.[31]

A number of laws regulate activities of foreign ships navigating in the territorial sea of Japan. These laws include: the Act on the Prevention of Collision at Sea;[32] the Maritime Traffic Safety Act;[33] the Navigational Aids Act;[34] the Telecommunications Business Act;[35] the Fisheries Act;[36] the Act on Regulation of Fishing Operation by Foreign Nationals;[37] the Act on Prevention of Marine Pollution and Maritime Disaster;[38] the Act on Services Related to Waterways;[39] the Customs Act;[40] the Foreign Exchange and Foreign Trade Act;[41] the Immigration Control and Refugee Recognition Act;[42] and the Quarantine Act.[43] These involve regulations permitted pursuant to the innocent passage provision (Article 21(1)) of the 1982 U.N. Convention on the Law of the Sea (LOSC).[44]

In 2008, the Act on Navigation of Foreign Ships through the Territorial Sea and Internal Waters[45] was adopted in order to clarify the prohibitions of certain activities of foreign ships within the territorial waters of Japan. Before this enactment, stopping, anchoring, mooring, or hovering of foreign vessels in the territorial waters of Japan was not illegal *per se*. In some cases, the JCG took action against foreign ships when they violated the Ship Act,[46] which prohibits a foreign ship navigating under a Japanese flag or the Immigration Control and Refugee Recognition Act,[47] which prohibits a ship carrying undocumented migrants.[48] In other cases, the JCG would arrest foreign vessels when they refused to stop for inspection under the Ship Act or the Fisheries Act.[49]

---

31 Massaki Kobashi, *Ryōkai tō ni okeru gaikoku senpaku no kōkō ni kansuru hōritsu ni tsuite*, 11(3) Unyu Seisaku Kenkyū 41 (2008), pp. 42–43.
32 Act No. 62 of 1 June 1977.
33 Act No. 115 of 3 July 1972.
34 Act No. 99 of 24 May 1949.
35 Act No. 86 of 25 December 1984.
36 Act No. 267 of 15 December 1949.
37 Act No. 60 of 14 July 1967.
38 Act No. 136 of 25 December 1970.
39 Act No. 102 of 17 April 1950.
40 Act No. 61 of 2 April 1954.
41 Act No. 228 of 1 December 1949.
42 Cabinet Order No. 319 of 4 October 1951.
43 Act No. 201 of 6 June 1951.
44 U.N. Convention on the Law of the Sea, 1833 *U.N.T.S.* 3.
45 Act No. 64 of 11 June 2008.
46 Act No. 46 of 8 March 1899, Art. 22(1).
47 Cabinet Order No. 319 of 4 October 1951.
48 Rekizo Murakami, *Ryōkai keibi no hōkōzō*, 2005, pp. 62–63.
49 *Id.* p. 63.

Under the 2008 Act on Navigation of Foreign Ships through the Territorial Sea and Internal Waters, foreign ships navigating in the territorial waters of Japan are prohibited to stop, anchor, moor, or hover unless they have legitimate reasons such as *force majeure*, distress or for the purpose of rendering assistance to persons, ships or aircraft in danger or distress.[50] They may also stop, anchor or moor only when they have a compelling reason in compliance with the 1977 Act on the Prevention of Collisions at Sea and other relevant laws and regulations of Japan.[51] Foreign ships are not allowed to navigate through the internal waters, except for the new internal waters, if they do not intend to enter a Japanese port.[52] If foreign ships have legitimate reasons to engage in any of these acts, they must provide prior notification to the JCG.[53]

The enactment of the 2008 Act facilitated control of so-called "suspicious vessels" (*fushin-sen*) in the Japanese territorial sea and internal waters. According to the 2008 Act, navigation of foreign ships through the Japanese territorial sea and some areas of internal waters which expanded by adopting straight baselines under the 1996 Territorial Sea Act[54] (hereinafter referred to as "new internal waters") shall be continuous and expeditious,[55] as prescribed under Article 18(2) of the LOSC.

Article 6 of the 2008 Act allows Coast Guard officers to inspect foreign vessels. If the captain and crew of a foreign vessel refuse, disturb or avoid an inspection or remain silent or make false statements, the captain or crew can be imprisoned for up to 6 months or receive a fine up to JPY 300,000.[56] If the Coast Guard finds that there was no legitimate reasons for the foreign vessel to stop, anchor, moor, or hover in the territorial sea or internal waters of Japan, the JCG may order the vessel to leave the territorial sea.[57] If the vessel does not follow the JCG order, the captain may be charged and receive up to one year of imprisonment or a fine of JPY 500,000.[58]

Article 18(2) of the LOSC stipulates that stopping and anchoring, which are "incidental to ordinary navigation," are considered to be within the meaning

50 Act on the Navigation of Foreign Ships through the Territorial Sea, supra note 45, Art. 4(2).
51 Act No. 62 of 1 June 1977.
52 Act on the Navigation of Foreign Ships through the Territorial Sea, supra note 45, Art. 4(2).
53 *Id.* Art. 5. In the past, Japan had requested foreign vessels entering the territorial sea as a result of *force majeure* or distress to give a prior notification to Japan Coast Guard, but only half of approximately 4,000 vessels followed this procedure. This resulted in a number of accidents such as damaging fishing nets, etc. See Kobashi, supra note 31, p. 43.
54 Territorial Sea Act, supra note 30.
55 Act on Navigation of Foreign Ships through the Territorial Sea, supra note 45, Art. 3.
56 *Id.* Art. 13.
57 *Id.* Art. 8.
58 *Id.* Art. 12.

of "passage." Although the phrase leaves room for interpretation, the scope of foreign ships' right of passage in the territorial sea in the LOSC appears to be broader than that set out in the 2008 Act which only permits vessels to stop and anchor in the case of *force majeure*, distress or the rendering of assistance to persons, ships or aircraft in danger or distress and when there is a compelling reason.

2 *Passage of Foreign Vessels in the Japanese Territorial Sea*

(a) Foreign Warships

In principle Japan allows foreign warships to exercise the right of innocent passage in the territorial sea of Japan.[59] The Self-Defense Forces, however, may take necessary actions based on the Prime Minister's decision in accordance with the government's policies and procedures expressed in the 1996 and 2015 Cabinet Decisions for cases when foreign submarines remain submerged and do not fly a flag, as well as for foreign warships in the territorial sea and internal waters of Japan whose navigation is considered to be non-innocent under international law.[60]

Japan prohibits the passage of foreign warships carrying nuclear weapons in its territorial sea based on the "Three Non-Nuclear Principles" of not possessing nuclear weapons, not producing them and not permitting their entry into the country.[61] When ratifying the LOSC in 1996, Japan made it clear that passage of vessels carrying nuclear weapons through the territorial sea cannot be considered "innocent."[62] The Japanese government justifies its position based on Article 19(1) of the LOSC which states that "[p]assage is innocent so long as it is not prejudicial to the peace, good order or security of the coastal State."[63]

This may raise a question as to whether this Japanese policy is consistent with Article 23 of the LOSC which explicitly allows the innocent passage of foreign nuclear-powered ships and ships carrying nuclear or other inherently dangerous or noxious substances as long as they carry documents and observe special precautionary measures established for such ships by international agreements.

59 Takane Sugihara et al., Gendai Kokusaihō Kōgi (5th edn, Yūhikaku, 2012), p. 124.

60 The explanation note can be found *at*: http://www.cas.go.jp/jp/gaiyou/jimu/pdf/gaikoku-gunkantaisho.pdf [Available only in Japanese].

61 Statement of 11 December 1967 by former Prime Minister Eisaku Sato, *see*, http://www.mofa.go.jp/policy/un/disarmament/nnp/index.html.

62 Toshihisa Takata, *The Conclusion by Japan of the United Nations Convention on the Law of the Sea (UNCLOS) and the Adjustment of Maritime Legal Regime*, 39 Japanese Annual of International Law 124 (1996), p. 133.

63 See Ichiro Komatsu, Jissen-Kokusaihō (2nd edn), 2015, p. 126.

On 21 August 1980, a Soviet nuclear-powered submarine was discovered afire on the high seas about 110 kilometers east of Okinawa. The JCG together with the Maritime and Air Self-Defense Forces undertook rescue measures. The Ministry of Foreign Affairs made inquiries to the Soviet Embassy concerning the risk of radioactive pollution and reiterated its Three Non-Nuclear Principles, as well as the prohibition on passage of nuclear-powered ships through its territorial sea. The USSR responded that there was no risk of radioactive pollution from the accident and that, in view of *force majeure*, it was desirable to shorten the submarine's course of navigation by towing it across Japanese territorial waters and into the East China Sea.[64]

When the submarine towed by a tugboat of the Soviet navy approached the Japanese territorial sea, the Japanese patrol boat warned that:

> the four Soviet ships including the nuclear-powered submarine will trespass in the Japanese territorial sea if you go on along this course. We do not consider that you will be exercising the right of innocent passage on the basis of the international Convention on the Territorial Sea and the Contiguous Zone, so we warn you not to trespass in the Japanese territorial sea.[65]

The Soviet convoy ignored the warning and entered Japan's territorial sea. The Ministry of Foreign Affairs gave a second warning, but the ships continued course and passed through the territorial sea around the Okinawa islands. This incident led the Japanese government to file a diplomatic protest with the USSR.[66]

Another example of a questionable passage of a foreign warship concerns the case of disguised submarines passing through the territorial waters of Japan. Such passage concerns the violation of Article 20 of the LOSC. On 10 November 2004, an unidentified submarine did not show its flag when it entered Japan's territorial waters off Okinawa near Sakishima Gunto and navigated without surfacing.[67] A maritime security operation was formed based

---

64 See Ko Nakamura, *The Passage Through the Territorial Sea of Foreign Warships Carrying Nuclear Weapons: An Interpretation of the Convention on the Territorial Sea and the Contiguous Zone and Its Application to the Broken Soviet Nuclear-Powered Submarine*, 25 Japanese Annual of International Law 1 (1982), p. 3.

65 *Id.* at 4.

66 *Id.*

67 Yukiya Hamamoto, *The Incident of a Submarine Navigating Underwater in Japan's Territorial Sea*, 48 The Japanese Annual of International Law 123 (2005); *State Practice of Japan*, 11 Asian Yearbook of International Law 187 (2003–2004), pp. 194–195. Article 20 of LOSC

on Article 82 of the Self-Defense Force Act[68] and tracked the submarine until it reached 500 kilometers northwest of Okinawa Island. The unidentified submarine turned out to be a Chinese nuclear submarine.[69] This marked the first time that Japan applied Cabinet Decision of 24 December 1996[70] that enabled the Self-Defense Forces to chase a submerged foreign submarine that does not fly a flag.

The Japanese government also considered the entry of a Chinese naval reconnaissance vessel into Japanese territorial water on 15 June 2016 not as being innocent.[71] A Maritime Self-Defense Force P-3C patrol aircraft identified the vessel entering the Japanese territorial waters west of Kuchinoerabu Island and warned it to exit the waters. Unlike in the case of the disguised submarine in 2004, no order was issued for the Self-Defense Forces to take maritime security measures because the vessel left the waters south of Yakushima Island in one and a half hours. On that occasion, the Defense Minister of Japan expressed his view that "[p]rior notifications should be made for a warship's entry into territorial waters."[72]

(b) "Suspicious Vessels"

Foreign vessels in the territorial sea are sometimes identified as being "suspicious vessels" (*fushin-sen*). The term suspicious vessels does not appear in Japanese law, but it is widely used in government documents and by the media. Suspicious vessels are often disguised with fraudulent vessel names, flags, or unnecessary equipment on board or which navigate in a suspicious manner. The navigation of such vessels is considered to be non-innocent.

On 23 March 1999, two fishing vessels were found hovering within the internal waters of Japan off Noto Peninsula and were chased by Japanese patrol boats. The vessels had disguised themselves by having Japanese fishing boat names but were equipped with unnecessary antennas.[73] The Japanese authorities chased the vessels on the grounds that the vessel had refused to be

---

requires submarines and other underwater vehicles to navigate on the surface and to show their flag in the territorial sea.

68 Act No. 165 of 9 June 1954.

69 Hamamoto, supra note 67, p. 126.

70 See supra note 60.

71 *Chinese naval ship enters Japan's territorial waters*, *The Japan Times*, (16 June 2016).

72 *China says it does not need Japanese permission to sail ships through Tokara Strait*, *The Japan Times*, (18 June 2016).

73 See Atsuko Kanehara, *The Japanese Legal System concerning Innocent Passage of Foreign Vessels*, 42 Japanese Annual of International Law 90 (1999), p. 92.

inspected as required under Article 74, paragraph 3, of the Fisheries Act.[74] The Japanese patrol boats delivered warning shots and the vessels left Japanese waters.[75]

This incident precipitated the revision of the Japan Coast Guard Act to allow JCG officers to use arms directly against foreign vessels in certain situations. The JCG and the Japan Maritime Self Defense Force undergo joint training and have created a manual for joint actions.[76] The primary role of JCG in reacting to suspicious vessels is acknowledged with the Japan Maritime Self-Defense Force being a supporting role when the JCG has difficulties reacting.[77]

3 *Temporary Suspension of Non-Innocent Passage and the Use of Force*

Article 20 of the Japan Coast Guard Act[78] stipulates that, when it is necessary to stop the passage of a foreign vessel navigating in the territorial sea, Coast Guard officers may use arms with Article 7 of the Police Duties Execution Act applying *mutatis mutandis*.[79]

However, Coast Guard officers are to refrain from using force except in the case of self-defense[80] or to avert clear danger.[81] The use of force is only authorized against a person who is committing a violent and dangerous crime, a person who is suspected of having committed a violent and dangerous crime, or a person who is resisting arrest.[82]

The 2001 revision of the Japan Coast Guard Act added paragraph 2 to Article 20, that allows Coast Guard officials to use arms directly against foreign vessels when they refuse to stop and resist inspection. To utilize this provision, the Coast Guard must demonstrate:

(1) the passage of the foreign vessel in question in the internal waters and territorial sea of Japan is not innocent in accordance with Article 19 of the LOSC;

(2) there is a probability that the same act will be repeated in the future if the navigation in question is left uncontrolled;

---

74 Fisheries Act, supra note 36, Article 74, paragraph 3 stipulates that fisheries surveillance officers may inspect a vessel and ask the person concerned questions when considered necessary.

75 Kanehara, supra note 73, p. 92.

76 Act No. 28 of 27 April 1948.

77 Junji Okuzono, Kaijyōhoanchō: Kaijyōjieitaikankei no henka to kaizokutaishohō, in Kaizokutaishohō no kenkyu (Jun Tsuruta ed., 2016), at 185.

78 Japan Coast Guard Act, supra note 76.

79 Act No. 136 of 12 July 1948.

80 Art. 36 of the Criminal Code, Act No. 45 of 24 April 1907.

81 *Id.* Art. 37.

82 Police Duties Execution Act, supra note 79, Art. 7.

(3) there is a to believe that the navigation in question is related to preparation to commit a serious crime in the territory of Japan;[83] and
(4) that the navigation must be temporarily suspended to allow the Coast Guard to inspect in order to prevent the commission of a serious crime.

There have been heated discussions regarding the possible use of weapons by the Self-Defense Forces in situations where there is no armed attack but is a threat to the peace and security of Japan such as in the case of submerged foreign submarines. The Cabinet Decision of 14 May 2015 indicates the government's policy that the Self-Defense Forces may take maritime security measures against foreign military vessels whose navigation in the Japanese territorial waters is not considered innocent.[84]

IV Navigation of Foreign Vessels in Straits

1 *Legislation on Straits in Japan*

The Appendix to the 1996 Act on the Territorial Sea and Contiguous Zone provides that "for the time being," a three nautical mile territorial sea is applied to the Sōya Strait, the Tsugaru Strait, the eastern and western channels of the Tsushima Strait, and the Ōsumi Strait.[85] Respecting the treatment of these straits, the 1977 Act on the Territorial Sea included the same provision.[86] When this provisional regime was established by the 1977 Act, it was considered that the State practice on international straits and the transit passage was inadequate.[87] Japan continues to limit the width of its territorial sea in this area opting not to adopt the regime of international straits under LOSC into its domestic law.

2 *Japan as a User State of International Straits*

Japan has protested when other States have planned to close their international straits or when military exercises have been conducted close to international straits.[88] This indicates Japan's support for freedom of navigation.

---

83 A serious crime means a crime which is punished by death penalty, life imprisonment, or imprisonment of more than 3 years under the Japanese Criminal Code, supra note 80 and see Japan Coast Guard Act, supra note 76, Art. 20(2).

84 Cabinet Decision of 14 May 2015, *available at*: www.cas.go.jp/jp/gaiyou/jimu/pdf/gaikoku-gunkantaisho.pdf.

85 Territorial Sea Act, 1996, supra note 30.

86 Territorial Sea Act, 1977, supra note 29.

87 Takata, supra note 62, p. 132.

88 When China held military exercises in 1995 north of Taiwan, the Japanese Foreign Ministry stated that this could imperil ships passing in the area. See Ko Swan Sik, *Chronicle*

Moreover, Japan cooperates with States bordering international straits as recommended in Article 43 of the LOSC.[89] Japan has been providing significant logistical and monetary support to the States bordering the Strait of Malacca since 1968. It is currently involved in two projects concerning the introduction of a system to automatically identify small vessels and the maintenance of facilities for navigational aids through private organizations such as the Strait of Malacca Council and the Nippon Foundation.[90]

V Navigation of Foreign Vessels in the EEZ

1 *Legislation That Affects Navigational Rights within the EEZ*

Japan established its 200 nautical mile EEZ pursuant to the 1996 Act on the Exclusive Economic Zone and Continental Shelf.[91] Article 3, paragraph 1, which corresponds to Article 56, paragraph 1 of the LOSC, stipulates that the relevant Japanese law and the punishment stipulated applies to the exploration, exploitation, conservation and management of the natural resources, the establishment and use of artificial islands, installations and structures, the protection and preservation of the marine environment, and marine scientific research in the EEZ and continental shelf.

An example of a Japanese law applicable to foreign vessels' activities in the EEZ is the 1996 Act on the Exercise of Sovereign Rights over Fishing and Other Activities in the Exclusive Economic Zone.[92] Article 3, paragraph 1 states that the Act is applicable to fishing, sampling and exploration activities by foreign nationals in the EEZ. However, under Article 3, paragraph 2, the application of the Fisheries Act[93] to foreign nationals in the EEZ is excluded except for Article 74 (Fisheries Supervising Public Officers), Article 141 (punishment of a person who violated the Act), and Article 145 (punishment of juridical person). Article 141 of the Fisheries Act provides that a person who violates the Act may be

of Events and Incidents Relating to Asia with Relevance to International Law July 1995–June 1996, 6 Asian Yearbook of International Law 331 (1996), p. 362.

89 LOSC, supra note 44, Article 43 urges user States and strait States to cooperate in the establishment and maintenance in a strait of necessary navigational and safety aids or other improvements in aid of international navigation as well as for the prevention, reduction and control of pollution from ships.

90 Japan Maritime Center, supra note 15, pp. 68–69.

91 Act No. 74 of 14 June 1996.

92 Act No. 76 of 14 June 1996.

93 Fisheries Act, supra note 36.

punished "by imprisonment with work for not more than six months or a fine of not more than 300,000 yen."

As to the protection and conservation of marine living resources in the EEZ, the 1996 Act on Preservation and Control of Marine Living Resources[94] mandates that the Minister of Agriculture, Forestry and Fisheries is to establish a basic plan for the preservation and control of marine living resources in the EEZ, including the total allowable catch (TAC) for each category of fisheries.

With regard to marine scientific research, Japan issued the Guideline for Conducting Marine Scientific Research in Areas under National Jurisdiction of Japan in 1996.[95] According to the Guideline:

> any foreign nationals or foreign institutions, whether private or public, are requested to obtain consent of the Government of Japan prior to conducting marine scientific research in the territorial sea or in the exclusive economic zone or on the continental shelf of Japan.

Such a request for consent is to be made through diplomatic channels to the Ministry of Foreign Affairs of Japan. If the research project involves catching, taking or exploration of marine animals and/or plants in the EEZ of Japan, a separate approval from the Ministry of Agriculture, Forestry and Fisheries of Japan under the 1996 EEZ Act[96] is necessary.

Problems remain in the implementation of the Guideline in the areas where the EEZs and continental shelf have not been delimited between Japan and China and between Japan and Korea. Japan and China exchanged *notes verbales* in 2001 to establish a prior notification system on marine scientific research in the East China Sea areas.[97]

The Act on Prevention of Marine Pollution and Maritime Disaster[98] applies to foreign vessels navigating in the EEZ of Japan under certain conditions.[99] The Act establishes a centralized mechanism for the protection of the marine

---

94 Act No. 77 of 14 June 1996.

95 Ministry of Foreign Affairs of Japan, *The Guideline for Conducting Marine Scientific Research in Areas under National Jurisdiction of Japan of July 20, 1996*, 33 Law of the Sea Bull. 38 (1997).

96 EEZ Act, supra note 92.

97 Ministry of Foreign Affairs of Japan, Press Release of 13 February 2001, available at: www.mofa.go.jp/mofaj/press/release/13/pdfs/rls_0213d.pdf.

98 Act on the Prevention of Marine Pollution and Maritime Disaster, supra note 38.

99 The Cabinet Order concerning the Application of the Act concerning the Prevention of Marine Pollution and Maritime Disaster in the Exclusive Economic Zone (Cabinet Order No. 102 of 26 June 1996, amended by Cabinet Order No. 297 of 12 December 2012) excludes certain kinds of foreign vessels conducting exploration and exploitation activities on the

environment from various sources of marine pollution. The Act prohibits the discharge of oil[100] and noxious liquid substances[101] as well as the dumping of wastes into the sea from ships, offshore facilities and aircraft. The Act also obliges ship owners and owners/managers of offshore facilities to take preventive and response measures against marine pollution from substances and wastes.

2 *Foreign Vessels within Japan's EEZ or Japanese Vessels in Other States' EEZs*

Foreign vessels enjoy the freedom of navigation in the Japanese EEZ in in principle. The following examples represent situations where Japan has needed to interfere with the navigation of foreign vessels in its EEZ or refrain from navigating in other States' EEZs in order to safeguard national and environmental interests.

(a) Vessel-Source Marine Pollution

Serious marine pollution serves as a reason for Japanese authorities to intervene in the navigation of foreign vessels in the EEZ. On the 2 January 1997, the Russian tanker *Nakhodka* was navigating from Shanghai to Petropavlovsk carrying 19,000kl of medium fuel oil. Because of stormy weather, the *Nakhodka* broke in two sections 57 n.m. (106 km) north-east of the Oki Islands in Shimane Prefecture. The stern soon sank and the upturned bow section grounded on rocks 200 meters from the shore in Fukui Prefecture. The accident resulted in a large amount of spilled oil which polluted the coast of 10 prefectures facing the Sea of Japan, over a distance of more than 1,000 km.[102] The JCG, the Maritime Self-Defense Force, the Ports and Harbors Bureau (of the then Ministry of Transport), the Maritime Disaster Prevention Center, local governments, the fishing industry, and local residents undertook clean-up operations. They

---

continental shelf of Japan and those navigating between Japanese ports from the application of the Act relating to the Prevention of Marine Pollution and Maritime Disaster.

100 Act on the Prevention of Marine Pollution and Maritime Disaster, supra note 38, Article 3(2) defines "oil" as including crude oil, heavy oil, lubricating oil, light oil, kerosene, volatile oil and other oils and oily mixture containing these oils.

101 *Ibid.*, Article 3(3) defines "noxious liquid substances" that includes liquid substances other than oil, which is carried as liquid cargo in bulk by a ship, and water ballast, tank washing water and other unnecessary liquid substances which has been generated in a ship containing these substances (excluding such substances as liquid petroleum gas and other substances that are not liquid at the normal temperature and excluding liquid substances loaded on a ship for the purpose of throwing and combustion for disposal in the sea area).

102 See International Oil Pollution Compensation Fund (IOPC Fund), Annual Report 2002, *available at:* http://www.iopcfunds.org.

collected about 6,240kl of oil.[103] The *Nakhodka* incident led Japan to revise the Act relating to the Prevention of Marine Pollution and Maritime Disaster[104] in order to respond better to large-scale oil pollutions occurring outside the territorial seas of Japan and to mandate the creation of contingency plans.

(b) Shipment of Highly Radioactive Materials

A series of shipments of highly radioactive materials, plutonium, high level nuclear wastes (HLW) and mixed plutonium/uranium oxide (MOX) fuel, from France to Japan starting in 1992 triggered protests by States in Africa, South America and the South Pacific.[105] The *Akatsuki Maru* first transported 2,200 pounds of plutonium from France to Japan in 1992, which was followed by a series of transportation of HLW and MOX fuel by the *Pacific Pintail*, the *Pacific Teal*, and the *Pacific Swan* in the following years.[106] Due to the protests, the Japanese government stated that its ships carrying highly radioactive materials would avoid entering the EEZs of all States.[107]

VI Routeing Arrangements

Japan has designated passage lanes within ports as well as outside ports and river areas for the purpose of safety, development and environmental preservation. The Act on Port Regulations[108] provides that if a vessel other than "miscellaneous vessels"[109] enters, leaves or passes through specified ports,[110] it must use the passage prescribed by the Ordinance of the Ministry of Land, Infrastructure, Transport and Tourism.[111] This rule does not apply if a vessel

103 The Ministry of Land, Infrastructure, Transport and Tourism, *Kaiyō osen ni taisuru torikumi*, Mar. 2004, at 15. According to the 2002 IOPC Funds Report, *ibid.*, the clean-up operations generated 40,000 tonnes of oily wastes.

104 Act on the Prevention of Marine Pollution and Maritime Disaster, supra note 38.

105 See Jon M. Van Dyke, *Sea Shipment of Japanese Plutonium under International Law*, 24 Ocean Dev. & Int'l L. 399 (1993).

106 Jon M. Van Dyke, *The Legal Regime Governing Sea Transport of Ultrahazardous Radioactive Materials*, 33 Ocean Dev. & Int'l L. 77, 78 (2002).

107 See Jon M. Van Dyke, *Balancing Navigational Freedom with Environmental and Security Concerns*, 2003 Colo. J. Int'l Envtl. Law & Pol'y 19, 22 (2003) and Van Dyke, supra note 105 at 399–400.

108 Act No. 174 of 15 July 1948.

109 Miscellaneous vessels include: a steam launch, barge, or boat, a ship that is operated solely using oars and paddles, or a ship that is operated mainly using oars and paddles.

110 A specified port is a port which a deep-draft vessel is able to enter and leave, or a port that a foreign vessel regularly enters and leaves, as specified by the Cabinet Order.

111 Act on Port Regulations, supra note 108, Art. 12.

is attempting to prevent a marine accident or if there are other compelling reasons.

There are currently no routeing arrangements based upon the protection of marine living resources. However, the marine protected areas have been designated under domestic law for the purposes of protecting natural parks and wild animals, aquatic animals and plants, and preserving world heritage sites. The 2008 Basic Plan on Ocean Policy promotes the establishment of marine protected areas for the protection of marine biodiversity and the sustainable use of aquatic resources in the light of the Convention on Biological Diversity[112] and other relevant international agreements.[113]

VII Conclusion

Considering the importance of the oceans for Japan in international trade, Japan has been consistent in maintaining freedom of navigation as a high priority.

Recent political and legislative developments, however, indicate a modest shift in Japan's priorities to focus on safeguarding maritime security interests. The 2008 Act on Navigation of Foreign Ships through the Territorial Sea and Internal Waters[114] was enacted as a consequence of difficulties in taking measures against "suspicious vessels" under the previous legislation. The recent legislation on peace and security has expanded the mandate of the Japan Self-Defense Forces to include the inspection of foreign vessels with the consent of the flag State within and beyond the Japanese territorial waters[115] unprecedented in the history of Japan after World War II.

It is difficult to evaluate in the abstract whether the Japanese laws concerning navigation of foreign vessels are in conformity or contravention with the

112 Convention on Biological Diversity, 1760 *U.N.T.S.* 57.

113 The 2008 Basic Plan on Ocean Policy formulated under the Basic Act on Ocean Policy (Act No. 33 of April 27, 2007) states that

> [a]s one of the means to ensure the biodiversity and realize sustainable use of fishery resources, the government should, in accordance with the Convention on Biological Diversity and other international agreements, clarify how to establish marine protected areas in Japan under coordination between related ministries and appropriately promote the establishment thereof (Chapter 2, Section 2(1)).

A provisional translation of the Basic Plan on Ocean Policy can be found *at*: http://www.kantei.go.jp/jp/singi/kaiyou/kihonkeikaku/080318kihonkeikaku_JE.pdf.

114 Act on the Navigation of Foreign Ships through the Territorial Sea, supra note 45.

115 Act on Ship Inspection Operations in Situations related to Peace and Security, Act No. 145 of 6 December 2000.

LOSC. It can be said, however, that the Japanese legislators have been careful since Japan has been a strong supporter of the LOSC while aware that the Convention contains scope for State practice.

Acknowledgement

The author would like to thank Ms. Katherine Cherry D. Bandanwal for her assistance in research. JSPS KAKENHI Grant Number 26780027.

CHAPTER 4

South Korea's Regulation on Navigation of Foreign Vessels

Seokwoo Lee and Young Kil Park

I Introduction

Conventional freedom of navigation was greatly restricted under the 1982 United Nations Convention on the Law of the Sea (hereinafter UNCLOS).[1] The boundary of territorial waters expanded to a maximum of 12 nautical miles and other restrictions on free navigation were introduced such as the requirement of coastal state approval before the conducting of marine scientific research in the exclusive economic zone (EEZ). Moreover, the UNCLOS does not include clear standards on the extent to which foreign military activities are permissible in a coastal states' EEZ without the coastal states' consent and whether conducting a marine survey should be recognized within the freedom of navigation.

Since Korea's ratification of the UNCLOS in 1996, Korea has sought to implement UNCLOS through the enactment of appropriate domestic law such as the establishment of the Korean EEZ through the enactment of Korea's Exclusive Economic Zone Act (the EEZ Act) in 1996.

This chapter will review Korea's domestic legislation on the navigation of foreign vessels in Korean waters and provide an assessment of Korea's implementation of the UNCLOS. The chapter examines the legal status and practices respecting Korea's territorial sea, EEZ, the passage of North Korean vessels, the Proliferation Security Initiative (PSI) and relevant UN Security Council resolutions.

II Regulation of Foreign Vessels in the Territorial Sea

The Territorial Sea and Contiguous Zone Act was enacted on 6 December 1995, prior to Korea's ratification of UNCLOS. Article 5(1) of the Territorial Sea and

1 U.N. Convention on the Law of the Sea, 10 December 1982, 1833 *U.N.T.S.* 397.

 | DOI:10.1163/9789004396272_005

Contiguous Zone Act permits the right of innocent passage in the territorial sea "so long as it is not prejudicial to peace, public order or security of the Republic of Korea," and provides, in paragraph 2, a list of 13 acts, including underwater activities, fishing activities and surveying, that are deemed to be "prejudicial to peace, public order or security." Vessel activities not covered by the 13 acts are seen as innocent. Paragraph 3 of the same Article provides for the temporary suspension of innocent passage in specified areas of the territorial sea "as prescribed by Presidential Decree if such suspension is essential for the security of the Republic of Korea." The Enforcement Decree of the Act places a narrow construction on the temporary suspension with the Minister of National Defense only to implement such a suspension where there has been advance deliberation by the State Council, approval of the President and due notice given of the temporarily suspended waters, including the period and grounds for suspension. Pursuant to Article 6 of the same Act, if a foreign ship (excluding foreign warships and government ships operated for non-commercial purposes) is deemed to have violated Article 5, the authorities concerned may stop, search or seize the ship, or issue other necessary orders or take other necessary measures. Further, pursuant to Article 8(1), the crew or others on board a foreign vessel who have violated Article 5(2) or (3) may be punished by imprisonment for not more than five years or a fine not exceeding 300 million won, and when necessary, the ship, its equipment, cargo, or other articles may be seized.

During the Third Conference on the Law of the Sea, the issue was raised as to whether it was necessary for foreign warships to give prior notice before entering a territorial sea. However, with no consensus on the matter, there is no such provision is in the UNCLOS. The Territorial Sea and Contiguous Zone Act provides in Article 5(1) in relevant part that:

> when a foreign warship or government ship operated for non-commercial purposes intends to pass through the territorial sea, it shall give prior notice to the authorities concerned as prescribed by Presidential Decree.

In accordance with this Article, the Enforcement Decree stipulates that applicable vessels must notify the Minister of Foreign Affairs "not later than three days" prior to its passage, giving the name, type and official number of the ship, the purpose of the passage, the passage route and schedule. Further, pursuant to Article 9, if a foreign warship or government ship operated for non-commercial purposes or its crew or passengers on board violate this Act or other relevant Acts and subordinate statutes, such a vessel may be required to remedy the violation or leave the territorial sea.

There has been criticism that the prior notice of foreign warships requirement implemented by Korea is not consistent with the UNCLOS. The U.S. Department of State has indirectly criticized Korea's prior notice requirement by noting that UNCLOS is silent on the issue of a prior notice requirement to coastal states for innocent passage, regardless of the nature of the vessel.[2] There are views within Korea questioning how much the three-day prior notice requirement contributes to national security.[3] This is based on the assumption that if a warship was passing through with hostile intent, it is unlikely to give prior notice.

The Territorial Sea and Contiguous Zone Act has recently been revised to add a number of matters unregulated by the 1995 Act concerning Korea's territorial sea or contiguous zone that are to be governed in accordance with treaties and customary international law.[4] This revision was intended to indicate a willingness by Korea to comply with international law in matters respecting the territorial sea and contiguous zone. The amendments can also be read as prioritizing the UNCLOS and customary international law over other laws (except for the Act).

The Maritime Safety Act regulates non-Korean vessels in order to ensure safety of navigation. Pursuant to Article 32(1), non-Korean vessels may not to pass through the internal waters of Korea without permission from the Minister of Oceans and Fisheries.[5] However, Article 32(2) recognizes an exception

2 United States, Dep't of State, *Limits in the Seas* No. 121, "Straight Baseline and Territorial Sea Baseline: South Korea", Sept. 30, 1988. For detailed discussion on innocent passage in general, see: D.H.N. Johnson, "Innocent Passage, Transit Passage", in *Encyclopedia of Public International Law*, Vol. 11; K. Hakapää and E.J. Molenaar, "Innocent passage – Past and Present," *Marine Policy*, Vol. 23, p. 131, 1998, R.R; and Churchill and A.V. Lowe, *The Law of the Sea*, 3rd ed., Manchester: Manchester Univ. Press, 1999.

3 Lee Chang-Wee, "A Study on the History and the Relevant Issues on the Territorial Sea of Korea", *Kangwon Law Journal*, Vol. 31 (Oct. 2010), pp. 219–220 (Korean).

4 Territorial Sea and Contiguous Zone Act, Article 7, Amended Mar. 21, 2017, Act No. 14607.

5 Maritime Safety Act, Article 32 (Passage of Non-Korean Vessels):

(1) No non-Korean vessel shall pass through inland waters of the Republic of Korea without permission there from the Minister of Oceans and Fisheries. (Amended by Act No. 11690, Mar. 23, 2013).

(2) Notwithstanding paragraph (1), a vessel may uninterruptedly and quickly pass through a sea area included in internal waters along the straight line defined in Article 2 (2) of the Territorial Sea and Contiguous Zone Act without anchoring, halting, mooring, or loitering: Provided, that the foregoing shall not apply to the following cases:

1. Where it is necessary due to a force majeure event or shipwreck;
2. Where it is necessary to rescue a human life or a vessel or aircraft in peril or in distress;
3. Other cases specified by Ordinance of the Ministry of Oceans and Fisheries, such as entry into a port or harbor of the Republic of Korea.

by allowing uninterrupted and quick passage through the sea area that are internal waters without the vessel anchoring, halting, mooring, or loitering on the basis of straight baselines defined in Article 2(2) of the Territorial Sea and Contiguous Zone Act,. This exception is in accordance with Article 8(2) of the UNCLOS.

Article 33 of the Maritime Safety Act designates as "special vessels" nuclear-powered vessels, vessels carrying hazardous cargo such as nuclear substances etc., and requires that these non-Korean vessels passing through Korea's territorial sea or its internal waters take extraordinary safety measures, such as carrying documents specified by the International Convention for the Safety of Life at Sea and other relevant international agreements or complying with special preventive measures prescribed by the Ordinance of the Ministry of Oceans and Fisheries.

III Navigation of Foreign Vessels in Korean Straits

Korea has two straits, the Korea Strait and the Jeju Strait, both of which have important strategic value.

The Korea Strait lies between the southern tip of the Korean peninsula and Japan's Tsushima Island. The narrowest breadth between the baselines of the two states is 22.75 nm. Within this area the two states have designated a minimum 3 nm as their territorial seas leaving about 17 nm for the EEZ. Thus, ships are able to navigate through the strait relying upon their high-seas right to freedom of navigation, which has few restrictions.

The well-known reasons for reducing the breadth of Korea's territorial sea to 3 nm in this area are twofold: first, because of the practical difficulty in exclusively regulating the Korea Strait and second, to avoid potential conflict with other states. There has been some criticism, however, that the territorial sea of the two states should be extended to the median line in order to strengthen sovereignty over the waters and to exercise corresponding control over foreign vessels.[6]

In contrast to the Korea Strait for which the government has clearly established a territorial sea to 3 nm, Korea has not been clear regarding a territorial sea for the Jeju Strait. If 12 nm from the straight baselines from the Korean

(3) Matters necessary for the submission of documents necessary for the permission under paragraph (1) and other measures shall be prescribed by Ordinance of the Ministry of Oceans and Fisheries. (Amended by Act No. 11690, Mar. 23, 2013).

6 See: Kim Myung Gi, "Problems of Transit Passage through the Korea Straits in the Convention on the Law of the Sea," *Journal of Korean Society of International Law* Vol.54 (Dec. 1983), 15–37 (in Korean).

peninsula and 12 nm from the normal baseline north of Jeju Island were applied to the Jeju Strait, it would eliminate the EEZ in the Jeju Strait. Thus, the Jeju Strait would be a strait used for international navigation between one part of the high seas or EEZ to another part of the high seas or EEZ in the Yellow Sea, the East China Sea or the East Sea. Transit passage could apply which, while increasing the possible scope of regulation and jurisdiction that could be exercised by Korea as the littoral state, would result in Korea bearing the burden of permitting the right of flight over the area by foreign aircraft. There is the argument that because there exists "a route through the high seas or through an EEZ of similar convenience" beyond Jeju Island, the Jeju Strait should not be considered an international strait to which "transit passage" applies pursuant to Article 38(1) of the UNCLOS. If so, the Jeju Strait would be subject to innocent passage and not transit passage. There is strong support for this argument as the routeing would only entail 40 miles of travel. An unclear interpretation exists since the Enforcement Decree of the Territorial Sea and Contiguous Zone Act provides in Article 4 that foreign warships or governmental ships operating for a noncommercial purpose must give three-day's prior notice to the Ministry of Foreign Affairs of Korea, "except in cases where the area of the sea through which the said ship navigates forms a strait used for international navigation in which no high seas lanes exist." It is apparent that this provision was written with the Jeju Strait in mind.

There is no clear guideline as to what a "route through the high seas or through an EEZ of similar convenience" means or who determines the existence of such a route.

IV Navigation of Foreign Vessels in the EEZ

After ratifying the UNCLOS, Korea enacted the Exclusive Economic Zone Act (EEZ Act) on 8 August 1996. Consisting of only five articles, the Act is a framework for which the specifics are provided in other statutes. The 1996 EEZ Act did not include provisions relating to the continental shelf. The Korean government recently amended the Act changing the title to the "EEZ and Continental Shelf Act" and indicating the boundaries and jurisdiction of Korea's EEZ and continental shelf.

The UNCLOS does not provide clear definitions of artificial islands, installments and structures though Article 60(1) distinguishes the three features. However, artificial islands, installations and structures have the same legal status. Korea's Maritime Safety Act uses the terminology "marine facility" to represent all three features and defines a marine facility as:

> a bridge, tunnel, cable, artificial island, or facility fixed to the ocean floor or a structure floating on the water for the purpose of exploration and development of resources, scientific marine surveys, mooring and repair of vessels, loading to and unloading from vessels, floating housing, tourism, leisure, etc., which is not a vessel.

The best known marine facility in Korea's EEZ is the Ieodo Ocean Research Station, which was completed in 2003. The underwater rock, Ieodo, is located 149 km from Marado, Korea's southernmost island and 287 km from China's Yushandao Island. The Ieodo Ocean Research Station is located approximately 700 m from the tip of Ieodo. China has expressed the view that the construction of the Korean research station was inconsistent with the UNCLOS.[7] The Korean government claims that it is an exercise of jurisdiction within the country's EEZ. The Station is clearly located on the Korean side of a provisional median line between Korea and China. The legal issue is whether a state has the right to build a scientific facility within an EEZ that overlaps with an adjacent state if the facility is built on the state's side of a provisional median line.

Although there is controversy surrounding the protection of the Ieodo Ocean Research Station and the potential designation of a protection zone for safe navigation in its surrounding waters, Korea has yet to designate a protection zone pursuant to the Maritime Safety Act. Maritime charts used in international navigation indicate a safe water zone within the 500 m radius of Ieodo.

Regarding protection zones, Article 8 of the Maritime Safety Act allows for the designation of a "zone for the safe navigation of vessels and the protection of a marine facility," and provides details for the same. The Enforcement Decree for the Act is consistent with the UNCLOS provision[8] stipulating in Article 5(2) that the protection zone is to be determined in consideration of the volume of vessel traffic in the waters around the maritime facility located in the EEZ and continental shelf and in consideration of the international standard provided for in the UNCLOS.

According to Article 12 of the Maritime Security Act, if there is a reason to believe that a vessel is: interfering with safe navigation of another vessel; or suspected of carrying weapons of mass destruction or other types of weapons or related materials; the Coast Guard may conduct a maritime inspection of the vessel. Maritime inspection within the meaning of this provision according to Article 2 includes: "ordering the concerned vessels etc. to stop, boarding of

---

7 *Yonhap News*, Oct. 6, 2004 (Korean), www.news.v.daum.net/v/20041006054928326?f=0.

8 U.N. Convention on the Law of the Sea, *supra* note 1, Article 60.

the ship, questioning, verifying facts, searching the ship, or taking other necessary measures." Further, pursuant to Article 13, if there is a reason to believe that the ship is uncooperative with the inspection, attempting flight, violating or about to violate a domestic law or treaty signed or ratified by Korea, then the Coast Guard may pursue or seize the ship.

Article 17(2) of the Maritime Security Act allows the use of machine guns in addition to personal firearms where it states that:

1. Where it undertakes operations related to national security such as counterespionage or counterterrorism operation
2. In case it belongs to any one of paragraph (1), where the vessel and the offender has attacked or intends to attack the security forces with a dangerous object such as body of the ship, weapon, deadly weapon, etc.
3. Where the vessel has not followed the order to stop or order to move more than three times and, as a group, has harmed or intended to harm the security forces.[9]

Also, in accordance with the Act on the Performance of Duties by Police Officers, Article 18 of the Maritime Security Act permits the use of police equipment such as handcuffs, ropes, police batons, and shields regularly used in performing police duties. Article 5(1) of the Presidential Decree of the Act[10] allows the use of water cannons. In order to prevent abuse in using this additional equipment and gear, Article 5(2) imposes a limit on their use, specifically to be used "in accordance with general usage, to use the minimum degree necessary to achieve its purpose, and to minimize harm to life or body." As the result of the killing of a Korean Coast Guard officer by Chinese fishermen who were engaged in illegal fishing in 2011, Korea expanded the use of machine guns to halt illegal fishing done by Chinese fishing vessels in Korean waters.

V Fishing Control in the West/Yellow Sea

As the title indicates, the Act on the Exercise of Sovereign Rights on Foreigner Fishing, etc. within the Exclusive Economic Zone (hereinafter Act on the Exercise of Sovereign Rights within the EEZ), deals with the fishing of foreigners. The Act provides in Article 4 that: "No foreigner may conduct fishery activities in an exclusive economic zone set by Presidential Decree for the purpose of protecting fishery resources or regulating fisheries (hereinafter referred to as 'Specifically Prohibited Zones')". Article 2 of the Enforcement Decree for the

9 The Maritime Security Act, Article 17(2), Amended Apr. 18, 2017, Act No. 14810.
10 The Enforcement Decree of the Maritime Security Act, Aug. 13, 2012, Decree No. 24040.

Act designates four Specifically Prohibited Zones: zones bordering North Korea in the East Sea and Yellow Sea; a zone of EEZ in the Korea Strait up to 12 nm from the nearest baselines; and a zone designated by the decree of the Ministry of Oceans and Fisheries for the purpose of the protection of fishery resources or fishery coordination as egg laying places or habitats of fishery resources.

The Act prescribes the imposition of fines and security payments. In an attempt to eradicate illegal Chinese fishing, the Korean government has continuously strengthened the penalties in the Act. According to Article 16(2) of the Act, as amended on December 27, 2016, unauthorized fishing activities may be punished with a fine not exceeding 300 million won. Violations of restrictions and conditions in a permit may be punished with a fine not exceeding 200 million won and the owner or the captain of a fishing vessel that does not comply with an order to stop may be fined up to 100 million won.[11]

In accordance with Article 23(1) of the Act, a public prosecutor or judicial police officer may:

> stop, board, search, seize the vessel that violates this Act or orders, restrictions or conditions issued or imposed under this Act or take other necessary measures with respect to the captain of such vessel or other violators.

According to Article 8(2) of the Enforcement Decree of the Act, "Where the captain of a violating vessel or other offender is sentenced to a penalty of a fine and such a sentence becomes final, the public prosecutor shall forthwith give a notice of the judgment to the State of registry of the violating vessel."

VI Marine Scientific Research within Korea's EEZ

Pursuant to Article 246 of the UNCLOS, consent by the coastal state is necessary for other States or competent international organizations to conduct MSR within an EEZ or on the continental shelf. Under "normal circumstances," coastal states are to grant their consent for MSR projects in their EEZ or on their continental shelf which are "to be carried out in accordance with this Convention exclusively for peaceful purposes and in order to increase scientific knowledge of the marine environment for the benefit of mankind."[12]

---

11 See Article 17 and Article 17(2) of the Act.

12 U.N. Convention on the Law of the Sea, *supra* note 1, Article 246(3).

Korea enacted the Marine Scientific Research Act on January 5, 1995, and it entered into force on July 6 of the same year. The Act's scope of application includes internal waters, territorial sea, the EEZ and continental shelf. While the UNCLOS provides no definition of MSR, Article 2(1) of the Korean Act defines MSR as "conducting research, exploration, etc. into the seabed, subsoil, superjacent waters, and lower atmosphere to study and discover the natural phenomena of the sea." When foreigners want to conduct MSR in the EEZ or continental shelf of Korea, they must submit a research plan to the Minister of Oceans and Fisheries through the Minister of Foreign Affairs six months in advance of the date of the desired activity. However, instead of listing the four grounds for rejection of approval set out in UNCLOS Article 246(5), the Marine Scientific Research Act lists seven grounds for refusal in Article 7(4).

Article 19(2) of the UNCLOS provides examples of what is prejudicial passage in the territorial sea, which includes "the carrying out of research or survey activities." No distinction is drawn between MSR and a hydrographic survey or hydrographic research, and whether these activities are consistent with innocent passage. In Korea's Act on the Establishment, Management, etc. of Spatial Data "hydrographic survey" is defined as "the survey of the depth of water, terrestrial magnetism, gravity, topography, geological features and the survey of the baseline and the land thereunder" and "hydrographic research" is defined as "hydrographical survey, oceanographic observation, sea lane research, sea surface name research for the purposes of maritime traffic safety; preservation, use, development of the ocean; securing of maritime jurisdiction; and prevention of marine disasters."[13] Article 4 of the Act excludes the following from its scope of application: regional surveys (excluding cadastral surveys); surveys that do not require a high degree of precision; surveys or hydrographical research conducted for pure academic research or military use; and exploratory hydrographical research pursuant to the Submarine Mineral Resources Development Act where the survey or hydrographic research has been officially announced by the Minister of Land, Infrastructure, and Transport and the Minister of Oceans and Fisheries. The Act, however, is silent on regulations applicable to foreign governments that undertake hydrographic surveys or research in Korean territorial waters or its EEZ. Thus, as with the UNCLOS, the domestic law is unclear as to whether foreign actors must obtain the consent of Korea before they can undertake hydrographic surveys or research in Korean waters.

13 Act on the Establishment, Management, etc. of Spatial Data, Article 2.

On 14 April 2006, Japan notified the International Hydrographic Organization (IHO) of its plans for a hydrographic survey in the waters near Dokdo.[14] This raised tensions between Korea and Japan. At the time, there was uncertainty within Korea as to the legal status of Japan's hydrographic survey and its relation to MSR, and whether a hydrographic survey should be permitted.[15] These matters have yet to be delineated in Korean domestic law.

VII Passage of North Korean Vessels

Passage of North Korean vessels through South Korean waters is another issue to be noted. The narrow area of South Korean waters adjacent to the Northern Limit Line (NLL),[16] where blue crab is plentiful, raises law enforcement and security issues. The area has been characterized by South Korea as a Special Maritime Zone under the Regulation for Safe Fishing of Vessel.[17] The Special Maritime Zone is designed to protect fishing vessels and control fishery activities in an area of military tension. Due to security concerns, particular requirements are imposed on fishing vessels within the Zone. These requirements, under the Regulation for Safe Fishing of Vessel, include the observation in Article 3 of a "No Fishing Line." However, the residents of the five West Islands are authorized to fish in designated fishing grounds off the islands even beyond the No Fishing Line. The South Korean Navy created a control line to prevent possible military clashes as a result of any accidental crossing of the NLL. Any naval or coast guard vessels intending to cross the line requires authorization from the Operational Command of the South Korean Navy.

The Specified Prohibited Zone represents the area where fishery activities by foreigners are prohibited under the Act on the Exercise of Sovereign Rights within the EEZ. This Zone is designed primarily to protect fishery resources in the EEZ, though it also includes security considerations.

14 *Yonhap News*, Apr. 14, 2006 (Korean), www.news.v.daum.net/v/20060414204413786?f=o.

15 For detailed discussion, see: Shin Chang-Hoon, "Survey/Research project of Japan in the East Sea from the perspective of the international law of the sea", *Seoul International Law Journal*, Vol. 13(1), 113–188 (2006) (Korean).

16 For discussions on legal status of the Northern Limit Line (NLL), see: Chung Min Jung, "International Law Issues and Challenges of the Northern Limit Line (NLL)," *Journal of Korean Society of International Law* Vol. 12, 2013 (Korean) and Yong Joong Lee, "A Study on the Northern Limit Line Dispute between the Two Koreas," *Kyungpook National University Law Journal* Vol.32, 2010 (Korean).

17 Article 4 of Regulation for Safe Fishing of Vessel, Order of Ministry of Oceans and Fisheries No. 251, revised on July 28, 2017.

The 2004 Agreement on Maritime Transportation between North and South Korea was designated to guarantee the operation of vessels in sea routes connecting Incheon, Gunsan, Yeosu, Busan, Ulsan, Pohang and Sokcho ports in the South and Nampo, Haeju, Goseong, Wonsan, Heungnam, Cheongjin and Najin ports of the North.[18] At the 15th Ministerial Meeting in June 2005, it was agreed that non-military vessels of the North could pass through the Jeju Strait;[19] and in August 2005, an "Amendment and Supplement agreement to implement and comply with the North and South Koreas Agreement on Maritime Transportation"[20] was reached that added the Jeju Strait sea route to the previously agreed routes.

As part of its 24 May 2010 response to North Korea's attack on the South Korean corvette *Cheonan* on 26 March 2010, South Korea prohibited the entry of all North Korean vessels into South Korean territorial and adjacent waters, thereby returning to the pre-August 2005 situation of prohibiting the operation of North Korean vessels in South Korean waters.

VIII UN Security Council Sanctions on North Korea

As a result of North Korea's nuclear weapons test on January 6, 2016, the United Nations Security Council (UNSC) adopted Resolution 2270 and indicated that the North Korean action was of the "gravest concern."[21] Paragraph 18 stated that:

> all States shall inspect the cargo within or transiting through their territory, including in their airports, seaports and free trade zones, that has originated in the DPRK, or that is destined for the DPRK, or has been brokered or facilitated by the DPRK or its nationals….

Paragraph 18 allows for the search of vessels passing through Korean territorial waters that originate from or are destined to North Korea, regardless of whether or not the vessel is suspected of engaging in prejudicial passage as

18 The document can be found at the homepage of the Ministry of Foreign Affairs. www.mofa.go.kr/www/brd/m_3984/view.do?seq=340958.

19 *Yonhap News*, June 23, 2005, www.news.naver.com/main/read.nhn?mode=LSD&mid=sec&sid1=100&oid=001&aid=0001034786.

20 *Yonhap News*, Aug. 10, 2005, www.news.naver.com/main/read.nhn?mode=LSD&mid=sec&sid1=100&oid=001&aid=0001072090.

21 UN Security Council Resolution 2270(2016), S/RES/2270 (2016), Adopted on March 2, 2016.

defined in Article 19(2) of the UNCLOS. Article 5(1) of the Korean Territorial Sea and Contiguous Zone Act permits foreign vessels the right of innocent passage in the Korean territorial sea "so long as it is not prejudicial to peace, public order or security of the Republic of Korea." According to the Constitution of the Republic of Korea, North Korea is not a recognized state and as such, North Korean vessels are not considered to be "foreign" vessels, and consequently, such vessels have no rights under international law and South Korean law.

IX Conclusion

This chapter has examined Korean legislation and the 2016 UN Security Council Resolution related to the navigation of foreign ships in the waters under Korean jurisdiction.

Korean law and practice regarding the navigation of foreign vessels in Korean territorial waters generally complies with international law (UNCLOS). There is a question as to whether Korea conforms with the UNCLOS by requiring notification three days prior to passage for foreign naval and non-commercial government vessels. It may be argued that Korea faces exceptional circumstances given the unique inter-Korea military security situation and that the UNCLOS is unclear as it relates to the prior notification regime.

Korea has two straits: the Korea Strait and Jeju Strait. Questions have been raised about the legal status of passage rights in the Jeju Strait which relates to whether or not the route south to Jeju Island can be recognized as a passage of similar convenience.

The navigation of foreign vessels in the Korean EEZ is regulated by numerous acts, such as the Korean Maritime Security Act. As Korea has not settled the delimitation of its maritime boundaries of its EEZ with China and Japan, there are tensions, particularly in the area surrounding Ieodo where the Ieodo Ocean Research Station is located.

The illegal fishing by Chinese vessels in Korean waters is a major problem that has caused harm to Korea and has proved difficult to resolve. Korea has introduced severe sanctions against illegal fishing and has recently resorted to the use of machine guns to crackdown on illegal activities. In addition, in order to enhance security and protect fishery resources, Korea has implemented measures such as the creation of specific sea areas, specified prohibited areas, and fishing line boundaries.

Marine scientific research conducted by foreign vessels is adequately regulated by the Marine Scientific Research Act. However, as with the UNCLOS and

Korean law, the classification of activities that fall under marine scientific research and military surveys is unclear.

Based on the 2004 South-North Maritime Agreement, North Korean vessels may pass through South Korean territorial waters and EEZ. However, since the sinking of the *Cheonan* in 2010, the passage of North Korean vessels in the waters of South Korea has been prohibited.

PART 2

Southeast Asia

CHAPTER 5

Navigation of Foreign Vessels in Indonesia

Hadyu Ikrami and Leonardo Bernard

I Introduction

Indonesia is the world's largest archipelagic state, comprising 17,504 islands[1] and having a population of more than 237 million people.[2] With a coastline of more than 54,000 kilometres, Indonesia's archipelagic and territorial waters encompass an area of 93,000 square kilometres.[3] The archipelago has long been an important trade route between China and India,[4] especially through the Straits of Malacca and Sunda.[5] Indonesia is a state party to the 1982 United

---

1 This figure was modified from 17,508 as reported in CIA, *The World Factbook, East & Southeast Asia: Indonesia* (Central Intelligence Agency, last updated on 3 November 2016), online: <https://www.cia.gov/library/publications/the-world-factbook/geos/id.html>. Indonesia lost the Sipadan and Ligitan islands to Malaysia pursuant to a 2002 decision of the International Court of Justice, and the islands of Arturo and Jaco were excluded from the figure after Timor-Leste's independence. See Kresna Buntoro, *An Analysis of Legal Issues Relating to Navigational Rights and Freedoms Through and Over Indonesian Waters* (University of Wollongong Thesis Collection, 2010) at 3.

2 237,641,326 people, based on the latest census in 2010 conducted by the Indonesian Statistic Board, with an almost 50:50 male-female ratio. Indonesian Statistics Board, online: <http://sp2010.bps.go.id/index.php/site/index>.

3 CIA, *supra* note 1.

4 Peter Church, ed., *A Short History of South-East Asia* (Singapore: John Wiley & Sons (Asia), 2003) at 41.

5 More than 80% of crude oil supplies for Japan and Korea are transported through the Strait of Malacca, with up to 60,000 vessels transiting the Strait per year, which in 2002 amounted to 10.3 million barrels of oil per day. See International Maritime Organization (IMO), "Protection of Vital Shipping Lanes," Note by the Secretary-General, IMO Document C 93/15, 7 October 2004, Annex, Profile of the Straits of Malacca and Singapore at 2.

The Japanese Ministry of Land Infrastructure and Transport estimated that in 2020, there would be 114,000 ships traversing the straits. See Joshua Ho, ed., *Realising Safe and Secure Seas for All: International Maritime Security Conference 2009* (Singapore: S. Rajaratnam School of International Studies, 2009); "Enhancing Safety, Security, and Environmental Protection of the Straits of Malacca and Singapore: The Cooperative Mechanism," *Ocean Development and International Law*, vol. 40 (2009) at 233–234; see also Sam Bateman, Joshua Ho, and Jane Chin, *Good Order at Sea in Southeast Asia* (Singapore: S. Rajaratnam School of International Studies, 2009) at 11–12, all three quoted in Sheldon W. Simon, "Safety and Security in the Malacca Straits: The Limits of Collaboration" (2011) 7:1 *Asian Security* at 27.

 | DOI:10.1163/9789004396272_006

Nations Convention on the Law of the Sea (UNCLOS)[6] and claims a 200 nautical miles exclusive economic zone (EEZ) from its archipelagic baselines.[7]

The Ministry of Marine Affairs and Fisheries (MMAF), created in 1999, is responsible for fisheries management at the national level,[8] while the Ministry of Transportation manages and regulates navigation through Indonesian waters.[9] In December 2014, a new Maritime Security Agency (BAKAMLA) was created with the authority to coordinate and deploy the assets of different agencies in order to strengthen the protection of Indonesian waters.[10] As a state party to UNCLOS, Indonesia recognizes the right of foreign vessels to exercise innocent passage through its territorial and archipelagic waters,[11] the right of transit passage through the Straits of Malacca and Singapore,[12] and the right of archipelagic sea lanes passage through its designated sea lanes.[13] This chapter will describe the key regulations regarding the passage and other activities of foreign vessels in Indonesian waters.

II Definition of Foreign Vessel and Vessel Registration

Article 1(39) of Indonesian Law No. 17 of 2008 on Shipping (Shipping Law) defines "foreign vessel" as "a vessel which flies the flag of a state other than Indonesia and is not registered in the Indonesian vessels register." Where a foreign vessel is to be registered in Indonesia, its flag state must first remove it from that state's vessels register.[14] By the same token, where a vessel loses its Indonesian nationality, such as if it is acquired by a foreign national or foreign

---

6 United Nations Convention on the Law of the Sea, 1833 *U.N.T.S.* 397.

7 Law No. 5 of 1983 on the Indonesian Exclusive Economic Zone (Indonesia) [*EEZ Law*], article 2.

8 Presidential Regulation No. 63 of 2015 on the Ministry of Marine Affairs and Fisheries (Indonesia), article 3.

9 Regulation of the Minister of Transportation No. PM 189 of 2015 on the Organization and Procedure of the Ministry of Transportation, as amended by the Regulation of the Minister of Transportation No. PM 86 of 2016 (Indonesia), article 259. See also Presidential Regulation No. 40 of 2015 on the Ministry of Transportation (Indonesia), article 3.

10 Presidential Regulation No. 178 of 2014 on the Maritime Security Agency (Indonesia), articles 3 and 4(c).

11 See below Part III.1.

12 See below Part III.3.

13 See below Part III.2.

14 Law No. 17 of 2008 on Shipping (Indonesia) [*Shipping Law*], article 160(2) and Government Regulation No. 51 of 2002 on Vessels (Indonesia) [*Vessels Regulation*], article 24(2).

corporation, it will no longer qualify as an Indonesian vessel and Indonesia will remove it from that state's vessels register.[15]

III Passage of Foreign Vessels

1 *Innocent Passage*

The right of innocent passage of foreign vessels through Indonesia's territorial and archipelagic waters is regulated by, *inter alia*, Government Regulation No. 36 of 2002 on the Rights and Obligations of Foreign Vessels in Making an Innocent Passage through Indonesian Waters (Innocent Passage Regulation),[16] which was adopted as an implementing legislation of Law Number 6 of 1996 on Indonesian Waters (Indonesian Waters Law).[17] Most of the provisions regarding innocent passage in Indonesian laws are derived from the UNCLOS.[18] For instance, the definition of passage in the Indonesian Waters Law replicates the definition of passage in Article 18(1) of the UNCLOS, namely:

> navigation through the territorial sea for the purpose of: (a) traversing that sea without entering internal waters or calling at a roadstead or port facility outside internal waters; or (b) proceeding to or from internal waters or a call at such roadstead or port facility.[19]

Under Indonesian law, all ships have the right of innocent passage through the territorial sea and archipelagic waters of Indonesia[20] and to navigate between the high seas, between different parts of the Indonesian EEZ, or between the

15 *Vessels Regulation, supra* note 14, article 32(1)(a)(5) and see Commercial Code, *Staatsblad* 1847:23 (Indonesia), article 313.

16 Government Regulation No. 36 of 2002 on the Rights and Obligations of Foreign Vessels in Making an Innocent Passage through Indonesian Waters (State Gazette Year 2002 No. 70, Supplementary State Gazette No. 4209) (Indonesia) [*Innocent Passage Regulation*].

17 Law No. 6 of 1996 on Indonesian Waters (State Gazette Year 1996 No. 73, Supplementary State Gazette No 3647) (Indonesia) [*Indonesian Waters Law*].

18 Indonesia deposited the ratification instrument for UNCLOS on 3 February 1986. "United Nations Convention on the Law of the Sea, Status as at: 25-05-2016 05:00:38 EDT," United Nations Treaty Collection, online, <https://treaties.un.org/pages/ViewDetailsIII.aspx?src=TREATY&mtdsg_no=XXI-6&chapter=21&Temp=mtdsg3&lang=en>.

19 According to *Indonesian Waters Law, supra* note 17, article 11(2), innocent passage in Indonesian waters applies not only to foreign vessels traversing the territorial sea, but also archipelagic waters. This is also in accordance with *UNCLOS, supra* note 6, article 52.

20 *Ibid.*, article 11(1) and *Innocent Passage Regulation, supra* note 16, article 2(1). This provision is essentially the same as *UNCLOS, supra* note 6, article 17.

high seas and the Indonesian EEZ.[21] Innocent passage must be continuous, direct, and prompt.[22] Stopping and anchoring are allowed, as long as they relate to normal navigation or are necessary because of *force majeure*, distress or to help other vessels or persons in danger.[23] Passage is deemed innocent if it does not pose a threat to the peace, order, or security of Indonesia, and is in accordance with international law.[24] Passage is deemed prejudicial to Indonesia if the vessel in question commits a prohibited act, such as espionage or intentional and grave pollution.[25] Submarines and other underwater vehicles are to navigate on the surface and show their flag during innocent passage.[26]

The Indonesian government may temporarily suspend the right of innocent passage in certain areas if it is necessary for the protection of its security, including for the performance of military drills.[27] The Indonesian Commander of Armed Forces can designate the areas and time period of a temporary suspension, which will be announced through the Indonesian Notices to Mariners and notified by the Ministry of Foreign Affairs to other states through diplomatic channels.[28] The suspension takes effect seven days after the notification and announcement.[29]

When exercising the right of innocent passage, foreign vessels powered by or transporting nuclear or other dangerous materials must bring documents to identify the vessel's specifications as well as the cargo and comply with special precautionary measures as stipulated in the relevant international agreements.[30] These measures are aimed at ensuring that humans and the environment will not be exposed to nuclear material and that dangerous goods will be

---

21 *Innocent Passage Regulation, supra* note 16, article 2(1).

22 *Indonesian Waters Law, supra* note 17, article 11(3), which is essentially the same as the *UNCLOS, supra* note 6, article 18(2).

23 *Ibid.* and *Innocent Passage Regulation, supra* note 16, article 3(4). This is essentially the same as *UNCLOS, supra* note 6, article 18(2).

24 *Indonesian Waters Law, supra* note 17, article 12(1), which is essentially the same as *UNCLOS, supra* note 6, article 19(1).

25 *Ibid.*, article 12(2) and *Innocent Passage Regulation, supra* note 16, articles 4(1) and 5(1)-(2). These provisions are essentially the same as those in *UNCLOS, supra* note 6, articles 19(2) and 21(1).

26 Ibid., article 15. This is essentially the same as *UNCLOS, supra* note 6, article 20.

27 *Ibid.*, article 13(1) and *Innocent Passage Regulation, supra* note 16, article 14(1). This is essentially the same as *UNCLOS, supra* note 6, article 25(3).

28 *Innocent Passage Regulation, supra* note 16, article 14(2).

29 *Ibid.*, article 14(3).

30 *Indonesian Waters Law, supra* note 17, article 16. This is fundamentally the same as *UNCLOS, supra* note 6, article 23.

A similar provision is of Government Regulation No. 37 of 2002 on the Rights and Obligations of Foreign Vessels and Aircrafts in Making an Archipelagic Sea Lanes Passage

packed and stowed safely.[31] In order to ensure navigational safety and protection of fisheries, the government may designate sea lanes and traffic separation schemes for foreign vessels carrying dangerous materials, foreign tankers, foreign fishing vessels, and foreign research or survey vessels.[32] These vessels may only exercise the right of innocent passage through the following sea lanes:[33]

1. Between the South China Sea and the Indian Ocean, the sea lane is: Natuna Sea-Karimata Strait-Java Sea-Sunda Strait and *vice versa*;
2. Between the Sulawesi Sea and the Indian Ocean, the sea lane is: Makassar Strait-Flores Sea-Lombok Strait and *vice versa*;
3. Between the Pacific Ocean and the Indian Ocean, the sea lane is: Maluku Sea-Seram Sea-Banda Sea-Ombai Strait-Sawu Sea and *vice versa*;
4. Between the Pacific Ocean and the Timor Sea or Arafura Sea, the sea lane is: Maluku Sea-Seram Sea-Banda Sea and *vice versa*.

In exercising the right of innocent passage through narrow straits, foreign vessels traversing the designated sea lane must not navigate closer than ten percent of the strait's width to the coast.[34] In the course of innocent passage, foreign fishing vessels must store their fishing gear in the cargo hold.[35] Foreign research and survey vessels must also store and deactivate all of their research and survey equipment and tools.[36] In traversing the sea lanes, foreign vessels must monitor the Indonesian Radio of Notices to Mariners and observe the navigational activities of other vessels traversing the islands.[37] Foreign vessels must also pay for any specific services provided to them while exercising the right of innocent passage,[38] such as pilotage or towing operations.[39] Failure to

---

through the Designated Archipelagic Sea Lanes (Indonesia) [*Archipelagic Sea Lanes Passage Regulation*], Article 9(3).

31 See IMO, *Implications of the United Nations Convention on the Law of the Sea for the International Maritime Organization, Study by the Secretariat of the International Maritime Organization (IMO)*, LEG/MISC.8 (30 January 2014), online: <http://www.imo.org/en/OurWork/Legal/Documents/LEG%20MISC%208.pdf>, at 36–37.

32 *Indonesian Waters Law, supra* note 17, article 14(1) and *Innocent Passage Regulation, supra* note 16, articles 11(1) and 12(1).

33 *Innocent Passage Regulation, supra* note 16, article 11(1)-(2).

34 *Ibid.*, article 6.

35 *Ibid.*, article 7(2).

36 *Ibid.*, article 8(2).

37 *Ibid.*, article 9.

38 *Ibid.*, article 10(1). The Elucidation of this Article stipulates that this Article implements *UNCLOS, supra* note 6, article 26(2).

39 See "Report of the International Law Commission covering the work of its eighth session (A/3159), Articles concerning the Law of the Sea with Commentaries 1956", Article 19 Commentary, para. (1), II *YB ILC* 1956 at 253 and 274, quoted in Center for Oceans Law and Policy, University of Virginia, "Article 26 – Charges Which May Be Levied upon Foreign

comply with the above may result in enforcement measures pursuant to the Indonesian civil procedure regulations.[40]

2 *Archipelagic Sea Lanes Passage*

Archipelagic sea lanes in Indonesian archipelagic waters have been designated as follows:[41]

1. between the South China Sea and the Indian Ocean: Natuna Sea-Karimata Strait-Java Sea-Sunda Strait and *vice versa*;
2. between the Sulawesi Sea and the Indian Ocean: Makassar Strait-Flores Sea-Lombok Strait and *vice versa*; and
3. between the Pacific Ocean and the Indian Ocean: Maluku Sea-Seram Sea-Banda Sea-Ombai Strait-Sawu Sea and *vice versa*.

The provisions on archipelagic sea lanes passage in Indonesian law largely follow the provisions of the UNCLOS, as can be seen in the 2002 Archipelagic Sea Lanes Passage Regulation. For instance, all foreign vessels and aircraft have the right of archipelagic sea lanes passage through Indonesian archipelagic waters to navigate between different parts of the high seas, different parts of the Indonesian EEZ, or between the high seas and the Indonesian EEZ.[42] Like innocent passage, archipelagic sea lanes passage must be continuous, direct, rapid and uninterrupted.[43] The government may designate traffic separation schemes to ensure the safe passage of vessels.[44]

Archipelagic sea lanes and air routes are determined by a series of continuous axis lines from the route's entry point to the exit point through adjacent archipelagic waters and the territorial sea.[45] Foreign vessels or aircraft exercising the right of archipelagic sea lanes passage are not to deviate more than 25 nautical miles to both sides of the archipelagic sea lane's axis lines, insofar as

---

Ships (II)," in *UN Convention on the Law of the Sea Commentary 1982 Online*, ed. Center for Oceans Law and Policy, University of Virginia (Leiden and Boston: Brill Nijhoff, 2013), at 235, retrieved from BrillOnline Reference Works, access provided by the National University of Singapore.

40 *Innocent Passage Regulation, supra* note 16, article 10(2).

41 *Archipelagic Sea Lanes Passage Regulation, supra* note 30, article 11. The designation of Indonesia's archipelagic sea lanes will be discussed below.

42 *Indonesian Waters Law, supra* note 17, article 18(2) and *Archipelagic Sea Lanes Passage Regulation, supra* note 30, article 2. This provision is essentially the same as *UNCLOS, supra* note 6, article 53(3).

43 *Ibid.*, article 18(1) and *Archipelagic Sea Lanes Passage Regulation, supra* note 30, article 4(1). This provision is essentially the same as *UNCLOS, supra* note 6, article 53(3).

44 *Ibid.*, article 19(1). This is essentially the same as *UNCLOS, supra* note 6, article 53(6).

45 *Ibid.*, 19(1)-(2). This is basically the same as *UNCLOS, supra* note 6, article 53(5).

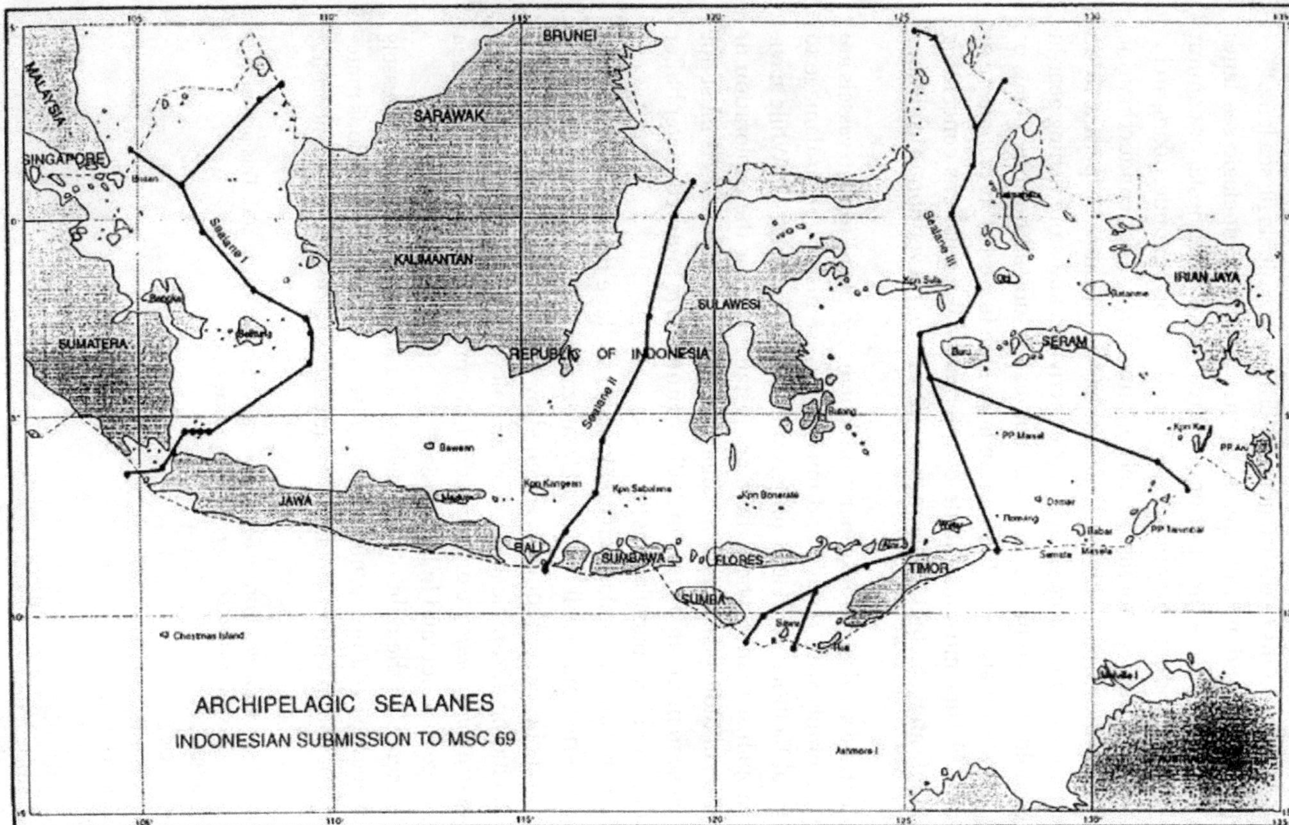

FIGURE 5.1 Indonesian Archipelagic Sea Lanes submitted to the IMO.
SOURCE: IMO MARITIME SAFETY COMMITTEE RESOLUTION MSC.72(69), *ADOPTION, DESIGNATION, AND SUBSTITUTION OF ARCHIPELAGIC SEA LANES*, ADOPTED ON 19 MAY 1998, ONLINE: <HTTP://WWW.IMO.ORG/BLAST/BLASTDATAHELPER.ASP?DATA_ID=15438&FILENAME=72(69).PDF>, ACCESSED ON 1 JUNE 2016 AT 9

they do not navigate to the coast closer than ten percent of the distance between the closest points to the islands bordering an archipelagic sea lane.[46]

Foreign vessels and aircraft exercising the right of archipelagic sea lanes passage must not pose a threat of or use force against Indonesia, or commit any other violations of international law.[47] Furthermore, in undertaking archipelagic sea lane passage, foreign vessels or aircraft must not conduct marine research or hydrographic surveys, unless they have acquired a permit to do so.[48] They may also not engage in fisheries activities and store fishing gear in the cargo hold.[49] In addition, they may not load or unload persons, goods or currency in ways that violate Indonesian laws, save in case of *force majeure* or an accident.[50] They must also abide by international regulations concerning navigational safety, including the regulations on the prevention of collisions at sea.[51]

Where there are designated separation schemes in place, foreign vessels are obliged to comply with them[52] and must not cause disruption or damage to navigational facilities as well as underwater cables and pipes.[53] While navigating through sea lanes where there are installations for the exploration or exploitation of biological or non-biological resources, foreign vessels must not sail too close to prohibited areas including within a five hundred-meter buffer zone around offshore installations.[54]

Foreign civil aircraft making an archipelagic sea lane passage must comply with the International Civil Aviation Organization (ICAO) safety regulations, and monitor the radio frequency assigned by the competent air traffic controllers, including the applicable radio frequency used in case of emergency.[55] Save in case of *force majeure* or an accident, aircraft exercising archipelagic sea lanes passage may not land in Indonesia.[56]

While exercising the right of archipelagic sea lanes passage, foreign vessels must not engage in dumping, must not dispose of oil or other hazardous materials at sea or commit other violations of international regulations concerning

46 *Archipelagic Sea Lanes Passage Regulation*, *supra* note 30, article 4(2). This provision is basically the same as *UNCLOS*, *supra* note 6, article 53(5).
47 *Ibid.*, article 4(3).
48 *Ibid.*, article 5.
49 *Ibid.*, article 6(1) and (2).
50 *Ibid.*, article 6(3).
51 *Ibid.*, article 7(1).
52 *Ibid.*, article 7(2).
53 *Ibid.*, article 7(3).
54 *Ibid.*, article 7(4).
55 *Ibid.*, article 8.
56 *Ibid.*, article 4(5).

pollution from vessels.[57] Foreign nuclear-powered vessels or foreign vessels transporting nuclear or other hazardous materials, while making an archipelagic sea lane passage, must carry documents identifying the cargo and the specifications of the vessel and comply with all precautionary measures as stipulated in the relevant international agreements.[58] Individuals or corporations responsible for the operation or cargo of a foreign commercial vessel may be held liable for violations of the Archipelagic Sea Lanes Passage Regulation[59] committed in the course of exercising the right of archipelagic sea lanes passage through Indonesian waters.[60] Meanwhile, where a foreign vessel or aircraft entitled to sovereign immunity violates the Archipelagic Sea Lanes Passage Regulation, the flag state of the vessel or aircraft is to bear the responsibility for such violation.[61]

3 *Transit Passage through Straits Used for International Navigation*

Article 20 of the Indonesian Waters Law stipulates that all foreign vessels and aircraft have the right of continuous, direct and rapid transit passage through straits used for international navigation between different parts of the high seas, between different parts of the Indonesian EEZ, and between the high seas and the Indonesian EEZ. The Elucidation of this Article provides that what is referred to as the right of transit passage is the right to make such passage through the Malacca and Singapore Straits. The Elucidation further sets out the requirements for transit passage that must be satisfied by foreign vessels or aircraft, which are essentially the same as those in UNCLOS Article 39, namely:

1. the vessel or aircraft must navigate promptly through or over the strait;
2. the vessel or aircraft must not threaten with or use force against Indonesia or commit any other violations of international law;
3. the vessel or aircraft must not stop during the passage save in case of *force majeure* or navigational disruption; and
4. the vessel or aircraft must comply with safety requirements at sea; take measures to prevent, reduce, and control pollution; abide by ICAO safety regulations; and monitor the designated radio frequency.

---

57 *Ibid.*, article 9(1) and (2).

58 *Ibid.*, article 9(3) and see *supra* note 30.

59 Specifically, *ibid.*, articles 7, 8, and 9.

60 *Ibid.*, 10(1).

61 *Ibid.*, article 10(2) and its Elucidation that specifically stipulates that this provision is an implementation of *UNCLOS*, *supra* note 6, articles 42(5) and 54, which respectively refer to foreign vessels and aircraft protected by sovereign immunity and the applicability of the provision to vessels and aircraft making archipelagic sea lanes passage.

Furthermore, in order to guarantee the safety of navigation in straits used for international navigation, the Minister of Transportation may designate archipelagic sea lanes as part of traffic separation schemes.[62] Examples of this are the lanes in the Phillips Strait, which are designed to enhance the safety of navigation of vessels making a transit passage from the Singapore Strait to the Malacca Strait.[63] Foreign vessels using such sea lanes are subject to the provisions of Indonesian law on innocent passage through archipelagic waters.[64]

IV Regulation of Foreign Vessel Activities

In addition to having rights of passage, foreign vessels are subject to various regulations as discussed below.

1 *Fishery Activities*

Under Indonesian Law No. 31 of 2004 on Fisheries, as amended by Law No. 45 of 2009 (Fisheries Law), there are three activities that the owners and/or operators of foreign vessels can engage in with regard to Indonesia's fishery resources: exploiting,[65] fishing,[66] and transporting.[67] The term exploiting fishery resources includes not only fishing, but also other commercial activities in relation to the fishing industry, such as pre-production, processing and marketing.[68] To exploit the fishery resources in Indonesia's EEZ,[69] the owners and/or operators of foreign vessels must obtain a License to Exploit Fishery Resources (*Surat Izin Usaha Perikanan* SIUP).[70] In order to obtain a SIUP, there

62 *Innocent Passage Regulation, supra* note 16, article 13(1) and see *Indonesian Waters Law, supra* note 17, article 21(1).

63 *Innocent Passage Regulation, supra* note 16, Elucidation of article 13(1).

64 *Innocent Passage Regulation, supra* note 16, article 13(2).

65 Law No. 31 of 2004 on Fisheries, as amended by Law No. 45 of 2009 (Indonesia) [*Fisheries Law*], articles 25 and 26.

66 *Ibid.*, articles 27(2), 27(3), and 29(2).

67 *Ibid.*, articles 28(2) and 28(3).

68 The term used in the *Fisheries Law, supra* note 65, is "*usaha*", which may also mean "commerce" or "trade". However, a close reading of the Fisheries Law yields an understanding that what is meant in the Fisheries Law is "exploitation." This interpretation is supported, for instance, by Article 25(1), which stipulates that "*usaha*" in the fishing industry consists of "pre-production, production, processing, and marketing." This shows that "*usaha*", within the meaning of the Fisheries Law, is much broader than trade in fish only. Therefore, the understanding of the term is "exploitation."

69 *Ibid.*, articles 29(2) and 30(1) and see *infra* notes 88–93 and accompanying text.

70 *Ibid.*, article 26(1).

has to be a fisheries agreement, access control or other types of arrangements between the government of Indonesia and the government of the flag state.[71]

In order to fish in the Indonesian EEZ,[72] the owners and/or operators of foreign vessels must possess a License to Fish (*Surat Izin Penangkapan Ikan*/ SIPI),[73] which is an integral part of a SIUP.[74] Foreign vessels must also ensure that at least seventy percent of its crew are Indonesians.[75] Furthermore, foreign vessels only have the right to fish if:[76]

1. Indonesia has the obligation to grant that right under an international agreement or an applicable international legal principle;
2. the allowable catch exceeds Indonesia's capacity to harvest the fishery resources; and
3. the foreign individuals, corporations, or states pay fees to Indonesia.

Foreign vessels may also transport fish within the fisheries management territory of Indonesia – which includes the territorial sea and EEZ[77] – if they possess a License for Vessels Transporting Fish (*Surat Izin Kapal Pengangkut Ikan*/ SIKPI).[78] A SIKPI is only issued to foreign vessels transporting bred fish, not caught fish.[79] SIKPI holders must land fish at the destination port as mentioned in the SIPI or SIKPI.[80] Failure to do so may result in the revocation of a SIPI or SIKPI.[81]

Foreign vessels with a fishing license may only carry one type of fishing gear when fishing in the EEZ[82] and must store the fishing gear in the cargo hold if they are not in possession of a fishing license but are traversing Indonesian waters.[83] The obligation to store fishing gear also applies to foreign vessels in

71 *Ibid.*, article 30(1).
72 *Ibid.*, articles 27(2) and 29(2) and see *infra* notes 88–93 and accompanying text.
73 *Ibid.*, article 27(2).
74 *Ibid.*, article 1(17).
75 *Ibid.*, article 35A(2).
76 *EEZ Law, supra* note 7, article 5(1) and (3) and the Elucidation of both paragraphs.
77 *Fisheries Law, supra* note 65, article 5(1).
78 *Ibid.*, article 28(2) and (3).
79 Regulation of the Minister of Marine Affairs and Fisheries No. 15/PERMEN-KP/2016 on Vessels Transporting Live Fish, as amended by the Regulation of the Minister of Marine Affairs and Fisheries No. 32/PERMEN-KP/2016 (Indonesia), article 4(3)(c) and article 7(6)(a).
80 Regulation of the Minister of Marine Affairs and Fisheries No. PER.30/MEN/2012 on Fishing in the Fisheries Management Territory of the Republic of Indonesia, as amended by the Regulations of the Minister of Marine Affairs and Fisheries No. 26/PERMEN-KP/2013 and No. 57/PERMEN-KP/2014 (Indonesia), article 37(6).
81 *Ibid.*, article 37(9).
82 *Fisheries Law, supra* note 65, article 38(2).
83 *Ibid.*, article 38(1).

possession of a fishing license when they are outside the permitted fishing areas.[84] Where crew members of a foreign vessel are accused of fishery crimes, they may be subject to the jurisdiction of the Fisheries Court,[85] and foreign crew members may be prosecuted and/or deported.[86]

Over the past few years, Indonesia has increased enforcement activities against foreign fishing vessels' operations in its EEZ without a license. As of 16 September 2016, the Indonesian government had destroyed 236 vessels that had committed illegal, unreported, and unregulated (IUU) fishing.[87] The government has also stopped issuing new fishing licenses or renewing expired fishing licenses for foreign vessels and Indonesian flagged vessels built outside Indonesia (*eks kapal asing*/"former foreign vessels").[88] While the Fisheries Law allows foreign vessels to fish in the EEZ,[89] the fact that they will not be able to obtain new fishing licenses suggests that Indonesia envisions a future where no foreign vessels can fish in Indonesia's EEZ.[90] This is also evidenced by, *inter alia*, the 2016 Presidential Regulation on Negative Investment List, which states that

---

84 *Ibid.*, article 38(3). The "fisheries management territory of the Republic of Indonesia" is defined in *ibid.*, article 5(1), as comprising: "(1) the Indonesian waters; (2) the Indonesian EEZ; and (3) rivers, lakes, reservoirs, swamps, and other puddles that can be commercialized as well as potential fish farms in the territory of the Republic of Indonesia."

85 *Ibid.*, article 71A.

86 *Ibid.*, articles 71A and 83A.

87 Fajar Pratama, "Menteri Susi Ajak Negara Lain Lebih Tegas Perangi Illegal Fishing", *DetikNews* (17 September 2016), online: <https://news.detik.com/berita/3300078/menteri-susi-ajak-negara-lain-lebih-tegas-perangi-illegal-fishing>, accessed on 4 October 2016.

88 See Regulation of the Minister of Marine Affairs and Fisheries No. 58/PERMEN-KP/2014 on the Discipline of Civil Servants at the Ministry of Marine Affairs and Fisheries in Enforcing Policies on Moratorium of Fishing License, Transhipment at Sea, and Employment of Foreign Sea Captains and Sailors (Indonesia), article 3(a)(1)-(2) and Regulation of the Minister of Marine Affairs and Fisheries No. 56/PERMEN-KP/2014 on the Moratorium on Licenses for Capture Fisheries in the Fishery Management Territory of the Republic of Indonesia, as amended by the Regulation of the Minister of Marine Affairs and Fisheries No. 10/PERMEN-KP/2015 (Indonesia) [*Licenses Moratorium Regulation*], articles 1 and 2.

Minister Susi Pudjiastuti decided not to extend the *Licenses Moratorium Regulation* after it expired on 31 October 2015. Irene Inriana, "Menteri Susi Pastikan Tak Perpanjang Moratorium Kapal", *CNN Indonesia* (3 November 2015), online: <www.cnnindonesia.com/ekonomi/20151103135800-92-89149/menteri-susi-pastikan-tak-perpanjang-moratorium-kapal/>. However, by virtue of the Letter of the Ministry of Marine Affairs and Fisheries Secretary-General No. B-195/SJ/11/2016 dated 11 February 2016, the moratorium has, in effect, become a permanent ban. See KKPNews, "Penghapusan Kapal Eks Asing dari Daftar Kapal Indonesia" (17 June 2016), online: Indonesian Ministry of Marine Affairs and Fisheries Website <www.kkp.go.id/2016/06/17/penghapusan-kapal-eks-asing-dari-daftar-kapal-indonesia/>.

89 *Fisheries Law*, *supra* note 65, articles 27(2), 27(3), 29(2), 30(1).

90 See KKPNews, *supra* note 88.

fishing in Indonesian waters may only be carried out using 100% Indonesian capital and must be licensed by the MMAF.[91] This policy, which has been reiterated on several occasions by the Minister of Marine Affairs and Fisheries,[92] is part of the government's policy to uphold Indonesia's sovereignty, ensure sustainable fisheries, and enhance the population's welfare.[93]

2 *Port Control*

Under Article 82 of the Regulation of the Minister of Marine Affairs and Fisheries No. PER.30/MEN/2012 on Fishing in the Fisheries Management Territory of the Republic of Indonesia, as amended by the Regulations of the Minister of Marine Affairs and Fisheries No. 26/PERMEN-KP/2013 and No. 57/PERMEN-KP/2014 (Fishing Regulation) and Article 36 of the Regulation of the Minister of Marine Affairs and Fisheries No. 3/PERMEN-KP/2013 on Fishery Port Masters, foreign vessels are subject to port state measures when entering and before exiting fishery ports in Indonesia. In addition, various provisions in the Regulation of the Minister of Transportation No. PM 36 of 2012 on the Organization and Operating Procedure of the Office of Port Master and Port Authority (Port Master and Port Authority Regulation) also stipulate that the Ministry of Transportation Office of the Port Master and Port Authority (OPMPA) has the power to exercise port state control over foreign vessels in Indonesian ports.[94] Neither port state control nor port state measures are defined in these Regulations. However, Article 82 of the Fishing Regulation stipulates that port state measures should be taken "in accordance with generally accepted international requirements and/or standards."

---

91 Presidential Regulation No. 44 of 2016 on the List of Businesses Which Are Closed and Conditionally Open to Investment (Indonesia), Annex III at 13.

92 Diko Oktara, "Menteri Susi: Sektor Penangkapan Ikan Tertutup untuk Asing", *Tempo.com* (21 June 2016), online: <https://m.tempo.co/read/news/2016/06/21/090781850/menteri-susi-sektor-penangkapan-ikan-tertutup-untuk-asing> and Yoga Sukmana and Aprillia Ika, "Susi: Kalau Perikanan Tangkap Diberikan ke Asing, Saya Siap Mundur…", *Kompas.com* (4 August 2016), online: <http://bisniskeuangan.kompas.com/read/2016/08/04/190000126/Susi.Kalau.Perikanan.Tangkap.Diberikan.ke.Asing.Saya.Siap.Mundur>.

93 Ministry of Marine Affairs and Fisheries of the Republic of Indonesia, Press Release, "Ini Pesan Menteri Susi kepada 476 Wisudawan STP" (26 August 2016), online: KKP <http://kkp.go.id/2016/08/26/ini-pesan-menteri-susi-kepada-476-wisudawan-stp/>, accessed on 7 October 2016.

94 Regulation of the Minister of Transportation No. PM 36 of 2012 on the Organization and Operating Procedure of the Office of Port Master and Port Authority (Indonesia) [*Port Master and Port Authority Regulation*], articles 1(1), 17(1), 21(1), 24(3), and 24(4), among other provisions.

Some of these international standards are embodied in the 2009 Agreement on Port State Measures to Prevent, Deter, and Eliminate Illegal, Unreported, and Unregulated Fishing (IUU Fishing Agreement),[95] to which Indonesia is a party. Article 13 of the Port State Agreement stipulates that one of the measures that may be taken by a port state is to inspect a vessel at the port. Annex B of the Agreement provides that the inspectors of a port state may board a vessel and take a number of measures, including:

1. inspecting the vessel documents to verify the vessel's identity and whether it is licensed to conduct its activities;
2. inspecting other relevant documents, including the manifest and description of the catch;
3. examining the fishing gear and the fish; and
4. assessing whether the vessel has engaged in IUU fishing.

Further, in 1996, Indonesia became a participant in the 1993 Memorandum of Understanding on Port State Control in the Asia-Pacific Region.[96] The Memorandum gives direction regarding the forms of port state control that Indonesia may exercise over foreign vessels, such as:

> [C]arry[ing] out inspections, which will consist of at least a visit on board a ship in order to check the certificates and documents, and furthermore satisfy themselves that the crew and the overall condition of the ship, its equipment, machinery spaces and accommodation, and hygienic conditions on board, meets the provisions of the relevant instruments.[97]

Some of the above measures have been stipulated in the Port Master and Port Authority Regulation, including the right to inspect vessel equipment and tools, as well as the vessel's compliance with seaworthiness requirements.[98] These measures also apply to national vessels.[99] Furthermore, foreign vessels that fish or transport fish are also subject to the following:

---

95 Agreement on Port State Measures to Prevent, Deter, and Eliminate Illegal, Unreported, and Unregulated Fishing, 22 November 2009, online: <http://www.fao.org/3/a-i5469t.pdf>.

96 Memorandum of Understanding on Port State Control in the Asia-Pacific Region, online: <http://www.tokyo-mou.org/doc/Memorandum%20rev15.pdf>, at 1, note 5.

97 *Ibid.*, article 3.1.

98 *Port Master and Port Authority Regulation*, *supra* note 94, articles 11(c), 15(d), and 24(2), among other provisions.

99 *Ibid.* The provisions apply to "vessels" in general, since they make no distinction between domestic vessels and foreign vessels.

1. they must notify the port master in a fishery port of their planned arrival at least 48 hours prior to arrival, and of their planned departure at least 24 hours before leaving the port;[100]
2. they must present the passports or seaman's books of foreign crew members, the License to Employ Foreign Manpower (*Izin Mempekerjakan Tenaga Kerja Asing* / IMTA), and Special Immigration Privileges documents (*Kemudahan Khusus Keimigrasian* / DAHSUSKIM) to the port master upon arrival;[101]
3. other documents that must be presented upon arrival at Indonesian ports include SIPI or SIKPI, an assignment letter confirming the nature of the vessel's work (i.e. whether to fish or transport fish), log book, seaworthiness certificate, certificate attesting to the qualifications of the crew members, health records, and radio certificate;[102] and
4. other documents that must be presented before departure from Indonesia include the Arrival Report, the initial page of the Result of the Catch Certificate for vessels having a capacity of more than 20 gross tonnage, and receipts of payment for port and cleaning services.[103]

Other important aspects of port control include environmental protection, control of hazardous and toxic waste, and safety at the port. Under the Port Master and Port Authority Regulation, the port master has competence to take measures to preserve the maritime environment, oversee and control the loading and unloading of dangerous and hazardous materials, prevent fires at the port, prevent pollution, engage in search and rescue, and verify compliance with the international ship and port facility security code.[104] Overall, the port master has the power to enforce the laws concerning maritime safety and security, coordination of governmental actions at ports, and port control.[105]

3 *Investigation into Incidents*

The Shipping Law stipulates that all incidents involving vessels must first be investigated by the port master, who has the competence to collect testimonies

---

100 Regulation of the Minister of Marine Affairs and Fisheries No. 3/PERMEN-KP/2013 on Fishery Port Masters (Indonesia), articles 6(2) and 9(3).

101 *Ibid.*, article 6(5)(j), (k), (m).

102 *Ibid.*, article 6(5). This obligation is imposed not only on foreign vessels, but also on national vessels.

103 *Ibid.*, article 9(4). This obligation is imposed not only on foreign vessels, but also on national vessels.

104 *Port Master and Port Authority Regulation*, *supra* note 94, articles 3(c)-(d), 10, and 14.

105 *Ibid*, article 2.

and preliminary pieces of evidence.[106] The result of that preliminary investigation may be passed onto the Maritime Court (*Mahkamah Pelayaran*) for further investigation.[107] The Maritime Court is a quasi-judicial body established by and answerable to the Minister of Transportation.[108] It is tasked with investigating marine incidents and enforcing the code of ethics for ships' captains and sailors.[109] The Court may carry out an investigation after the port master completes their preliminary investigation.[110] The Court has the competence to investigate collisions between vessels, fire aboard ships, shipwrecks, and other serious incidents involving vessels.[111] It is entrusted with determining whether or not captains or crew of a ship are negligent or at fault for marine incidents.[112]

By law, sea captains are responsible for any incident involving their vessels unless proven otherwise.[113] Upon finding a sea captain or a sailor guilty of violations of the code of ethics, the Court may recommend that the Minister of Transportation impose administrative penalties, such as a warning or temporary revocation of the master mariner license (*Sertifikat Keahlian Pelaut*).[114] The Court has decided on a number of cases involving foreign vessels. In 2014, the Court decided that the Second Officer of the *MV Vishva Prerna*, a vessel flying the Indian flag, was negligent in the collision between that vessel and an Indonesian vessel that was being towed in the Java Sea.[115] The Court also decided on an incident involving the *MT Star Asia*, a vessel flying the Thai flag which collided with an Indonesian vessel. In its judgment, the Court acquitted the captains of both vessels and attributed the responsibility for the collision to the maritime pilot.[116] Furthermore, in a case involving the *MT Norgas*

---

106 *Shipping Law, supra* note 14, article 220(1)-(2).

107 *Ibid.*, article 221(3).

108 *Ibid.*, articles 250(1) and 1(64) and Decision of the Minister of Transportation No. KM 15 of 1999 on the Organization and Procedure of the Maritime Court (Indonesia), article 1(1).

109 *Shipping Law, supra* note 14, article 251.

110 *Ibid.*

111 *Ibid.*, articles 252 and 245; Regulation of the Minister of Transportation No. KM.55 of 2006 on the Procedure for Investigation into Marine Incidents (Indonesia), article 2(2) and Government Regulation No. 1 of 1998 on the Investigation into Marine Incidents (Indonesia), article 2(2).

112 *Ibid.*, article 253(1)(a).

113 *Ibid.*, article 249.

114 *Ibid.*, articles 253(1)(b) and (2).

115 Maritime Court Judgment No. HK.2010/48/XII/MP.14, 19 December 2014 (collision between MV. Vishva Prerna and TK. Sahabat Kapuas Mandiri XXXII while towed by KT. Mega Prima II in the vicinity of Masalembu Island, Java Sea), online: <http://mahpel.dephub.go.id/putusan/_shared/upload/putusan/pdf/e8ea60f218dd75c5d5b1b8de7f15ab6b.pdf>.

116 Maritime Court Judgment No HK.2010/26/VIII/MP.13, 22 August 2013 (collision between MT Medelin Atlas and MT Star Asia in the Fairway of the Dumai Port, between Buoy 22

Cathinka, the Court found that the negligence of the Singaporean vessel's Chief Officer resulted in the collision between that vessel and an Indonesian vessel in the Sunda Strait.[117] The Court consequently passed its judgment to the Embassy of China, which had issued the competence certificate to the Chief Officer, without handing down a punishment.[118]

One of the challenges faced by the Maritime Court is that the general Indonesian courts have concurrent jurisdiction over marine incidents.[119] This means that while the Maritime Court has the power to decide upon the administrative liability of seafarers, the general courts have the competence to decide upon criminal and civil liability.[120] This leaves open the possibility of contradictory judgments.[121] The Shipping Law also confers the competence to investigate marine incidents to the National Transportation Safety Committee (*Komite Nasional Keselamatan Transportasi*).[122] The difference between its function and that of the Maritime Court is that the Safety Committee does not have the power to determine liability for any incidents.[123]

4 *Foreign Vessels and Aircraft Protected by Sovereign Immunity*

Foreign vessels and aircraft that enjoy sovereign immunity, such as warships and military aircraft,[124] are subject to, *inter alia*, the Innocent Passage Regulation, the Archipelagic Sea Lanes Passage Regulation, and the Indonesian Waters Law. They have the rights of innocent passage and archipelagic sea lanes passage,[125] and are prohibited from using military equipment and conducting military drills.[126] This prohibition may be waived with the consent of

---

and Buoy 23), online: <http://mahpel.dephub.go.id/putusan/_shared/upload/putusan/pdf/7fia979bdboocfea3a5b734527593b92.pdf>.

117 Maritime Court Judgment No HK.2010/34/XII/MP.12, 11 December 2012 (collision between MT Norgas Cathinka and KMP Bahuga Jaya in the Sunda Strait), online: <http://mahpel.dephub.go.id/putusan/_shared/upload/putusan/pdf/b80d169697b44c15c993978102ec-c46b.pdf>.

118 *Ibid.*, at 612, para. v.

119 Public Communication Center of the Ministry of Transportation, "Peran Mahkamah Pelayaran Perlu Dioptimalkan", (9 November 2011), online: Indonesian Ministry of Transportation Website <http://dephub.go.id/welcome/readPost/peran-mahkamah-pelayaran-perlu-dioptimalisasi-7691>.

120 *Ibid.*

121 Public Communication Center of the Ministry of Transportation, *supra* note 119.

122 *Shipping Law, supra* note 14, article 256(1) and (2).

123 *Ibid.*, article 256(3).

124 See *UNCLOS, supra* note 6, articles 29–32, 42(5), and 236.

125 *Innocent Passage Regulation, supra* note 16, article 2(1) and *Archipelagic Sea Lanes Passage Regulation, supra* note 30, article 2.

126 *Ibid.*, article 4(1)(f); *Archipelagic Sea Lanes Passage Regulation, supra* note 30, article 4(4) and *Indonesian Waters Law, supra* note 17, article 12(2) and its Elucidation.

Indonesia, as shown by a recent naval exercise held in West Sumatra involving 32 countries.[127] If the exercise of the right of archipelagic sea lanes passage by immunity-protected foreign vessels or aircraft results in a loss, injury, or damage to Indonesia, the flag state bears international responsibility.[128]

5 *Submarine Cables, Electric Generation, and Marine Scientific Research*

Pursuant to Indonesian Law No. 5 of 1983 on the Indonesian Exclusive Economic Zone (EEZ Law), foreign vessels have the freedom of navigation and freedom to lay submarine cables and pipelines in Indonesia's EEZ, subject to the applicable provisions of international law.[129] Foreign vessels may also engage in economic exploration and/or exploitation in the EEZ, such as generating electricity from hydropower, wave power, and wind power, insofar as the government has licensed such activities or if those activities are based on any international agreement to which Indonesia is a party.[130] A license from the government is required for creating and/or making use of artificial islands and other installations,[131] as well as conducting scientific research in the EEZ.[132] If the government does not deny an application four months after it is received, the research project may be carried out six months after the date of receipt.[133]

6 *Other Regulations*

Foreign vessels are prohibited from transporting passengers and/or goods between islands or ports in Indonesia,[134] must not fly the Indonesian flag,[135]

127 Nani Afrida, "Komodo Military Exercise Kicks Off in West Sumatra," *The Jakarta Post* (12 April 2016), online: <http://www.thejakartapost.com/news/2016/04/12/komodo-military-exercise-kicks-west-sumatra.html>.

128 *Archipelagic Sea Lanes Passage Regulation, supra* note 30, article 10(2). The Elucidation of this Article stipulates that this provision implements *UNCLOS, supra* note 6, articles 42(5) and 54, which respectively refer to foreign vessels and aircraft protected by sovereign immunity and the applicability of the provision to vessels and aircraft making archipelagic sea lanes passage.

129 *EEZ Law, supra* note 7, article 4(3).

130 *Ibid.*, article 5(1).

131 *Ibid.*, article 6.

132 *Ibid.*, article 7.

133 *Ibid.*, Elucidation of article 7.

134 *Shipping Law, supra* note 14, article 8(2).

135 *Ibid.*, article 165(2).

and must only fly the Indonesian flag in addition to their respective state flags when they are about to enter, exit and while they are at any Indonesian port.[136] They may also engage in activities other than transporting passengers and/or goods in the Indonesian waters, such as oil and gas surveying, drilling, offshore construction, supporting offshore operations, dredging and salvage, and underwater work, provided that: (1) there are not or not enough Indonesian vessels to carry out those activities; and (2) such activities are licensed by the Minister of Transportation.[137]

Those activities may only be carried out where the government has failed to procure an Indonesian vessel or a foreign vessel purchased by an Indonesian national or corporation by way of leasing.[138] Where a foreign vessel for the above activities is purchased by an Indonesian corporation, the corporation must be 100% owned by Indonesians.[139] The procurement rules do not apply in case of an emergency or urgency, such as when there is an incident or disruption to the safety of shipping.[140] Furthermore, foreign vessels may be subject to arrest and destruction by the Indonesian authorities for violations of the law based on sufficient evidence[141] and may be subject to hot pursuit by the Indonesian authorities if they violate provisions relating to the EEZ.[142]

Where a foreign vessel or a foreign national on board is arrested by the authorities, representatives of the flag state, the owner of the vessel, the ship's captain, or whomever has a professional or commercial affiliation with the vessel may file a request for the release of the vessel or person.[143] The request may be granted if the applicant posts bail, the amount of which will be determined by the court.[144]

---

136 *Ibid.*, article 166(2).

137 Regulation of the Minister of Transportation No. 10 of 2014 on the Procedure and Requirements for Granting the License to Use Foreign Vessels for Activities Other Than Transporting Passengers and/or Goods in Domestic Sea Transport Activities, as amended by the Regulations of the Minister of Transportation No. 79 of 2014, No. 10 of 2015, and No. 200 of 2015 (Indonesia), articles 2(1)-(3) and 9(3).

138 *Ibid.*, articles 9(2)-(2a) and 11(4)-(4a).

139 *Ibid.*, articles 9(2a)(b)(2) and 11(4a)(b)(2).

140 *Ibid.*, article 13A.

141 *EEZ Law, supra* note 7, article 13 and its Elucidation; *Fisheries Law, supra* note 65, article 69(4).

142 *Ibid.*, article 4(1)(c) and its Elucidation.

143 *Ibid.*, article 15(1) and its Elucidation.

144 *Ibid.*, article 15(2).

V IMO-Approved Routeing Arrangements in National Waters

The IMO has adopted a wide range of measures, including traffic separation schemes, archipelagic sea lanes, and ship reporting systems.[145] The IMO approved the partial designation of archipelagic sea lanes in Indonesian archipelagic waters in 1988.[146] The Annex to the IMO Resolution (MSC. 72 (69)) sets out the Indonesian archipelagic sea lanes as follows (see figure 5.1):

1. *Sea Lane I*: South China Sea-Natuna Sea-Karimata Strait-Western Java Sea-Sunda Strait-Indian Ocean.
   – Sea Lane IA: Spur from North of P. Merapas to Point I-3 (00° 50'.00 N; 106° 16'.33 E).
2. *Sea Lane II:* Celebes (Sulawesi) Sea-Makassar Strait-Lombok Strait-Indian Ocean.
3. *Sea Lane IIIA:* Pacific Ocean-Maluku Sea-Seram Sea-Banda Sea-Ombai Strait-Sawu Sea-Indian Ocean.
   – Sea Lane IIIB: Spur from Point IIIA-8 (03° 20'.00 S; 125° 30'.00 E) – IIIB-2 (08° 31'.00 S; 127° 33'.00 E); Banda Sea-Leti Strait-Timor Sea.
   – Sea Lane IIIC: Spur from Point IIIA-8 (03° 20'.00 S; 125° 30'.00 E) – IIIC-2 (06° 44'.00 S; 132° 35'.00 E); Banda Sea-Arafuru Sea.
   – Sea Lane IIID: Spur from Point IIIA-11 (09° 23'.00 S; 122° 55'.00 E) – IIID-1 (10° 58'.00 S; 122° 11'.00 E); Sawu Sea-Sea between Sawu and Roti Islands-Indian Ocean.
   – Sea Lane IIIE: Spur from Point IIIA-2 (01° 40'.00 N; 126° 57'.50 E) – IIIE-2 (04° 32'.20 N; 125° 10'.40 E).[147]

---

145 IMO Maritime Safety Committee Resolution MSC.72(69), *Adoption, Designation, and Substitution of Archipelagic Sea Lanes*, adopted on 19 May 1998, online: <http://www.imo.org/blast/blastDataHelper.asp?data_id=15438&filename=72(69).pdf>, accessed on 1 June 2016 [*Resolution MSC.72(69)*], preamble, para. 3; IMO Maritime Safety Committee Resolution MSC.71(69), *Adoption of Amendments to the General Provisions on Ships' Routeing (Resolution A.572(14) as amended)*, adopted on 19 May 1998, online: <http://www.imo.org/blast/blastDataHelper.asp?data_id=15437&filename=71(69).pdf>; IMO Assembly Resolution A.572(14), *General Provisions on Ships' Routeing*, adopted on 20 November 1985, online: <http://www.imo.org/blast/blastDataHelper.asp?data_id=22369&filename=A572(14).pdf>; and see also The Convention on the Safety of Life at Sea, (SOLAS) *U.N.T.S.*, Chapter V, Regulation 10, online: <http://www.imo.org/en/OurWork/facilitation/documents/solas%20v%20on%20safety%20of%20navigation.pdf>.

146 *Resolution MSC.72(69), supra* note 145.

147 *Ibid.*

This designation may also be found in the Archipelagic Sea Lanes Passage Regulation[148] and its Annex.[149] As shown by the title of the Annex to Resolution MSC.72(69), this is a partial designation of the Indonesian archipelagic sea lanes since Article 53(4) of the UNCLOS requires that archipelagic sea lanes encompass: "all normal passage routes used as routes for international navigation or overflight through or over archipelagic waters."[150] The archipelagic sea lanes designated above are between northern and southern Indonesia. Indonesia has not proposed east-west lanes.[151]

The IMO has adopted a number of traffic separation schemes[152] and ship reporting systems[153] to ensure the safety of navigation in the Malacca and Singapore Straits, which are situated between Indonesia, Malaysia and Singapore, and are among the world's busiest waterways.[154] The IMO traffic separation for the Malacca and Singapore Straits are 250 nautical miles long and lie between Permatang Sedepa (One Fathom Bank) and just before the South China Sea, near Horsburgh Lighthouse.[155] The overall traffic management scheme involves detailed coordinates of the traffic separation schemes, inshore traffic zones, and precautionary areas in the Malacca and Singapore Straits.[156]

The IMO has adopted a mandatory ship reporting system for vessels traversing the Malacca and Singapore Straits.[157] Vessels that have a capacity of at least 300 gross tonnage or are 50 metres long or more; carrying hazardous

148 *Archipelagic Sea Lanes Passage Regulation, supra* note 30, article 11.

149 *Ibid.,* Annex I. This Annex provides detailed coordinates of the designated archipelagic sea lanes in Indonesian waters.

150 See United States, Bureau of Oceans and International Environmental and Scientific Affairs, "Limits in the Seas, No. 141, Indonesia: Archipelagic and Other Maritime Claims and Boundaries", at 5, U.S. Department of State, online: <http://www.state.gov/documents/organization/231912.pdf>.

151 *Ibid.,* at 4.

152 See IMO, *Ships' Routing, 2015 Edition,* 12th ed. (London: IMO Publishing, 2015), Part B, Section V.

153 IMO Maritime Safety Committee, *Resolution MSC.73(69), Mandatory Ship Reporting Systems,* adopted on 19 May 1998, Annex 1, [*Resolution MSC.73(69)*], online: <http://www.imo.org/blast/blastDataHelper.asp?data_id=15439&filename=73(69).pdf>.

154 See BIMCO and the Maritime Authorities of Indonesia, Malaysia, and Singapore (Cooperative Mechanism for the Straits of Malacca and Singapore), *Safe Passage: The Straits of Malacca and Singapore* (Bagsvaerd, Denmark: *BIMCO*), at 2, online: <https://www.bimco.org/~/media/Products/Manuals-Pamphlets/Safe_Passage_Straits_of_Malacca_and_Singapore/Safe_Passage_-_The_Straits_of_Singapore_and_Malacca_2014-05_Pamphlet.ashx>.

155 *Ibid.,* at 8.

156 IMO, *Ships' Routing, supra* note 145.

157 *Resolution MSC.73(69), supra* note 145.

materials; or fitted with Very High Frequency ("VHF") are required to report before traversing the Straits.[158] The report is to be made to the Vessel Traffic Service (VTS) authorities complete with the name, call sign, IMO identification number, position, hazardous cargo and class (if any) of the vessel.[159] Vessels must also report when navigating into or from certain areas as described in the IMO Resolution.[160] Each vessel must have a VHF radio telephone and monitor the relevant VHF channel.[161] If it wishes to call the VTS authorities, it should do so through a specific VHF channel, depending on the sector and location of the vessel.[162]

VI Conclusion

As the largest archipelagic state in the world and with important archipelagic sea lanes, monitoring Indonesian waters is not an easy task. The Malacca and Singapore Straits especially present a unique challenge due to their special status as straits used for international navigation. In 2007, Indonesia, Malaysia, and Singapore, implementing Article 43 of UNCLOS agreed to establish a Cooperative Mechanism to enable user states and other stakeholders to cooperate with the littoral states in enhancing navigational safety and environmental protection in those Straits.[163]

Despite the challenges, the Cooperative Mechanism is a historic breakthrough,[164] and in some ways goes beyond what is mandated in Article 43.[165] The Mechanism expressly recognizes the role of the IMO and also welcomes participation of not only user states, but also private entities and other

158 *Ibid.,* clause 1.

159 *Ibid.,* clause 3.2.

160 *Ibid.,* clause 3.2(.3).

161 *Ibid.,* clause 4.2.

162 *Ibid.,* clause 5.1.

163 See Cooperative Mechanism, "Establishment," online: <http://www.cm-soms.com/?p=td&id=6>.

164 Tommy Koh, "New Milestone in Better Straits Cooperation: Article 43 of UNCLOS Helps Keep Malacca, Singapore Straits Safe, Secure and Clean", *Business Times* (28 September 2007), online: Lee Kuan Yew School of Public Policy <http://lkyspp.nus.edu.sg/ips/wp-content/uploads/sites/2/2013/04/pa_tk_bt_New-milestone-in-better-straits-cooperation_2809071.pdf>.

165 See Leonardo Bernard, "The Cooperative Mechanism in the Straits of Malacca and Singapore" in Robert C. Beckman et al., eds., *Freedom of Navigation and Globalization,* (Leiden and Boston: Brill Nijhoff, 2015) at 217.

stakeholders.[166] It is intended to be simple, so that it can accommodate other forms of cooperative arrangements or consider special circumstances of certain users.[167] Most importantly, it addresses the challenges in managing the Straits by involving user states and other stakeholders without infringing upon the sovereignty of the littoral states.[168]

---

166 See Robert Beckman, "The Establishment of Cooperative Mechanism" in Aldo Chircop et al., eds., *The Future of Ocean Regime-Building* (Leiden: Martinus Nijhoff Publishers, 2009) at 252.

167 "The Co-operative Mechanism between the Littoral States and User States on Safety of Navigation and Environmental Protection in the Straits of Malacca and Singapore," Submission by Indonesia, Malaysia and Singapore to the IMO, IMO/SGP 2.1/1, 16 August 2007, also quoted in Bernard, *supra* note 165, at p. 217.

168 *Ibid.*

CHAPTER 6

Navigation of Foreign Vessels in Malaysian Waters: between Compliance with International Law and National Regulation of Discretion

David M. Ong

1 Introduction

The modern international law of the sea is characterized by the need to balance the traditional freedoms of the sea, foremost among these the freedom of navigation, and on the other hand, the progressive enclosure of the seas by increased maritime jurisdiction afforded to coastal States. The international legal framework for this balancing act between maritime freedoms and coastal State enclosure is in the 1982 UN Convention on the Law of the Sea (UNCLOS),[1] which sets out both the quantitative (distance) and qualitative (jurisdiction) legal constraints to coastal State expansion of their control over marine areas adjacent to their coastlines.

This maritime jurisdiction is provided to the coastal States through the 12 nautical mile (nm) territorial seas, 24 nm contiguous zones, 200 nm exclusive economic zones (EEZs) and finally, continental shelves that can extend to 350 nm or 100 nm beyond the 2,500 meter (m) isobath, which is a line connecting the depth of 2,500 m. Within the interstices of these spatial and jurisdictional constraints, coastal States navigate between complying with their international obligations upholding the traditional freedoms of the sea and their regulatory discretion to exercise their sovereignty in the territorial sea and sovereign rights and jurisdiction in the EEZ and continental shelf. A collective assessment of individual State practice on how coastal States implement their regulatory discretion within these designated maritime jurisdictional zones goes a long way to establishing where the balance lies between coastal State control and the freedoms of foreign-flagged State vessels within these zones.

This chapter will examine the regulation of foreign vessel navigation within Malaysian waters with a view to assessing first, whether Malaysia is in compliance with its international obligations to ensure innocent passage and freedom of navigation within waters under its jurisdiction, and second, the extent

1 U.N. Convention on the Law of the Sea, 1833 *U.N.T.S.* 397.

 | DOI:10.1163/9789004396272_007

to which Malaysia exercises its discretion on this issue. This discussion will then look at whether and how Malaysia is either upholding the navigational freedoms enunciated in UNCLOS or constraining them because of their perceived impingement upon Malaysian national interests. Finally, where Malaysian domestic law is at variance with its obligations under UNCLOS, but is not enforced by Malaysian authorities, this chapter will consider whether the existence of such incompatible national law nevertheless constitutes a breach of international law for the purpose of possible attribution of State responsibility.

In this chapter navigational freedoms include not only the freedom of navigation itself, but also associated maritime freedoms, such as: the freedom of fishing, subject to relevant provisions within the UNCLOS; the freedom to conduct marine scientific research; and the freedom to lay pipelines and cables. All these navigational and maritime freedoms are listed in Article 87(1) of the UNCLOS. These associated maritime freedoms are subject to the condition that they "shall be exercised by all States with due regard for the interests of other States in their exercise of the freedom of the high seas, and also with due regard for the rights under this Convention with respect to activities in the Area."[2]

II Geographical Characteristics and Historical Practice

Malaysia's geographical position is unique. It is arguably a hydrographically divided country with peninsular Malaysia being separated by the southern part of the South China Sea from the two Malaysian (federal) states of Sabah and Sarawak on Borneo island. The Indonesian island of Natuna lies in-between peninsular Malaysia and its two federal states on Borneo island. Natuna has been incorporated into the archipelagic baselines system of Indonesia,[3] exacerbating the hydrographically separated nature of Malaysia. This unique geographical position of Malaysia was the basis for the negotiation of Article 47(6) in the UNCLOS within Article 47 which deals with archipelagic baselines. Article 47(6) was specifically drafted to allow Malaysia to maintain its internal maritime communication links between peninsular Malaysia, on the

2 *Ibid.*, Article 87(2).

3 See: Annex I, The List of Geographical Coordinates of Points of The Indonesian Archipelagic Baselines Based on the Government Regulation of the Republic of Indonesia Number 38 of 2002, As Amended By The Government Regulation of the Republic of Indonesia Number 37 of 2008, in *Limits In The Seas*, No. 141, "Indonesia Archipelagic and Other Maritime Claims and Boundaries," Office of Ocean and Polar Affairs, Bureau of Oceans and International Environmental and Scientific Affairs, U.S. Department of State, September 15, 2014.

one hand, and Sabah and Sarawak on Borneo island on the other hand. Article 47(6) provides:

> If a part of the archipelagic waters of an archipelagic State lies between two parts of an immediately adjacent neighbouring State, existing rights and all other legitimate interests which the latter State has traditionally exercised in such waters and all rights stipulated by agreement between those States shall continue and be respected.

Malaysia is also adjacent to a major international shipping lane – the Malacca Straits. In November 1971, the three littoral States of the Malacca Straits – Malaysia, Indonesia and Singapore – issued a "Statement on the Malacca Straits",[4] wherein, *inter alia*, Malaysia and Indonesia adopted a common position purporting to deny the Straits of Malacca its legal status as "international straits," with Singapore taking note of their joint decision.[5] Specifically, the two countries objected to the Malacca Straits being designated as "international straits" due to their concerns that the control and management of these Straits would become internationalized. Instead, Malaysia and Indonesia preferred the application of the innocent passage regime for international shipping through the Straits and hoped to retain control over such shipping. Their efforts were ultimately not successful as a new passage regime "transit passage" was adopted in Part III of the UNCLOS, and it is this regime that applies to the Malacca Straits.

Indonesia, Malaysia and Singapore held consultations with the States that constituted the major users of the Straits during the course of the Third U.N. Conference on the Law of the Sea (UNCLOS III) and reached a common understanding regarding the purpose and meaning of Article 233,[6] in relation to its application to the Straits of Malacca and Singapore, to take into account the peculiar geographic and traffic conditions in those Straits. Article 233 provides:

> Nothing in Sections 5, 6 and 7 (of Part XII on "Protection and Preservation of the Marine Environment") affects the legal regime of straits used

4 The text of this Statement can be found in Phiphat Tangsubkul, *ASEAN and the Law of the Sea*, Singapore: Institute of Southeast Asian Studies (ISEAS) (1982) Appendix J, at 134. For a discussion on the background and consequences of this Joint Statement, see Michael Leifer, *Malaysia, Singapore and Indonesia*, Sijthoff & Noordhoff, Netherlands: Alphen aan de Rijn (1978) at 48.

5 See: Paragraph 5 of the (Joint) 1971 Statement, *ibid.*

6 UNCLOS, *supra* note 1, Article 233 is entitled: "Safeguards with respect to straits used for international navigation."

> for international navigation. However, if a foreign ship other than those referred to in Section 10 has committed a violation of the laws and regulations referred to in article 42, paragraph 1(a) and (b), causing or threatening major damage to the marine environment of the straits, the States bordering the straits may take appropriate enforcement measures and if so shall respect mutatis mutandis the provisions of this section.

This common understanding was transmitted to the President of the Conference by a letter from the representative of Malaysia.[7] The Annex to this letter sets out that:

> 1. Laws and regulations enacted by States bordering the Straits under article 42, paragraph 1 (a) of the convention, refer to laws and regulations relating to traffic separation schemes, including the determination of under keel clearance for the Straits provided in article 41.
> 2. Accordingly, a violation of the provision of resolution A.375(X), by the Inter-Governmental Maritime Consultative Organization adopted on 14 November 1977, whereby the vessels referred to therein shall allow for an under keel clearance of at [east 3.5 metres during passage through the Straits of Malacca and Singapore, shall be deemed, in view of the peculiar geographic and traffic conditions of the Straits, to be a violation within the meaning of article 233. The States bordering the Straits may take appropriate enforcement measures, as provided for in article 233. Such measures may include preventing a vessel violating the required under keel clearance from proceeding. Such action shall not constitute denying, hampering, impairing or suspending the right of transit passage in breach of articles 42, paragraph 2 or 44 of the draft convention.
> 3. States bordering the Straits may take appropriate enforcement measures in accordance with article 233, against vessels violating the laws and regulations referred to in article 42, paragraph 1 (*a*) and (6) causing or threatening major damage to the marine environment of the Straits.

7 Dated 28 April and received 29 April, 1982. Doc A/CONF.62/L.145. In *Official Records of the Third United Nations Conference on the Law of the Sea, Volume XVI* (*Summary Records, Plenary, First and Second Committees, as well as Documents of the Conference, Eleventh Session*) at: <http://legal.un.org/diplomaticconferences/lawofthesea-1982/docs/vol_XVI/a_conf-62_l-145.pdf>.

4. States bordering the Straits shall, in taking the enforcement measures, observe the provisions on safeguards in Section 7, Part XII of the draft convention.
5. Articles 42 and 233 do not affect the rights and obligations of States bordering the Straits regarding appropriate enforcement measures with respect to vessels in the Straits not in transit passage. ...

The letter shows a modification of the previous Malaysian position in this regard. This modified position was reflected in subsequent government policy statements and academic commentary. A recent Statement by the Permanent Representative of Malaysia to the United Nations, provides, *inter alia*, as follows:

> Closer to home, the Straits of Malacca is one of the most important international waterways which connect the Indian Ocean to the Pacific Ocean. Due to the positive growth and relevance of the Straits in facilitating international trade, it continues to pose a variety of challenges in balancing the economic viability and environmental sustainability of the area. As such, in line with Part III of UNCLOS 1982, on the Straits Used for International Navigation, Malaysia has put in place its Traffic Separation Scheme and Aids to Navigation in maintaining safety and security of the passage through the Straits. A Cooperative Mechanism on Safety and Navigation and Environmental Protection in the Straits of Malacca was also established with two other littoral States, as practical and effective framework for international cooperation in the Straits of Malacca and Singapore.[8]

Mohd Rusli has observed that in terms of maritime navigation, the Malacca Straits have always been regarded as a single strait, even though the international watercourse is formed by two different Straits, namely the Strait of Malacca and the Strait of Singapore.[9] It is then suggested that the Straits of Malacca and Singapore fulfil the criteria for the application of the transit passage regime if

8 See: paragraph 8 of Statement by H.E. Ambassador Hussein Haniff, Permanent Representative of Malaysia to the United Nations, at the Plenary Meeting of the General Assembly, devoted to the commemoration of the thirtieth anniversary of the opening for signature of the 1982 United Nations Convention on the Law of the Sea, New York, USA, 11 December 2012, at: <https://www.un.int/malaysia/sites/www.un.int/files/Malaysia/67th_session/2012-12-11_unclos.pdf>.

9 Mohd Hazmi bin Mohd Rusli, "The Application of Transit Passage Regime in Straits Used for International Navigation: A Study of the Straits of Malacca and Singapore", *Asian Politics and Policy*, Volume 4, October 2012, 549–569, at 549.

they are considered as a single strait(s), but not if each strait is considered a separate strait.[10] According to Rahman, recognition of the application of the transit passage regime of the Malacca Straits paves the way for a multilateral, rather than trilateral, approach to the management of these Straits.[11] Rahman explains this change of emphasis by observing that prior to 2001 the maritime cooperation regime for the Straits of Malacca was mainly trilateral in nature but there was a change to international cooperation regime following 9/11,[12] to incorporate an enhanced security element. Subsequently, she notes that the International Maritime Organization (IMO) adopted a multilateral approach to the Straits of Malacca and Singapore based on the generalized principles of conduct, incorporating respect for the sovereignty of the littoral States, alongside compliance with the burden sharing principle under Article 43 of the UNCLOS.[13] Rahman concludes that the multilateralism approach of the IMO has transformed the previous trilateral cooperation into multilateral cooperation in the Straits of Malacca, combining the efforts of State actors (littoral States and user States) as well as non-State actors (non-governmental organizations and the international shipping industries).[14]

III Regulation of Navigational Freedoms

1 *Malaysian Declaration upon Ratification of* UNCLOS

Having signed the treaty text of the 1982 UNCLOS when it was opened for signature on 10 December 1982, Malaysia followed this with the deposit of its instrument of ratification on 14 October 1996. Article 310 of the UNCLOS allows States to make declarations or statements regarding its application at the time of signing, ratifying or acceding, which do not purport to exclude or modify the legal effect of the provisions of the UNCLOS. Malaysia exercised its right under Article 310 and attached a Declaration to its ratification of the UNCLOS. The Declaration states:

> In accordance with article 310 of the United Nations Convention on the Law of the Sea, the Government of Malaysia makes the following declarations:
>
> …

10 *Ibid.*

11 Nazira Abdul Rahman, "Multilateralism in the Straits of Malacca and Singapore", *Marine Policy*, Volume 44, February 2014, 232–238, at 232.

12 *Ibid.*

13 *Ibid.*

14 *Ibid.*

> 3. The Malaysian Government also understands that the provisions of the Convention do not authorize other States to carry out military exercises or manoeuvers, in particular those involving the use of weapons or explosives in the exclusive economic zone without the consent of the coastal State.
> 4. In view of the inherent danger entailed in the passage of nuclear-powered vessels or vessels carrying nuclear material or other material of a similar nature and in view of the provision of article 22, paragraph 2, of the Convention on the Law of the Sea concerning the right of the coastal State to confine the passage of such vessels to sea lanes designated by the State within its territorial sea, as well as that of article 23 of the Convention, which requires such vessels to carry documents and observe special precautionary measures as specified by international agreements, the Malaysian Government, with all of the above in mind, requires the aforesaid vessels to obtain prior authorization of passage before entering the territorial sea of Malaysia until such time as the international agreements referred to in article 23 are concluded and Malaysia becomes a party thereto. Under all circumstances, the flag State of such vessels shall assume all responsibility for any loss or damage resulting from the passage of such vessels within the territorial sea of Malaysia.
> 5. The Malaysian Government also wishes to reiterate the statement relating to article 233 of the Convention in its application to the Straits of Malacca and Singapore which has been annexed to a letter dated 28 April 1982 transmitted to the President of the Third United Nations Conference on the Law of the Sea.[15]

One of the most contentious issues raised by Malaysia in its Declaration is in paragraph 3, namely, that the provisions of the Convention do not authorize other States to carry out military exercises or manoeuvers, in particular those involving the use of weapons or explosives, in the EEZ without the consent of the coastal State. Pedrozo has stated that:

> All nations have an absolute right under international law to conduct military activities beyond the territorial sea of another nation. …Efforts by a handful of nations to expand coastal State authority in the EEZ to

15 Accessible from the UN Department of Ocean Affairs and the Law of the Sea (UNDOALOS) website, at: <http://www.un.org/depts/los/convention_agreements/convention_declarations.htm>.

> include residual competencies and rights in the zone were rejected by a majority of the States participating in the UNCLOS negotiations.[16]

He continues stating that "(m)ost nations agreed with the position advocated by the major maritime powers, that [m]ilitary operations, exercises and activities have always been regarded as internationally lawful uses of the sea. The right to conduct such activities will continue to be enjoyed by all States in the exclusive economic zone."[17] He goes on to conclude that:

> In the end, the Conference negotiators finally agreed on Articles 55, 56, 58 and 86, all of which accommodate the various competing interests of coastal States and user States in the EEZ without diminishing freedom of navigation and other internationally lawful uses of the sea. Dissatisfied with the outcome of the negotiations, however, a few nations have sought to unilaterally expand their control in the EEZ, particularly by imposing restrictions on military operations and other lawful activities. These efforts impinge on traditional uses of the oceans by other States and are inconsistent with international law and State practice.[18]

This debate is ongoing with recent exchanges by commentators on the status of military exercises being conducted within Malaysian waters. Specifically, Malaysia's domestic legal requirements for prior authorization for the passage of nuclear-powered ships within its territorial sea and the prior consent necessary for military exercises or manouevres within its EEZ have been listed as examples of "excessive maritime claims" challenged during the period of October 1, 2015 through September 30, 2016, as part of the long-standing U.S. Department of Defense, Freedom of Navigation (FON) program,[19] as set out

16 Raul (Pete) Pedrozo, "Military Activities in the Exclusive Economic Zone: East Asia Focus", *International Legal Studies*, Vol.90 (2014) 514–543, at 515, citing Satya N. Nandan and Shabtai Rosenne, eds., *United Nations Convention on the Laws of the Sea 1982: A Commentary*, Vol. II 491–821 (1993) at 529–530. at: <https://www.usnwc.edu/getattachment/973bec67-9225-4dde-9550-26279c600e2f/Military-Activities-in-the-Exclusive-Economic-Zone.aspx>.

17 *Ibid.*, at 515–516, citing *Third UN Conference on the Law of the Sea, Plenary Meetings, Official Records*, Vol.17, U.N. Doc. A/CONF.62/WS/37 and ADD.1–2, 244 (1973–1982).

18 *Ibid.*, at 516.

19 A summary of the historical background and practice of the U.S. Freedom of Navigation program, at: <http://policy.defense.gov/Portals/11/DoD%20FON%20Program%20Summary%2016.pdf?ver=2017-03-03-141350-380>.

in its Report for Fiscal Year 2016.[20] This categorization by the United States has been challenged by the pre-eminent Malaysian maritime security policy academic, B.A. Hamzah, who argues that the absence of any explicit prohibition against the Malaysian exercise of its jurisdiction in its territorial sea and EEZ on foreign military activities allows Malaysia to institute such prior authorization requirements, based on a wide definition of what such activities constitute.[21] He comments further that: "As long as the activities are military in nature and the activities result in the production of data to serve the military needs and can be used against its security, they are not allowed in the Malaysian EEZ, without its expressed consent. Unauthorised military activities are deemed not 'peaceful' and prejudicial to the security (of) Malaysia."[22] This broad justification for Malaysia's restrictions has been criticized by a prominent regional commentator Robert Beckman who counters that, while it is true that UNCLOS does not explicitly prohibit a coastal State from regulating military activities by foreign warships in its EEZ, neither is there any provision in UNCLOS giving coastal States jurisdiction to govern military or security matters in their EEZ.[23] Beckman acknowledges, however, that pursuant to Article 58(3) of the UNCLOS:

> the right of foreign warships to conduct military activities in the EEZ of another State is not unlimited. UNCLOS provides that in exercising their rights in the EEZ, States must have "due regard" for the "rights and duties" of the coastal State.[24]

Within this context, it should be noted that the term "due regard," albeit as provided in Article 56(2), rather than Article 58(3), of UNCLOS has been interpreted by the Arbitral Tribunal in the case brought by Mauritius against the United Kingdom over the unilateral establishment by the United Kingdom of the Chagos Marine Protected Area (MPA), as follows:

---

20 U.S. Department of Defense, Freedom of Navigation Program, "Report for Fiscal Year 2016", 28 February, 2017, at: http://policy.defense.gov/Portals/11/FY16%20DOD%20FON%20Report.pdf?ver=2017-03-03-141349-943.

21 BA Hamzah, "Unauthorised Manoeuvres in Waters: US Chides M'sia Restrictions", S Rajaratnam School of International Studies (RSIS) Commentary, No. 088, 9 May, 2017. at: https://www.rsis.edu.sg/wp-content/uploads/2017/05/CO17088.pdf.

22 *Ibid.*

23 Robert Beckman, "Unauthorised Manoeuvres in Waters: US Chides M'sia Restrictions – A Rejoinder to B.A. Hamzah", RSIS Commentary, No.092, 12 May, 2017, at: https://www.rsis.edu.sg/wp-content/uploads/2017/05/CO17092.pdf.

24 *Ibid.*

> In the Tribunal's view, the ordinary meaning of "due regard" calls for the United Kingdom to have such regard for the rights of Mauritius as is called for by the circumstances and by the nature of those rights. The Tribunal declines to find in this formulation any universal rule of conduct. The Convention does not impose a uniform obligation to avoid any impairment of Mauritius' rights; nor does it uniformly permit the United Kingdom to proceed as it wishes, merely noting such rights. Rather, the extent of the regard required by the Convention will depend upon the nature of the rights held by Mauritius, their importance, the extent of the anticipated impairment, the nature and importance of the activities contemplated by the United Kingdom, and the availability of alternative approaches. In the majority of cases, this assessment will necessarily involve at least some consultation with the rights-holding State.[25]

The final sentence of this extract is most pertinent to the issue of foreign flag-State military exercises within a coastal State's EEZ, *i.e.*, the requirement for consultation between the States involved in any such dispute. This suggests that although Malaysia cannot insist on prior authorization or consent over the exercise of foreign military activities within its EEZ, it has a right to be consulted on any plan or intention to do so by another State.

2 *Inferred Baselines: Implications for Innocent Passage*

Pursuant to Article 7 of the UNCLOS, States are entitled to construct straight baselines joining appropriate coastal base points, from which the breadth of the territorial sea is to be measured, subject to certain geographical criteria being fulfilled. Malaysia has not formally utilized straight baselines around its coasts, although such baselines can be inferred from an examination of official maps.[26] Of particular importance in this context is the map issued by the Malaysian Directorate of National Mapping on 21 December 1979, which illustrates

---

25 *Chagos MPA* (*Mauritius v UK*), Arbitral Tribunal established under Annex VII of the 1982 UNCLOS, *Award*, 18 March, 2015, at para.519, at: http://www.pcacases.com/pcadocs/MU-UK%2020150318%20Award.pdf.

26 See: Sam Bateman and Clive Schofield, "State Practice Regarding Straight Baselines in East Asia – Legal, Technical and Political Issues in a Changing Environment", paper presented at *Difficulties In Implementing The Provisions Of UNCLOS*, conference organised by the Advisory Board on the Law of the Sea (ABLOS), in Monaco, at the International Hydrographic Bureau on 16–17 October 2008, text to fn.64, citing Kriangsak Kittichaisaree *The Law of the Sea and Maritime Boundary Delimitation in South-East Asia,* (Singapore, Oxford University Press: 1987) 17–18. https://www.iho.int/mtg_docs/com_wg/ABLOS/ABLOS_Conf5/Papers/Session7-Paper1-Bateman.pdf.

Malaysia's agreed maritime boundaries and the (then) limits of Malaysia's maritime jurisdiction claims.[27] This "Peta Baru" ("New Map") delineated both its 12 nm territorial sea and 200 nm EEZ limits around both the peninsular and Borneo island parts of Malaysia.[28] The outer limits of both these maritime jurisdiction zones were drawn from inferred, rather than specified, base points connecting straight baselines around the Malaysian coastline.

In 2006 Malaysia enacted the Baselines of Maritime Zones Act.[29] According to Bateman and Schofield, this legislation provides for the declaration of geographical coordinates of base points for the straight baselines from which the territorial sea of Malaysia is determined.[30] Section 4(1) of the Act provides for the declaration of the geographical coordinates of base points from which the straight baselines of Malaysia may be determined under Section 5. Under Section 5(2), in respect of any area for which geographical co-ordinates of base points have been declared under Section 4, the method of straight baselines may be employed for determining the maritime zones of Malaysia. However, it would seem that such geographical coordinates have not yet been specified. Article 16(1) of the UNCLOS requires that "the baselines for measuring the breadth of the territorial sea ... shall be shown on charts of a scale or scales adequate for ascertaining their position. Alternatively, a list of geographical coordinates of points, specifying the geodetic datum, may be substituted."

The legal significance of this non-compliant behavior for the navigation of foreign-flagged vessels within the maritime spaces around the inferred base points for the Malaysian straight baselines relates to the fact that the legal status of the waters on the landward side of these straight baselines are to be regarded as internal waters and thus assimilated to the land territory of the coastal State.[31] However, Article 7(3) of the Convention states, *inter alia*, that: "the sea areas lying within the lines must be sufficiently closely linked to the land domain to be subject to the regime of internal waters." Moreover, Article 8(2) states that:

---

27 Full title (in Bahasa Malaysia): *Peta Baru Menunjukkan Sempadan Perairan dan Pelantar Benua Malaysia*. 1979. Map. Rampaian 97, Cetakan 1 – PPNM, Syit 1. Kuala Lumpur: Directorate of National Mapping Malaysia.

28 *Ibid.*

29 Baselines and Maritime Zones Act, 2006, Laws of Malaysia, Act 660. at: faolex.fao.org/docs/texts/mal70074.doc.

30 Bateman and Schofield, *supra* note 26, text following fn.68, citing Forbes, V.L. (2007) "The Territorial Sea Datum of Malaysia," *Maritime Institute of Malaysia* (MIMA) *Bulletin,* Vol.14, No. 4: 3–8.

31 UNCLOS, *supra* note 1, Article 8(1) of the Convention provides that "waters on the landward side of the baseline of the territorial sea form part of the internal waters of the State."

> Where the establishment of a straight baseline in accordance with the method set forth in article 7 has the effect of enclosing as internal waters areas which had not previously been considered as such, a right of innocent passage as provided in this Convention shall exist in those waters.

Although the combined legal effect of these two provisions would continue to allow for the innocent passage of foreign-flagged vessels within the maritime areas landward of the straight baselines of the coastal State, the Malaysian practice of not specifying its base points for its straight baselines raises concerns as such uncertainty could result in confusion. On the other hand, as Bateman and Schofield have noted:

> Almost all East Asian coastal countries ... have implemented a straight baseline system. In most cases, the use of straight baselines has been controversial and judged by the United States, in particular, to be "excessive", and thus subject to diplomatic protest, as well as the operational assertion of navigational rights by U.S. ships under the Freedom of Navigation (FON) program.[32]

Bateman and Schofield have observed that in the Malaysian legislation there appears to be a qualification that allows the outer limits of the territorial sea to be declared based on the recommendation of the relevant Minister.[33] This relates to Section 6 of the 2006 Baselines and Maritime Zones Act, entitled: "Limits of maritime zones." Section 6(1) initially provides that the maritime zones of Malaysia are to be measured from the baselines. However, Sub-section (2) then provides that: "Notwithstanding Subsection (1), [Malaysia] may by order published in the *Gazette*, declare the outer limit lines or the lines of delimitation of the whole or any part of any of the maritime zones of Malaysia." According to Bateman and Schofield, this allows for the relevant Malaysian maritime jurisdiction zones such as the territorial sea and EEZ limits in the 1979 Peta Baru (New Map) to be preserved.[34]

---

32 Bateman and Schofield, (2008) *supra* note 26, text to fn.33, citing J.A. Roach and R.W. Smith, *United States Responses to Excessive Maritime Claims*, The Hague, Martinus Nijhoff (1996) and also Roach and Smith "Straight Baselines: The Need for a Universally Applied Norm", *Ocean Development and International Law*, Vol. 31 (2000) 47–80.

33 Bateman and Schofield, *supra* note 26, text following fn. 68.

34 *Ibid.*, text following fn. 68.

3 *Exclusive Economic Zone (EEZ) Act: Implications for Navigational Freedoms*

The main piece of legislation governing maritime activities within the 200 nm EEZ proclaimed by Malaysia is the 1984 Exclusive Economic Zone Act.[35] Taking its cue from the sovereign rights and jurisdiction provided for coastal States in Part V of the 1982 UNCLOS on the EEZ, Malaysia has undertaken through this Act to consolidate its powers in this regard. For example, Section 5 of the 1984 EEZ Act, entitled "Prohibition of activities in the exclusive economic zone or on the continental shelf except where authorized," provides that:

> Except where authorized in accordance with the provisions of this Act or any applicable written law, no person shall in the exclusive economic zone or on the continental shelf:
> (a) explore or exploit any natural resources, whether living or non-living;
> (b) carry out any search, excavation or drilling operations;
> (c) conduct any marine scientific research: or
> (d) construct or authorize and regulate the construction, operation and use of:
> (i) any artificial island;
> (ii) any installation or structure for any of the purpose provided for in Section 4 or for any other economic purpose; or
> (iii) any installation or structure which may interfere with the exercise of the rights of Malaysia in the zone or on the continental shelf.

This provision captures many of the sovereign rights over natural resources and jurisdiction over related activities accorded to coastal States in the UNCLOS. The focus here is the balance between the sovereign rights of the coastal State and navigational freedoms. This balance is demonstrated in UNCLOS Article 56(2) which provides that: "In exercising its rights and performing its duties under this Convention in the exclusive economic zone, the coastal State shall have due regard to the rights and duties of other States and shall act in a manner compatible with the provisions of this Convention." As well there is Article 58 on "the rights and duties of other States in the exclusive economic zone", paragraph 3 which sets out that:

> In exercising their rights and performing their duties under this Convention in the exclusive economic zone, States shall have due regard to the rights and duties of the coastal State and shall comply with the laws and

35 Laws of Malaysia, Act No. 311, 1984.

> regulations adopted by the coastal State in accordance with the provisions of this Convention and other rules of international law in so far as they are not incompatible with this Part.

The first aspect of this balancing act to be assessed concerns the promulgation of both prescriptive and enforcement jurisdiction by Malaysia regarding vessel-source pollution discharges within its EEZ. In this respect, it should first be noted that Section 2 of the 1984 Malaysian EEZ Act provides a broad definition of a pollutant which is defined as:

> any substance which, if introduced into the sea, is liable to create hazards to human health or to harm living resources in the sea or other marine life, or to damage amenities or interfere with other legitimate uses of the sea and, without limiting any of the generality of the foregoing, includes any substance that is prescribed by the Minister charged with responsibility for the environment by order in the *Gazette* to be a pollutant for the purposes of this Act.

However, Section 10(1) provides that:

> if any oil, mixture containing oil or pollutant is discharged or escapes into the exclusive economic zone from any vessel, land-based source, installation, device or aircraft, from or through the atmosphere or by dumping – (a) the owner or master of the vessel, if the discharge or escape is from a vessel … shall be guilty of an offence and shall be liable to a fine not exceeding one million (Malaysian) ringgit (RM).' (approximately USD $250,000). (emphasis added)

Thus, the marine pollution offence is contingent only on the fact of an unauthorised discharge, without the requirement of any proof of contamination or pollution. Within this context, "Mixture containing oil" means:

> (a) a mixture with an oil content of one hundred parts or more in one million parts of the mixture; or
> (b) a mixture with such oil content as is prescribed by the Minister charged with responsibility for the environment by order in the Gazette to be a mixture containing oil for the purposes of this Act;

(and) "oil" means:

> (a) crude oil, diesel oil, fuel oil or lubricating oil; or

(b) any other description of oil which is prescribed by the Minister charged with responsibility for the environment by order in the Gazette to be oil for the purposes of this Act; ...[36]

Articles 42(1)(b) and 211(5) of the UNCLOS allow coastal States to have prescriptive jurisdiction to adopt laws for the prevention, reduction and control of pollution from vessels that give effect to applicable international regulations regarding the discharge of oil, oily wastes and other noxious substances in the Straits of Malacca and the Malaysian EEZ generally. The applicable international standards are those laid down in the 1973/78 International Convention for the Prevention of Pollution by Ships (MARPOL).[37] As Birnie and Boyle note: "there are strong grounds for treating the MARPOL Convention as a customary standard to be complied with by the vessels of all States, whether or not they have chosen to ratify (this convention.)"[38] These standards do not provide for the imposition of strict liability offences. Small amounts of oil discharge are permitted when en route and if more than 50 nm from land, except in select "Special Areas," where virtually all discharges are proscribed.[39] Thus, the Malaysian legislation would appear to be inconsistent with the permitted scope of prescriptive maritime jurisdiction in the UNCLOS

Moreover, the Malaysian EEZ Act sets out comprehensive powers for the relevant Malaysian government authorities in the enforcement of these provisions. Section 15(1) provides that: "The Director-General may detain any vessel from which the oil, mixture containing oil or pollutant escaped or was discharged in the circumstances mentioned in Subsection (1) of Section 14." Section 24(1) states that:

For the purpose of ensuring compliance with the provisions of this Act or any applicable written law, any authorized officer may, where he has reason to believe that an offence has been committed under this Act or such written law, without a warrant-

(a) stop, board and search any vessel within the exclusive economic zone and inspect any licence, permit, record, certificate or any other document required to be carried on board such vessel under

36 *Ibid.*, Section 2.

37 International Convention for the Prevention of Pollution by Ships, 1973 (1973) 12 ILM 1319, amended by 1978 Protocol (1978) 17 *ILM* 546.

38 Patricia Birnie and Alan Boyle, *International Law and the Environment* (Oxford: Clarendon Press, 1992), at 267.

39 See MARPOL, *supra* note 37, 1973/78, Annex I, Regulations 9 and 10.

this Act such written law or any generally accepted international rules and standards, and make copies of the same;

(b) make such further enquiries and physical inspection of the vessel, its crew, equipment, gear, furniture, appurtenances stores and cargo as may be necessary to ascertain whether or not a suspected violation of the provisions of this Act or such written law has been committed;

(c) enter and search any place in which he has reason to believe that an offence under this Act or such written law is about to be or has been committed;

(d) arrest any person who he has reason to believe has committed any offence under this Act or such written law;

(e) detain any article which he has reason to believe has been used in the commission of any offence under this Act or such written law;

(f) detain any vessel, including its equipment, gear, furniture, appurtenances, stores and cargo, which he has reason to believe has been used in the commission of any offence or in relation to which any offence has been committed under this Act or such written law.

However, Malaysia's enforcement jurisdiction in respect of marine pollution offences pursuant to Article 220 of the UNCLOS extends to vessel inspection only where there are clear grounds for believing that the vessel has committed a violation resulting in a "substantial discharge" causing or threatening "significant pollution" of the marine environment,[40] and allows the detention of a vessel only where there is "clear, objective evidence" of a discharge causing "major damage or threat of major damage" to the coastline, or related interests or resources of the coastal State.[41] As Bodansky notes: "(I)n essence, coastal state enforcement of EEZ vessel-source pollution standards is the least favoured option under (the 1982) UNCLOS III and is permitted only when a vessel has committed a discharge violation (of an internationally prescribed standard) that results in, or threatens substantial damage to the coastal state."[42] Again, Malaysian legislation appears to be in excess of the enforcement jurisdiction accorded to a coastal State under the UNCLOS.[43]

---

40 UNCLOS, *supra* note 1, Article 220(5).

41 Ibid., Article 220(6).

42 Daniel Bodansky, "Protecting the Marine Environment from Vessel-Source Pollution: UNCLOS III and Beyond" (1991) 18 *Ecological Law Quarterly*, 719 at 757–758.

43 For a general description of the jurisdiction of Malaysian and Singaporean courts over Admiralty matters, see Li and Elsworth, "Arrest of Ships in Far East Jurisdictions", in Peter

The 1984 EEZ Act also contains a "requirement for discharge or escape of certain substances to be reported". Section 12(1):

> If any oil, mixture containing oil or pollutant is discharged or escapes into the exclusive economic zone from any vessel, land-based source, installation, device or aircraft, the owner or master of the vessel, the owner or occupier of the place on land, the owner or person in charge of the installation or device or the owner or pilot of the aircraft, as the case may be, shall immediately report the occurrence of such discharge or escape to the Director-General.

Section 12(2) provides that: "Any person who fails to comply with this section shall be guilty of an offence and shall be liable to a fine not exceeding ten thousand Malaysian ringgit" (approximately, USD$2,500). Assessing this reporting requirement in light of the navigational freedoms within the Malaysian EEZ are (assimilated to the high seas regime under international law) also raises important interpretation and implementation issues.

4 *Regulation of Marine Scientific Research (MSR): Implications for Navigational Freedoms*

Article 246(1) and (2) of the UNCLOS on marine scientific research (MSR), *inter alia*, in the EEZ provides that: "Coastal States, in the exercise of their jurisdiction, have the right to regulate, authorize and conduct marine scientific research in their exclusive economic zone ... in accordance with the relevant provisions of this Convention" and that such research "shall be conducted with the consent of the coastal State." Further, Article 246(3) states that: "(c)oastal States shall, in normal circumstances, grant their consent for marine scientific research projects by other States ... to be carried out in accordance with this Convention exclusively for peaceful purposes and in order to increase scientific knowledge of the marine environment for the benefit of all mankind. To this end, coastal States shall establish rules and procedures ensuring that such consent will not be delayed or denied unreasonably."

Section 16 of the Malaysian EEZ Act, 1984 entitled: "Government consent required for conduct of marine scientific research", in Sub-section (1) provides that: "No marine scientific research may be conducted in the exclusive economic zone or on the continental shelf without the express consent of and subject to conditions imposed by the Government." Sub-section (2) of Section

---

Wetterstein and Anders Beijer (eds) *Essays in Honour of Hugo Tiberg*, Stockholm: Jurisforlaget (1996) at 466–474.

16 provides that: "Subject to Section 17, the Government shall give its consent where the marine scientific research would be carried out by any State or competent international organization for peaceful purposes and to increase scientific knowledge of the marine environment."

Section 17 of the Malaysian EEZ Act provides that Malaysia has the right to withhold consent in situations that mirror the provisions in Article 246(5) of the UNCLOS. The lack of detailed regulation on what constitutes marine scientific research (MSR) for the purposes of requiring the consent (or otherwise) of Malaysian authorities means that there is continuing uncertainty for States in relation to such activities when these are conducted by foreign-flagged vessels within the Malaysian EEZ or on its continental shelf. George noted in 2008 that there was "no law that proffers a definition of MSR and there is no comprehensive legislation on Research that includes clear provisions on MSR in Malaysia governing national/regional scientists, international scientists or international scientific organizations within Malaysia in all of her maritime zones."[44]

5 *The Fisheries Act: Navigation of Foreign Fishing Vessels through* EEZ

Section 16 of the Malaysian Fisheries Act, 1985 entitled: "Passage of foreign fishing vessel through Malaysian fisheries waters", Sub-section (1) provides that, "subject to Sub-sections (2) and (3), a foreign fishing vessel may enter Malaysian fisheries waters, for the purpose of passage through such waters in the course of a voyage to a destination outside such waters."[45] Sub-section (3) of Section 16 requires that:

> The master of a foreign fishing vessel entering Malaysian fisheries waters for the purpose mentioned in Subsection (1) shall notify by radio, telex or facsimile in the English or Malay Language an authorized officer of the name, the flag State, location, route and destination of the vessel, the types and amount of fish it is carrying and of the circumstances under which it is entering Malaysian fisheries waters.

There are a number of points to be made regarding the compatibility of the above Malaysian law with the rights and obligations in the 1982 UNCLOS. First, the current Section 16(1) is the result of a 1993 amendment, made to the

44 Mary George, "Regulating Marine Scientific Research: A Correlation Between the Law of the Sea, Science and National Sovereignty", *Malaysian Journal of Science*, Vol 27 (2008) 137–153, at 145.

45 Fisheries Act, 1985, Laws of Malaysia, Act 317.

original 1985 provision.[46] The 1985 provision stated that: "a foreign fishing vessel may enter Malaysian fisheries waters, for the purpose of innocent passage through such waters in the course of a voyage to a destination outside such waters." The original provision in the 1985 Act was clearly at variance with the implicit inclusion that all fishing vessels enjoy the freedom of navigation in the EEZs of coastal States, as evidenced by UNCLOS Article 58(1) of which states:

> In the exclusive economic zone, all States, whether coastal or land-locked, enjoy, subject to the relevant provisions of this Convention, the freedoms referred to in article 87 of navigation and overflight and of the laying of submarine cables and pipelines, and other internationally lawful uses of the sea related to these freedoms, such as those associated with the operation of ships, aircraft and submarine cables and pipelines, and compatible with the other provisions of this Convention.

Moreover, although Article 86 establishes that:

> The provisions of this Part apply to all parts of the sea that are not included in the exclusive economic zone, in the territorial sea or in the internal waters of a State, or in the archipelagic waters of an archipelagic State," it then provides that: "This article does not entail any abridgement of the freedoms enjoyed by all States in the exclusive economic zone in accordance with article 58.

Second, this original provision regarding "innocent passage" for foreign-flagged fishing vessels in the 1985 Malaysian Fisheries Act was an inversion of the navigational freedom otherwise enjoyed by such vessels within an EEZ involving an expansive interpretation of Malaysian sovereign rights and jurisdiction over living resources within its EEZ, coupled with a discriminatory approach to any foreign-flagged fishing vessels found within its EEZ. A justification for this position arises from the multiple incursions by fishing vessels from Thailand within the Malaysian EEZ, as well as other neighbouring Southeast Asian countries, from the late 1970s to the present day. Valencia, for example, has noted in relation to the 1985 Act, that "the problem of access primarily concerns Thai fishermen who were fishing in Malaysian waters before Malaysia declared an EEZ (in 1980)."[47] A more recent study observes that:

---

46 Fisheries Amendment Act, 1993, Section 9(b), Laws of Malaysia, Act A854, 15 July, 1993.

47 Mark J Valencia, *Malaysia and the Law of the Sea: The Foreign Policy Issues, the Options and Their Implications*, Kuala Lumpur, Malaysia: Institute of Strategic and International Studies (ISIS) (1991) at 96.

> Thailand's reconstructed catch totalled 266 million t(onnes) from 1950–2010, which was 2.8 times the reported landings of 95 million t(onnes). Of total reconstructed catch, 176 million t(onnes) originated from outside the Thai(land) EEZ, of which approximately 75% was caught by industrial fishing vessels either operating illegally in foreign waters or not properly reporting their catches. This suggests a failure of flag-state control, and indicates that stricter monitoring and enforcement of the Thai industrial fishing fleet should be pursued to mitigate un-controlled fishing effort both in the Thai EEZ and in the EEZs of other countries (as well as) in the High Seas.[48]

IV Regulation of Navigational Freedoms: Non-Compliance or State Responsibility?

The issue in this section concerns how international law responds to State non-compliance with its international obligations that exists in its national legislation, whether or not the State enforces such incompatible provisions against other States. Specifically, this relates to the non-compliance by Malaysia with its UNCLOS obligations within its domestic laws. First, in so far as this issue can be characterized as relating to the "interpretation and application" of the 1982 UNCLOS, then it is arguable that the domestic provisions can be challenged by other State parties to the Convention under the dispute settlement provisions in Part XV. This challenge can be undertaken irrespective of whether the interests of the State making this challenge has suffered harm or loss to its interests as a direct result of the Malaysian encroachments into the traditional navigational freedoms of the sea set out in its legislation.

Second, the doctrine of State Responsibility under international law needs to be examined. The 2001 International Law Commission (ILC) Draft Articles on State Responsibility for Internationally Wrongful Acts[49] provides in its first

48 Lydia Teh, Dirk Zeller and Daniel Pauly, *Preliminary Reconstruction of Thailand's Fisheries Catches: 1950–2010*, Fisheries Centre, The University of British Columbia, Working Paper Series, Working Paper #2015-01 (2015) 14 pp., Abstract, at 1, at: http://www.seaaroundus.org/doc/publications/wp/2015/Teh-et-al-Thailand.pdf.

49 Draft Articles on Responsibility of States for Internationally Wrongful Acts, with Commentaries, 2001, text adopted by the International Law Commission at its fifty-third session, in 2001, and submitted to the General Assembly as a part of the Commission's report covering the work of that session (A/56/10). The Report, which also contains commentaries on the draft articles, appears in the *Yearbook of the International Law Commission, 2001*, vol. II, Part Two, as corrected. Report of the International Law Commission on the work of its fifty-third session, at 91–92, at: http://legal.un.org/ilc/texts/instruments/english/commentaries/9_6_2001.pdf.

two provisions: "Article 1: Every internationally wrongful act of a State entails the international responsibility of that State," and "Article 2: There is an internationally wrongful act of a State when conduct consisting of an action or omission: (*a*) is attributable to the State under international law; and (b) constitutes a breach of an international obligation of the State." These provisions suggest that it is an internationally wrongful act (or omission to act) by a State in relation to an international obligation owed by that State, rather than the promulgation of domestic laws in breach of that obligation, that gives rise to State responsibility under international law. On the other hand, Article 12 on the "existence of a breach of an international obligation," states: "There is a breach of an international obligation by a State when an act of that State is not in conformity with what is required of it by that obligation, regardless of its origin or character." This suggests that when a State adopts domestic law that does not conform with an international obligation on that State, the act of law-making is in itself a breach of that international obligation. This is buttressed by Article 42, which provides for the invocation of responsibility by an injured State where: "A State is entitled as an injured State to invoke the responsibility of another State if the obligation breached is owed to (a) that State…" This implies that if the original act of a State consists of adopting a domestic law that goes beyond what is permitted under the UNCLOS, then any State to which the international obligation under UNCLOS is owed is entitled to invoke the responsibility of the non-compliant State under international law, provided the claimant State can show that it is an injured State in this regard.

Attention therefore shifts to what is meant by an injured State. Draft Articles, Article 31 of the "Reparation", provides:

1. The responsible State is under an obligation to make full reparation for the injury caused by the internationally wrongful act.
2. Injury includes any damage, whether material or moral, caused by the internationally wrongful act of a State.

This provision clearly suggests that a State can claim to be injured without having to show actual, material damage to its interests as a result of the breach of an international obligation owed to that State. In other words, moral injury arising from the incompatibility of a provision of national law in relation to an international legal obligation may be sufficient to constitute an internationally wrongful act by that State and, therefore, trigger State responsibility on the part of that non-compliant State. On the other hand, the ILC Commentaries notes that:

> This formulation (of paragraph 2 of article 31) is intended both as inclusive, covering both material and moral damage broadly understood, and as limitative, excluding merely abstract concerns or general interests of a State that is individually unaffected by the breach. "Material" damage here refers to damage to property or other interests of the State and its nationals which is assessable in financial terms. "Moral" damage includes such items as individual pain and suffering, loss of loved ones or personal affront associated with an intrusion on one's home or private life.[50]

On the basis of the ILC Commentaries, it would appear that the requirement of some form of material, as opposed to moral, damage is required, at least for the purposes of restitution or compensation. Article 36 of the ILC Draft Articles on "Compensation" provides that:

> 1. The State responsible for an internationally wrongful act is under an obligation to compensate for the damage caused thereby, insofar as such damage is not made good by restitution.
> 2. The compensation shall cover any financially assessable damage including loss of profits insofar as it is established.

The ILC Commentary to Article 36 notes that: "The qualification 'financially assessable' is intended to exclude compensation for what is sometimes referred to as 'moral damage' to a State, i.e. the affront or injury caused by a violation of rights not associated with actual damage to property or persons: this is the subject matter of satisfaction, dealt with in article 37."[51]

Article 37 on "Satisfaction" indicates that:

> 1. The State responsible for an internationally wrongful act is under an obligation to give satisfaction for the injury caused by that act insofar as it cannot be made good by restitution or compensation.
> 2. Satisfaction may consist in an acknowledgement of the breach, an expression of regret, a formal apology or another appropriate modality. …

Notably, however, the withdrawal of non-compliant domestic legislation incompatible with the applicable international law is not envisaged by Article

50 *Ibid.*

51 *Ibid.*, at 99.

37(2) nor is it explicitly mentioned in the accompanying ILC Commentary which remarks, *inter alia*, that:

> Paragraph 2 describes, in a non-exhaustive fashion, some modalities of satisfaction. ...Material and moral damage resulting from an internationally wrongful act will normally be financially assessable and hence covered by the remedy of compensation. Satisfaction, on the other hand, is the remedy for those injuries, not financially assessable, which amount to an affront to the State. These injuries are frequently of a symbolic character, arising from the very fact of the breach of the obligation, irrespective of its material consequences for the State concerned. ...The forms of satisfaction listed in the article are no more than examples. The appropriate form of satisfaction will depend on the circumstances and cannot be prescribed in advance. ...Paragraph 2 does not attempt to list all the possibilities, but neither is it intended to exclude them. Moreover, the order of the modalities of satisfaction in paragraph 2 is not intended to reflect any hierarchy or preference. Paragraph 2 simply gives examples which are not listed in order of appropriateness or seriousness. The appropriate mode, if any, will be determined having regard to the circumstances of each case.'[52]

Having said this, the ILC refers back to Article 30 on "Cessation and non-repetition," which provides as follows:

> The State responsible for the internationally wrongful act is under an obligation:
> (a) to cease that act, if it is continuing; (and)
> (b) to offer appropriate assurances and guarantees of non-repetition, if circumstances so require.

The Commentary notes that: "Assurances or guarantees of non-repetition may be sought by way of satisfaction (e.g. the repeal of the legislation which allowed the breach to occur) and there is thus some overlap between the two in practice."[53]

What is arguably still unclear is whether the injured State must be able to point to some form of harm or damage that it has suffered as a result of the breach or violation of an international legal obligation found to exist

52 *Ibid.*, at 105–106.
53 *Ibid.*, at 90.

between the injured State and the State responsible for this breach/violation. Moreover, if indeed some form of tangible (whether material or moral) damage or harm must be proved, then what is the required threshold of material or moral damage needed to meet the definition of an injured State for the purpose of claiming the responsibility of the State that has breached/violated the applicable international legal obligation between the two States?

While these questions may appear to be far removed from the specific legal issues involving navigation within Malaysian waters explored, they must be addressed to ensure a comprehensive international legal examination of the consequences of: 1) the exercise of prescriptive jurisdiction by a coastal State within its maritime zones, possibly resulting in non-compliant domestic legislation in relation to the different navigational rights and freedoms enjoyed by other States within these maritime zones; as well as 2) the enforcement jurisdiction exercised by a coastal State over foreign-flagged vessels within these maritime zones on the basis of non-compliant domestic legislation, which may give rise to international disputes between a coastal State and the flag States of these vessels under Part XV of UNCLOS, or even coastal State responsibility for breaches of common international obligations between these (coastal and flag) States, as canvassed above.

V Conclusions

This chapter has examined Malaysian national regulation of the full suite of navigational freedoms within its maritime jurisdiction zones with a view to assessing whether Malaysia has acted in compliance with its international obligations, especially in relation to the 1982 UNCLOS. Several discrepancies have been noted, ranging from categorization issues in relation to the notion of international straits; the initial provision of innocent passage (rather than freedom of navigation) within its 200nm EEZ for foreign fishing vessels (now withdrawn); and finally, an expansive definition of the marine pollution offence, as well as extensive enforcement jurisdiction over vessels allegedly committing this widely defined offence. It has also been observed that Malaysia has addressed its most egregious non-compliance issues, notably by 1) allowing the claim that the Malacca Straits is not an international straits to lapse over time; as well as 2) amending its 1985 Fisheries Act to allow for the passage of foreign fishing vessels through its EEZ.

Overall, Malaysia has shown a propensity to address its non-compliance with applicable international norms to ensure that it is within the limits of the law. However, questions remain regarding certain Malaysian domestic law provisions that are incompatible with Malaysia's international legal obligations under the 1982 UNCLOS and whether they may be subject to challenge by other States parties to UNCLOS through the dispute settlement mechanisms under Part XV or whether other States may make claims against Malaysia pursuant to the State responsibility doctrine.

CHAPTER 7

Archipelagic States and Maritime Navigation: Perspectives and State Practice of the Philippines

Jay L. Batongbacal

1 Introduction

The introduction of the archipelagic State concept in the early stages of the negotiation of the modern law of the sea represented a challenge to the navigational interests of the maritime powers. The "archipelago concept," as it was called, was first expressed in the 1950s in response to the call for the position of coastal States on the breadth of the territorial sea. Indonesia and the Philippines, the two largest mid-ocean archipelagoes and both former colonies with long histories of affinity with the sea, during the first UN Conference on the Law of the Sea in 1958 put into question the application of the normal and straight baseline methods devised for continental coastal States. The challenge was not finally met until 20 years later with the drafting and incorporation of Part IV detailing the concept of the Archipelagic State in the 1982 UN Convention on the Law of the Sea.[1]

The archipelagic State, comprised of "a group of islands, including parts of islands, interconnecting waters and other natural features which are so closely interrelated that such islands, waters and other natural features form an intrinsic geographical, economic and political entity, or which historically have been regarded as such",[2] is a concept that holds great significance symbolically, politically, economically, and culturally to the two largest mid-ocean archipelagic States Indonesia and the Philippines. Between them, and neighboring Malaysia (technically a coastal archipelago), the Southeast Asian archipelagoes encompass numerous straits used for international navigation and straddle numerous sea lines of communication across a vital part of the Asia Pacific. The Southeast Asian maritime region can be considered to have essentially defined the archipelagic sea lane passage regime incorporated in the UNCLOS as an attempt to differentiate the allocation of navigational rights

1 U.N. Convention on the Law of the Sea, 1833 *U.N.T.S.* 397.
2 *Ibid.*, Art 46.

 | DOI:10.1163/9789004396272_008

and freedoms in a way that accounts for the more extensive usage of the sea by Southeast Asian peoples.

II Background to UNCLOS Part IV

The seed for the question of archipelagoes and related navigational rights was laid in the *Corfu Channel*[3] and *Anglo-Norwegian Fisheries Cases*.[4] The International Court *Corfu Channel Case* established the right of innocent passage in favor of warships through straits used for international navigation; while the *Anglo-Norwegian Fisheries Case* validated the use of straight baselines by coastal States with highly irregular coastlines, including coastlines with coastal archipelagoes created by outlying islands and rocks (in Norway's case, these were formed by the *skjaergaards*). While discussions of the status and treatment of archipelagoes had been ongoing since 1911,[5] the two *Cases* gave incentives for some governments and scholars to advocate the use of straight baselines to enclose mid-ocean archipelagoes during the 1950s deliberations of the International Law Commission (ILC) prior to the First U.N. Conference on the Law of the Sea in 1958. However, the proposal eventually became too contentious and was not adopted in the ILC draft articles.[6] The application of straight baselines was important since their use could turn inter-island waters into internal waters that could be closed to foreign vessel passage.

In 1955, responding to the U.N. Secretary General's call for opinions on the breadth of the territorial sea, the Philippines expressed its claim to archipelagic State status in a *Note Verbale* which stated that it considered as its territorial waters "all waters around, between and connecting the different islands belonging to the Philippine Archipelago," circumscribed by the irregular-rectangular limits of the cession treaties between its former colonial administrators Spain and the United States.[7] The rationale for the expansive claim

3 *Corfu Channel (United Kingdom v. Albania)* [1949] *I.C.J. Rep.* 4.

4 *Anglo-Norwegian Fisheries (United Kingdom v. Norway)* [1951] *I.C.J. Rep.* 116.

5 See: Phiphat Tangsukbul, "The Southeast Asian Archipelagic States: Concept, Evolution and State Practice," Research Report No 15. East-West Environment and Policy Institute: Honolulu, 1984, at 14–16.

6 Division on Ocean Affairs and the Law of the Sea (DOALOS), "The Law of the Sea: Archipelagic States, Legislative History of Part IV of the United Nations Convention on the Law of the Sea," Sales No. E.90.V.2. United Nations: New York, 1990 at 1–2.

7 Philippines, *Note Verbale*, 20 January 1955, in Report of the International Law Commission to the General Assembly, UN Doc A/2934, *Yearbook of the International Law Commission 1955*, Vol. II. United Nations: New York, at 52–53.

can be gleaned from the purposes attributed to the treatment of the territorial waters "for purposes of protection of fishing rights, conservation of fisheries resources, enforcement of its revenue and anti-smuggling laws, defense and security, and protection of such other interests as the Philippines may deem vital to its welfare and security."[8] In addition, the Philippines reiterated its claim to "[a]ll mineral deposits and occurrences of petroleum or natural gas in public and/or private lands within the territorial waters or on the continental shelf, or its analogue in an archipelago, seaward from the shores of the Philippines which are not within the territories of other countries."[9] However, the Philippines also recognized that these waters were subject to innocent passage rights by friendly foreign vessels.[10] Thus, external security and resource access were the primary considerations for the archipelagic State claim, which reinforced long-standing historical concerns over the Philippines' territorial integrity.[11]

In 1957, Indonesia in the Djuanda Declaration expressed its claim as an archipelagic State based on history, geopolitics, and economics. Declaring that "the Indonesian archipelago has been an entity since time immemorial," and as such it was "necessary to consider all waters between the islands an entire entity."[12] It also declared "all waters around, between and connecting the islands or parts of islands belonging to the Indonesian archipelago irrespective of their width or dimension" to be part of its inland or national waters subject to absolute sovereignty, although it also permitted the peaceful passage of foreign vessels "insofar as it is not contrary to the sovereignty of the Indonesian State or harmful to her security."[13] Unlike the Philippines, which relied on the arbitrarily drawn treaty limits, Indonesia used straight baselines connecting the outermost points of its islands to describe its archipelagic waters claim.

---

8 *Ibid.*

9 *Ibid.*

10 *Ibid.*

11 The insecurities about and need to establish and maintain, territorial integrity has been a constant theme in Philippine legal and political discourse since the 1930s. All three of the principal Constitutions of the Philippines (ratified in 1935, 1973, 1987 respectively) have been headed by an Article describing and defining the "National Territory." This concern originates from the historical formation of the Philippine nation-State as an aggregation of the Luzon and Visayas islands conquered and colonized by Spain from the 1560s to 1898, and the Mindanao and Sulu islands pacified and assimilated by the United States from 1898 to the 1920s. During the 1935 Constitutional Convention, delegates were concerned about reported plans to separate the Mindanao and Sulu islands from the rest of the archipelago.

12 Proclamation on the Territorial Waters of the Republic of Indonesia, excerpted in Tangsukbul, *supra* note 5, at 32.

13 *Ibid.*

Both the Philippines and Indonesia endorsed proposals for the special treatment of archipelagoes to the first and second Law of the Sea conferences in 1958 and 1960, but these were not supported.[14] The opportunity to focus attention on archipelagos arose in 1971 with the preparatory work for the Third U.N. Conference on the Law of the Sea. In 1972, the Philippines, together with Indonesia, Fiji, and Mauritius submitted to the Seabed Committee a statement of archipelagic principles[15] that included the recognition of the archipelagic State concept together with basic passage rights in favor of foreign vessels within archipelagic waters. The passage proposal stated:

> 3. Innocent passage of foreign vessels through the waters of the archipelagic State shall be allowed in accordance with national legislation, having regard to the existing rules of international law. Such passage shall be through sea lanes as may be designated for that purpose by the archipelagic State.

This was elaborated into five draft articles on archipelagoes with numerous sections.[16] Passage rights in favor of foreign vessels were proposed to be recognized "in sea lanes suitable for the safe and expeditious passage of ships through its archipelagic waters" and the archipelagic State "may restrict the innocent passage by foreign ships through those waters to those sea lanes."[17] The original intention of the archipelagic States respecting passage rights can be properly described as restrictive and this set off alarm bells for the maritime powers in view of potential impact on submarine and carrier group operations. In the years that followed, a flurry of diplomatic activity, particularly between the United States and Indonesia in 1974, over the text submitted by the "archipelago group" introduced at the joint session of the Seabed Committee in Caracas,[18] led to the formulation and finalization of text that became Part IV of the UNCLOS.

---

14 DOALOS, "Archipelagic States," *supra* note 6, at 2.

15 Fiji, Indonesia, Mauritius and the Philippines: Archipelagic Principles. UN Doc A/AC.138/SC.II/L.15, 14 March 1973, in S. Oda, *The International Law of the Ocean Development: Basic Documents*, Vol. II. Shijtoff: Leiden, 1975, at 323.

16 Fiji, Indonesia, Mauritius and the Philippines: Draft Articles on Archipelago, UN Doc A/AC.138/SC.II/L.48, 6 August 1973, in Oda, *supra* note 15, at 323–325.

17 *Ibid.*, Article V.

18 Fiji, Indonesia, Mauritius and the Philippines: Draft Articles relating to Archipelagic States, UN Doc A/CONF. 62/C.2/L.49, 9 August 1974, in Third United Nations Conference on the Law of the Sea, 1973–1982, First and Second Session (New York, 3–15 December 1973 and Caracas, 20 June to 29 August 1974), Vol. III: Documents, United Nations: New York, 2009, at 226–227.

Throughout these discussions, the interests of archipelagic States and user States were diametrically opposed. The exchange of proposals demonstrated that archipelagic States were willing to concede or accept only innocent passage rights in favor of foreign vessels; while user States demanded unrestricted passage rights.[19] However, the archipelagic states also had internal differences with Indonesia and the Philippines on the one side and the smaller archipelagic States, like Fiji and Mauritius, not sharing their concerns about foreign vessels. The absence of solidarity among the archipelagic States undermined their ability to pressure possible concessions from the maritime powers. In August 1974, the United States was willing to concede only that "the archipelago State could require notification for any vessel or aircraft departing from these archipelagic sea lanes because of force majeure, distress or other circumstances" and was willing to discuss extending this notification requirement to areas outside archipelagic sea lanes.[20] In the end, however, no agreement on this was reached, and, instead, the dual regime for passage within archipelagic waters in UNCLOS Part IV was adopted.

III Two Passage Regimes in Archipelagic Waters

Two passage regimes exist in archipelagic waters enclosed by straight archipelagic baselines drawn in accordance with the technical requirements of UNCLOS Article 4. The first is that of innocent passage laid out in UNCLOS Part II, enjoyed by ships of all States through archipelagic waters.[21] This makes archipelagic waters analogous to the territorial sea, except that "the archipelagic State may, without discrimination in form or in fact among foreign ships, suspend temporarily in specified areas of its archipelagic waters the innocent passage of foreign ships" for purposes of security after due publicity.[22]

The second regime is that of archipelagic sea lanes passage, contained in Article 53, which is comprised of two elements: archipelagic sea lanes and the right of archipelagic sea lanes passage. Within archipelagic waters subject to innocent passage, an archipelagic State may designate "sea lanes and air routes above them suitable for continuous and expeditious passage of foreign ships and aircraft" from one part of the high seas to another part of the high seas,

19 See generally DOALOS, "Archipelagic States," *supra* note 6.

20 United States, National Archives and Records Administration, Access to Archives Database (NARA AAD). Document 1974CARACA06493, US Embassy Caracas to US Embassy Singapore, 30 July 1972.

21 UNCLOS, *supra* note 1, Art. 52(1).

22 *Ibid*, Art. 52(2).

crossing both the archipelagic waters and adjacent territorial seas.[23] These sea lanes are to be designated by axis lines through archipelagic waters, on either side of which vessels and aircraft may deviate by no more than 25 nautical miles (i.e. the sea lane is up to 50 nautical miles wide) as long as they "do not navigate closer to the coasts than 10 per cent of the distance between the nearest points on islands bordering the sea lane."[24] An archipelagic sea lane "shall include all normal passage routes used as routes for international navigation or over flight through or over archipelagic waters."[25] To manage the maritime traffic, archipelagic States may establish traffic separation schemes or substitute sea lanes in accordance with generally accepted international regulations.[26] The regulations for substitution of sea lanes are currently dealt with in the "General Provisions for the Adoption, Designation, and Substitution of Archipelagic Sea Lanes (GPASL)" adopted by the International Maritime Organization (IMO),[27] with traffic separation schemes also adopted in accordance with IMO procedures.[28]

Within the archipelagic sea lanes, ships have archipelagic sea lanes passage, defined as "the exercise in accordance with [UNCLOS] of the rights of navigation and overflight in the normal mode solely for the purpose of continuous, expeditious, and unobstructed transit between one part of the high sea or an exclusive economic zone and another part of the high seas or an exclusive economic zone."[29] In theory, these rights are to be exercised while traversing the archipelagic sea lanes designated by the archipelagic State. However, indicative of the desire of the maritime powers to preserve freedom of the seas through archipelagic waters, and as part of the concessions made to ensure acceptance of the broader regime of the archipelagic State, paragraph 12 of UNCLOS Article 53 expressly provides that "[i]f an archipelagic State does not designate sea lanes or air routes, the right of archipelagic sea lanes passage may be exercised through the routes normally used for international navigation."

As a result, in order for the two passage regimes to be geographically segregated, the archipelagic State is to designate archipelagic sea lanes. This allows

23 *Ibid*, Art. 53(1).

24 *Ibid*, Art. 53(5).

25 *Ibid.*, Art. 53(4). However, duplication of routes of similar convenience in crossing the archipelagic waters is not necessary.

26 *Ibid.*, Art. 53(6) and 53(7).

27 See Annex 2: General Provisions for the Adoption, Designation and Substitution of Archipelagic Sea Lanes, in Resolution MSC.72(69), Adoption of Amendments to the General Provisions on Ships' Routeing (Resolution A.572(14) as amended), 19 May 1998, IMO Doc MSC 69/22/Add. 1.

28 See General Provisions on Ships' Routeing. Resolution A.572(14), 20 November 1985, as amended.

29 UNCLOS, *supra* note 1, Art. 53(3).

an archipelagic State to distinguish between waters that are subject to innocent passage and waters where the right of archipelagic sea lanes passage also applies. The right of archipelagic sea lanes passage, for all practical purposes, applies only to military vessels and aircraft, despite the attempt in the UNCLOS to characterize the passage rights as available to all ships without discrimination. Passage "in the normal mode" bears no relevance to commercial vessels and aircraft which are adequately accommodated by the innocent passage regime,[30] the term was designed and negotiated specifically to accommodate navigation by submarines and aerial operations of carrier-borne aircraft.[31] In the absence of archipelagic sea lanes, all archipelagic waters used for international navigation are subject to the right of archipelagic sea lanes passage,[32] i.e., submarines may claim the right to navigate while submerged, and military aircraft may claim the right to overflight, through any part of a State's archipelagic waters.

Whether an archipelagic State has designated archipelagic sea lanes that enables the segregation of archipelagic waters and passage regimes described above is determined by the IMO GPASL, formulated in the course of Indonesia's designation of archipelagic sea lanes in 1994–1996. The GPASL introduced the concept of a "partial designation" which substantially reduces the ability of an archipelagic State to decide on archipelagic sea lane routing through the archipelagic waters. A "partial designation" is defined as a proposal "which does not meet the requirements to include all normal passage routes and navigational channels as required by UNCLOS."[33] Such a designation does not prevent the continuous use of the right of archipelagic sea lanes passage in other routes normally used for international navigation located in archipelagic waters,[34] which means that a partial designation does not accomplish the purpose of prescribing and limiting the areas through which military ships and aircraft may pass. This effectively renders the designation ineffective until the archipelagic State has carried out a complete designation, which means a designation that satisfies all the demands of the user States for routes through the archipelago.

30 B. Kwiatkowska and Etty Agoes, "Archipelagic Waters Regime in the Light of the 1982 United Nations Convention on the Law of the Sea: Convention and State Practice," *Bandung: Netherlands Cooperation with Indonesia in Legal Matters*, 1991 at 44.

31 B. Kwiatkowska and Etty Agoes, "Archipelagic Waters: An Assessment of National Legislation," in R. Wolfrum (ed). *Law of the Sea at a Crossroads: The Continuing Search for a Universally Accepted Regime*, Proceedings of an interdisciplinary symposium, July 10–14, 1990, Berlin: Dunker and Humblot, 1991, 107–151.

32 UNCLOS, *supra* note 1, Art. 53(12).

33 GPASL, *supra* note 28, Art. 2.2, para. 2.

34 *Ibid.*, Art. 6.6.

The problem that arises, which makes the concept of "partial designation" a substantial change to the UNCLOS "package deal" between archipelagic States and maritime powers, is that routing and navigation through the seas change over time depending on factors such as the nature of ships, efficiency of propulsion, maritime risks, type of cargo, and trade patterns. Routes commonly used in the 19th Century, for example, differ from those in use at present due to the difference in the volume and extent of maritime trade. Whether a designation is "complete", therefore, becomes the prerogative of user States to decide, rather than the archipelagic State. The requirement of "completeness" also nullifies the power of substitution of archipelagic sea lanes, as a substitution is no longer be necessary if all available routes are required to be designated. The original purpose of archipelagic States in seeking to limit foreign vessel passage to specified areas of the archipelagic waters within which archipelagic sea lanes are designated is no longer achievable. As stated by former Ambassador Hashim Djalal:

> ... it would be difficult to determine "all normal passage routes", because the normal passage routes used by a particular country or company may be different from the normal passage routes used by a other countries or companies, depending on their location or from where they start the passage. If "all normal passage routes" used by "all" countries in the world would be regarded as routes used for international navigation that would be designated as archipelagic sea lanes, then the whole archipelagic waters could be regarded as falling under the regime of archipelagic sea lanes passage, thus defeating the purposes of establishing the archipelagic sea lanes...[35]

Despite Indonesia's designation of sea lanes in 1996,[36] which user States have deemed to be a partial designation,[37] two principal issues of interpretation of

35 H. Djalal, "The 1982 UN Convention on the Law of the Sea and Navigational Regimes," presented at the International Conference on Maritime Transit Issues Revised. Manila, Philippines, 17–18 November 1999, in D. Johnston and A. Sirivivatnanon (eds.). *Maritime Transit and Port State Control: Trends in System Compliance*, (Southeast Asian Programme in Ocean Law, Policy and Management: Bangkok, 2000), at 79–80.

36 Act No. 6 of 08 August 1996 regarding Indonesia Waters, Division on Ocean Affairs and Law of the Sea, United Nations: New York, 2017, at www.un.org/Depts/los/LEGISLATIONANDTREATIES/PDFFILES/IDN_1996_Act.pdf.

37 R. Warner, "Implementing the Archipelagic Regime in the International Maritime Organization," in D. Rothwell and S. Bateman (eds.), *Navigational Rights and Freedoms and the New Law of the Sea*, (Kluwer Law International: The Hague, 2000), at 176.

UNCLOS Art. 53 remain unsettled. The first concerns the placement of the axis lines to designate an archipelagic sea lane. During the Indonesian designation process, differences in opinion arose between the United States, Australia, and Indonesia. The United States argued in favor of placing the axis lines in a way that maximized the sea room available for the user State's vessels and aircraft,[38] i.e., emphasizing the need for the full 50 nautical mile swath, even if the sea lane included islands within it. This was not acceptable to Indonesia since it meant surrendering parts of its land territory and territorial airspace to the user States. Australia argued that axis lines should follow safe routes for navigation,[39] while Indonesia argued that the archipelagic State was not obliged to ensure and guarantee navigational safety, but only suitability for international navigation.[40]

The second issue relates to the implementation of the 10% buffer zone around bordering islands, which is intended to prevent foreign vessels and aircraft from coming too close to the island territories of the archipelagic State. The United States argued that islands within 25 nautical miles of the axis lines were not on the "border" of the archipelagic sea lane and were not entitled to a 10% buffer zone and were even subject to overflight.[41] This was not acceptable to Indonesia. Instead of a technical solution, however, it was agreed that Indonesia would designate in its navigational charts which islands had a buffer zone for maritime and air navigation.[42]

IV Philippine State Practice

From the beginning, the Philippine position with respect to foreign vessels travelling through the archipelago has been to accept only the regime of innocent passage. As noted above, in its 1956 *Note Verbale*, the Philippines laid claim to "[a]ll waters around, between and connecting the different islands belonging to the Philippine Archipelago, irrespective of their width and dimension" as its territorial waters, while conceding that such claim was "without prejudice to the exercise by friendly foreign vessels of the right of innocent passage over those waters."[43] The innocent passage rightly, however, was

38 *Ibid.*, at 178–179.
39 *Ibid.*
40 *Ibid.*, at 179.
41 Indonesia, Summary of US-Indonesian Consultations on Archipelagic Sea Lanes, Jakarta, 23–27 October 1997, IMO Doc MSC 69/7/x (25 October 1997).
42 Warner, *supra* note 37, at 184.
43 *Note Verbale*, *supra* note 7.

limited to commercial vessels plying customary routes. For non-commercial vessels including warships, the Philippines would allow innocent passage and overflight only in specific sea lanes designated for that purpose, and subject to prior notification and consent.[44]

The Philippines maintained this position throughout the Law of the Sea negotiations, from the introduction of the Archipelagic Principles in 1972 through the Caracas and Geneva Sessions at which the substance of the Archipelagic State proposal was discussed. The United States assessed that Philippine concerns at the time over Muslim secessionism, the Spratly islands, and suspected links between the insurgent communist New People's Army and People's Republic of China made it sensitive to free passage of vessels,[45] resulting in a "rather rigid" position.[46]

The Philippine position on navigation put it at odds with Indonesia, which was willing to accept the U.S. proposal of free passage and overflight of submarines, warships and aircraft without notification through archipelagic sea lanes and straits in exchange for recognition of the archipelagic State concept.[47] At one point, the Philippines risked isolation from the other archipelagic States, and Indonesia even considered separating from the Philippines and presenting its own working paper.[48] In the end, however, Indonesia and the United States reached a confidential understanding for the latter to be silent about the archipelagic State concept in exchange for Indonesia's acceptance of the U.S. proposal for passage through archipelagic sea lanes.[49] The Philippines, however, maintained the view that the draft provisions were "unreasonable if not oppressive" as they placed the country in a worse situation than if archipelagic principles were not applied on account of the overflight rights granted to aircraft. Furthermore, while it was willing to recognize innocent passage rights, the Philippines reserved its rights regarding the passage of warships.[50] Presumably these rights refer to the requirement of notification and consent.

44 United States, NARA AAD, Document 1975GENEVA031167, US Embassy Geneva to State Department, May 2, 1975.

45 NARA AAD, Document 1974MANILA04294, US Embassy Manila to State Department, 15 April 1974.

46 NARA AAD, Document 1974MANILA06080, US Embassy Manila to State Department, 23 May 1974.

47 NARA AAD, Document 1974STATE128398, US Embassy State Department to US Embassy Caracas, 15 June 1975.

48 NARA AAD, Document 1974MANILA06080, 23 May 1974, *supra* note 46 and NARA AAD, Document 1974STATE115667, State Department to US Embassy Jakarta, 3 June 1974.

49 NARA AAD, Document 1974CARACA07810, US Embassy Caracas to State Department, 17 August 1974.

50 NARA AAD, Document 1978STATE226188, State Department to US Mission New York, 6 September 1978.

The above accounts for the Philippines' interpretation of the archipelagic sea lanes provisions, set forth in its Statement accompanying its signature to the UNCLOS in 1982, wherein it is emphasized that the Part IV provisions "do not nullify or impair the sovereignty of the Philippines as an archipelagic State over the sea lanes and do not deprive it of authority to enact legislation to protect its sovereignty, independence, and security," adding that "the concept of archipelagic waters is similar to the concept of internal waters under the Constitution of the Philippines, and removes straits connecting these waters with the economic zone or high seas from the rights of foreign vessels to transit passage for international navigation."[51] This was apparently designed to preserve the regulatory prerogatives applicable to the territorial sea and ensure their equal application to archipelagic waters and sea lanes.

In its desire to control vessel traffic through archipelagic waters, the Philippines entered a into a number of bilateral arrangements concerning passage of foreign ships and aircraft. In 1988, after bilateral talks, the Philippines unilaterally designated two special sea lanes for Taiwanese fishing vessels crossing the Balintang and Bashi Channels.[52] These sea lanes were not in accordance with the UNCLOS, nor were they some form of traffic separation scheme. Controversy over their alleged use of the sea lanes for Taiwanese fishing in Philippine waters led to the express repeal of the Executive Order and the abolition of the sea lanes in 1998 with the enactment of the Philippine Fisheries Code.[53]

The Philippines has attempted to control legislatively the passage of foreign vessels in Philippine waters, targeting fishing vessels specifically. In 1998, the Philippine Fisheries Code made it unlawful for any foreign fishing vessel to fish in Philippine waters and incidentally established that the entry of a foreign fishing vessel into Philippine waters without permission constituted a *prima facie* presumption that the vessel intends to engage in illegal fishing in Philippine waters.[54] The Code also requires that commercial and other passage that is not in the conduct of fisheries to take place only in "designated sea lanes."[55]

---

51 U.N. DOALOS, Declarations and Statements: Philippines, paras. 6 and 7, at www.un.org/depts/los/convention_agreements/convention_declarations.htm.

52 Philippines, Executive Order no. 473, Establishing of sea lanes for the use of fishing vessels proceeding to and from their fishing areas in the South Pacific Ocean, and for other purposes, Manila: Official Gazette, 5 August 1991.

53 Philippines, Republic Act No. 8550, An Act providing for the development, management, and conservation of the fisheries and aquatic resources, integrating all laws pertinent thereto and for other purposes, Manila: *Official Gazette*, 25 February 1998, at s. 131. Also available at FAOLex: <faolex.fao.org/docs/pdf/phi16098.pdf>.

54 *Ibid.*, s. 87.

55 *Ibid.*, s. 41.

The Philippines' prospective attitude toward archipelagic sea lanes and archipelagic sea lanes passages may be seen by looking at House Bill no. 4153 and its counterpart Senate Bill no. 2738, filed during the 14th Congress in 2011.[56] The archipelagic sea lanes bill before Congress purports to unilaterally designate three sea lanes through the archipelago and expressly attempts to limit all foreign vessel passage only to those sea lanes. This designation was to be legislated without the requisite consultation with the IMO in accordance with the GPASL. The proposal was opposed by only one person (the author of this article) at the public hearings in the House of Representatives at the time, as being ill-advised and constituting a partial designation.

The 2017 version of the bill eliminated the unilateral designation of sea lanes and authorized the President to carry out the designation process.[57] However, the legislative intent appears to be to ensure that the Philippines is, like Indonesia, able to limit foreign vessel passage to only the designated sea lanes. Speaking on the passage of the bill on Third Reading at the 16th Congress, sponsor Congressman Ace Acedillo stated that "[t]he ASL law will now delimit maritime areas that foreign ships can pass through without inviting suspicion," and leaves it to the President to define the sea routes where foreign vessels can pass through.[58] The draft law also expressly attempts to regulate the exercise of archipelagic sea lane passage by specifying the rights and obligations of vessels and aircraft exercising archipelagic sea lanes passage rights.

Overall, the Philippines assumes that implementation of the UNCLOS passage regime allows for the regulation of foreign vessels exercising passage rights. Recently, in a case that challenged the constitutionality of the Philippines' 2009 archipelagic baselines law,[59] the Supreme Court stated that "the political branches of the Philippine government, in the competent discharge of their constitutional powers, may pass legislation designating routes within

---

56 The bills, not having passed, were subsequently re-filed in succeeding Congresses. At the start of the 17th Congress in June 2016, the archipelagic sea lanes bill was refiled as Senate Bill no. 92 and House Bill no. 3285, and the maritime zone bill as Senate Bill no. 93 and House Bill no. 3286.

57 See House of Representatives, House Bill no 3285, 13 January 2017, at <www.congress.gov.ph/legisdocs/basic_17/HB03285.pdf>.

58 "House bill assigning routes for foreign ships, planes approved on 2nd reading," Businessworld online, 23 March 2015, at <www.cab.gov.ph/news/2250-house-bill-assigning-routes-for-foreign-ships-planes-approved-on-2nd-reading>.

59 Republic Act No. 9522, An Act to amend certain provisions of Republic Act No. 3046, as amended by Republic Act No. 5446, to define the archipelagic baselines of the Philippines and for other purposes. 10 March 2009, at <senate.gov.ph/republic_acts/ra%209522.pdf>.

the archipelagic waters to regulate innocent and sea lanes passage."[60] However, the Court accepted that "[n]o modern State can validly invoke its sovereignty to absolutely forbid innocent passage that is exercised in accordance with customary international law without risking retaliatory measures from the international community." It also recognized that the imposition of the dual regime of passage rights under the UNCLOS "was a concession by archipelagic States, in exchange for their right to claim all the waters landward of their baselines, regardless of the depth or distance from the coast, as archipelagic waters subject to their territorial sovereignty."[61]

V Challenges for the Archipelagic Sea Lanes Regime

As the 21st Century marches on, it is clear the archipelagic sea lanes regime will continue to experience challenges despite the specification of the regime's rules in UNCLOS Part IV. The archipelagic States persist in reserving the prerogative to manage foreign vessel traffic by attempting to limiting these vessels to designated sea lanes. The Philippines has attempted to constrict the maritime traffic in its archipelagic waters to only a few identifiable routes and is debating legislation indicating an intent to regulate the exercise of passage rights through these waters, such as limiting them to only designated sea lanes.

60 *Magallona v. Executive Secretary, et al.* G.R. No. 187167, 16 July 2011, at <sc.judiciary.gov.ph/jurisprudence/2011/august2011/187167.html>.

61 *Ibid.*

CHAPTER 8

Regulation on Navigation of Foreign Vessels: Singapore's Practice

Zhen Sun

1 Introduction

Located at the crossroads of the East-West trade and with extensive connectivity to the emerging Asian market, Singapore is the trading hub that connects Asia and the world.[1] Singapore borders the Straits of Malacca and Singapore (SOMS), a strait used for international navigation as defined under the 1982 United Nations Convention on the Law of the Sea (UNCLOS).[2] The SOMS is the main shipping channel linking the East-West trade for oil, natural gas, and raw and manufactured goods. As the major trading hub in Asia, there are about 1,000 vessels at any given time within Singapore port, and more than 130,000 ships call at Singapore annually.[3] Singapore is an island State that is separated from Malaysia by the Strait of Johor with a width of 0.8 to 2.6 nautical miles (M), and separated from Indonesia by the Singapore Strait with the widest point of less than 10 M.[4] These geographic factors determine that the waters under Singapore's jurisdiction is limited to internal waters, as defined under the Port Limits Notification 2010, and a very narrow territorial sea, with much part of the latter forming the Singapore Strait that is subject to the regime of transit passage.[5]

1 Maritime and Port Authority Singapore (MPA), "A Maritime Gateway to Key Asian Markets," <www.mpa.gov.sg/web/portal/home/maritime-singapore/introduction-to-maritime-singapore/gateway-to-asia> (all web links in this chapter were valid on 10 September 2018).

2 United Nations Convention on the Law of the Sea (UNCLOS), 10 December 1982, 1833 *U.N.T.S.* 3.

3 MPA, "Maritime Singapore: Facts and Trivia," <www.mpa.gov.sg/web/portal/home/maritime-singapore/introduction-to-maritime-singapore/facts-and-trivia>.

4 Michael Leifer, *Malacca, Singapore, and Indonesia* (Sijthoff & Noordhoff, 1978), 53. United States National Geospatial-Intelligence Agency, Pub.174, *Sailing Directions (Enroute), Strait of Malacca and Sumatera* (14th Edition, 2016), Sector 9. Singapore Strait and Approaches, Johor Strait, 160, <msi.nga.mil/MSISiteContent/StaticFiles/NAV_PUBS/SD/Pub174/Pub174bk.pdf>.

5 MPA, (Port Limits) Notification 2010 (MPA Port Limits Notification). All Singapore legislation is available at "Singapore Statutes Online," sso.agc.gov.sg/.

 | DOI:10.1163/9789004396272_009

This chapter will discuss Singapore's practice of regulating foreign ships and identify the gaps that need to be filled. It will first chart the marine areas that are under Singapore's jurisdiction, including internal waters, the limited territorial sea and the potential claim to an exclusive economic zone (EEZ). It will then review the regulation of foreign vessels within waters under Singapore's sovereignty, including the criteria and procedures for foreign vessels to re-register to obtain the Singapore flag, and the scope and processes of port regulation and port State control. This chapter will then discuss Singapore's rights to and practice of regulating foreign ships relating to innocent passage within its territorial sea and transit passage through the Singapore Strait. The last part of this chapter will discuss the measures that have been adopted by the International Maritime Organization (IMO) based on the joint proposals from the three littoral States Indonesia, Malaysia, and Singapore, respecting the Singapore Strait. The chapter concludes with recommendations.

II Singapore's Maritime Jurisdiction

Singapore ratified UNCLOS and the Agreement relating to the Implementation of Part XI of UNCLOS on 17 November 1994 and became its 68th State Party.[6] It is, however, geographically restrained from having the full extent of the maritime areas set out in the UNCLOS. Singapore has indicated that it has a territorial sea that extends up to 12 M and an EEZ, but has not adopted legislation to clarify its maritime claims.[7]

The Singapore Island is surrounded by the Malaysia Peninsula from the north semi-sphere with a narrow Johor Strait, and facing Indonesian islands across the Singapore Strait. The Johor Strait is about 27 M long that connects to the Strait of Malacca on the west, and the Singapore Strait on the southeast. The Singapore Strait is about 52.1 M long with a width of 8.7 M at the West entrance and 17.4 M at the East entrance.[8] Singapore has settled its territorial sea boundaries with Malaysia in the Johor Strait, and the main parts

6 United Nations, Division for Ocean Affairs and the Law of the Sea (DOALOS), "Chronological Lists of Ratifications of, Accessions and Successions to the Convention and the Related Agreements," <www.un.org/Depts/los/reference_files/chronological_lists_of_ratifications.htm#> The United Nations Convention on the Law of the Sea.

7 No. 1485 – Singapore Maritime Zones, AG/S/0014/78Pt. 3 Vol. 78; MFA 072-711/23/02, Republic of Singapore Government Gazette (2008), at 2176.

8 *Sailing Directions*, *supra* note 4, Sector 9, Singapore Strait and Approaches, 127.

in the Singapore Strait with Indonesia.[9] Nonetheless, the maritime boundary lines among the three neighbouring States are not connected. The States will need to work out the tri-points at both the west and east ends of the Singapore Strait.[10]

A remaining issue with Singapore's maritime jurisdiction is with regard to the legal status of the Pedra Branca land feature that is 24 M to the east of the Singapore Island.[11] On two occasions in 1980 and 2008 respectively, both related to the sovereignty claim over Pedra Branca, Singapore declared that it may claim a 12 M territorial sea and an EEZ generated from Pedra Branca.[12] Pedra Branca is a small naturally formed area of land that is above water at high tide, with an area of about 8560 square meters (m^2) at low tide. It is 137 meters long and has an average width of 60 meters.[13] It is not clear whether Pedra Branca can sustain human habitation or economic life of its own and hence be entitled to an EEZ or/and a continental shelf. According to the reasoning by the Arbitral Tribunal in the *South China Sea Arbitration* on the definition of an island in Article 121(3) of the UNCLOS, "human habitation entails more than the mere survival of humans on a feature and that economic life entails more than the presence of resources", in particular, the Arbitral Tribunal notes that "a purely official or military population, serviced from the outside, does not constitute evidence that a feature is capable of sustaining human habitation."[14] Given

9 Singapore, "Maritime Boundary Delimitation Agreements and Other Material," <www.un.org/Depts/los/LEGISLATIONANDTREATIES/STATEFILES/SGP.htm>.

10 For more details of Singapore's maritime areas refer to Zhen Sun, "Implementation of the United Nations Law of the Sea Convention in Singapore," in Seokwoo Lee and Warwick Gullett (eds.), *Asia-Pacific and the Implementation of the Law of the Sea: Regional Legislative and Policy Approaches to the Law of the Sea Convention* (Brill, 2016), 117–124.

11 Ministry of Foreign Affairs Singapore (MFA), at "Pedra Branca," <www1.mfa.gov.sg/SINGAPORES-FOREIGN-POLICY/Key-Issues/Pedra-Branca>.

12 MFA Press Statement: "International Court of Justice awards sovereignty of Pedra Branca to Singapore," 23 May 2008. The Singapore MFA declared that:

> Singapore has a territorial sea limit that extends up to a maximum of 12 nautical miles and an Exclusive Economic Zone. ... The precise coordinates of Singapore's territorial sea and Exclusive Economic Zone will be announced at an appropriate time. Should the limits of its territorial sea or Exclusive Economic Zone overlap with claims of neighbouring countries, Singapore will negotiate with those countries with a view to arriving at agreed delimitations in accordance with international law.

See: <www.mfa.gov.sg/content/mfa/media_centre/special_events/pedrabranca/press_room/mfa_pr/2008/200805/press_200805_11.html>.

13 *Sovereignty over Pedra Branca/Pulau Batu Puteh, Middle Rocks and South Ledge (Malaysia/Singapore)*, [2008] *I.C.J. Reports*, para. 16, <www.icj-cij.org/en/case/130>.

14 Permanent Court of Arbitration (PCA), *The South China Sea Arbitration (The Republic of Philippines v. The People's Republic of China), Award* 12 July 2016, para. 546 and 550, <pca-cpa.org/en/cases/7/>.

that Pedra Branca has no vegetation or fresh water, and only a few person stationed there for official duties, it is unlikely that either Malaysia or Indonesia would accept the position that Pedra Branca is an island that is entitled to an EEZ and continental shelf if Singapore were to insist on its claim. The uncertainty concerning the legal status of Pedra Branca affects the maritime division in the eastern part of the Singapore Strait.

Pursuant to Maritime and Port Authority of Singapore (MPA) Port Limit Notification 2010, the Minister for Transport announced that the waters and any place or premises which is under the control of or used by the MPA for the purpose of carrying out its duties or functions are declared to be a port.[15] The port water limits follows the boundary with Malaysia in the Johor Strait, and goes very close to the traffic separation system in the Singapore Strait (see Figure 8.1 in the Annex). This means that except for port waters, which are internal waters, Singapore's maritime jurisdiction is limited to a narrow territorial sea forming a strait used for international navigation, and the potential of a territorial sea and EEZ generated from Pedra Branca subject to delimitation with both Malaysia and Indonesia.

Singapore played an active role in the negotiations at the Third United Nations Conference on the Law of the Sea (UNCLOS III) which began in 1973 and lasted for nine years. Of particular relevance to Singapore was the regime on straits used for international navigation established in Part III. With the extension of the maximum breadth of the territorial sea to 12 M, half of the SOMS including the entire Singapore Strait falls within the territorial sea of Malaysia, Indonesia and Singapore.[16] Maintenance of the freedom of navigation through the SOMS, among other straits, was not only a matter of interests to the major maritime States, but also of concern to many user States whose international sea-borne trade has to pass through such straits, to flag States with large merchant fleets, and to States like Singapore bordering a strait and relying on it for communication and development. Singapore was a member of an informal private group led by Fiji and the United Kingdom that negotiated and produced the text on the regime of straits used for international navigation.[17] As a compromise, all ships enjoy the right of transit passage, the exercise of the freedom

15 MPA Port Limits Notification, *supra* note 5.

16 Treaty between the Republic of Indonesia and Malaysia Relating to the delimitation of the Territorial Seas of the Two Countries in the Strait of Malacca, 17 March 1970, <www.un.org/Depts/los/LEGISLATIONANDTREATIES/STATEFILES/IDN.htm>.

17 Myron H. Nordquist (ed.), *United Nations Convention on the Law of the Sea 1982: A Commentary* (Vol. I) (Virginia Commentary Vol. I), (Martinus Nijhoff, 1985), 107 and Satya N. Nandan and Shabtai Rosenne (eds.), *United Nations Convention on the Law of the Sea 1982: A Commentary* (Vol. II) (Virginia Commentary Vol. II), (Martinus Nijhoff, 1993), 288.

of navigation solely for the purpose of continuous and expeditious transit, in international straits; while States bordering such straits may adopt laws and regulations in respect of the safety of navigation, marine pollution, fishing and its control of customs, fiscal, immigration or sanitary matters.[18]

There are a few provisions in Part III of the UNCLOS that were crafted to reflect the specific concerns in the SOMS. For example, considering the specific geographic features of Singapore, the definition of the right of transit passage was clarified to ensure that it would not unfairly affect navigation into Singapore waters. This clause became known as the "Singapore Clause" and provides that: "the requirement of continuous and expeditious transit does not preclude passage through the strait for the purpose of entering, leaving or returning from a State bordering the strait, subject to the conditions of entry to that State."[19] Hence, vessels that call at the Singapore port do not lose their right of transit passage through the SOMS merely because they enter the port waters of Singapore. Moreover, Article 43 was inserted to address the burden on the States bordering a strait, expressed by Malaysia among others, to ensure the safe use of the strait by calling for cooperation between user States and States bordering a strait to provide aids to navigation and prevent, reduce and control of pollution from ships.[20] In addition, Singapore along with its two neighbours and other major users of the SOMS, submitted a "statement relating to Article 233 of the draft convention on the law of the sea in its application to the Straits of Malacca and Singapore" before the conclusion of UNCLOS III to clarify their enforcement jurisdiction over foreign ships in relation to the laws and regulations adopted.[21]

According to the Interpretation Act, "Singapore" means the Republic of Singapore and is deemed to include the Island of Singapore and all islands and places which on 2 June 1959 were administered as part of Singapore and all territorial waters adjacent thereto.[22] Therefore, all Singapore domestic legislation applies to its territorial waters, including the Criminal Law (Temporary Provisions) Act, the Customs Act, the Fisheries Act, and the Public Order Act. The maritime legislation of Singapore includes Acts of Parliament and subsidiary legislation that is made by the MPA that affects the port of Singapore and ships registered under the Singapore flag. Much of Singapore's maritime legislation

---

18 UNCLOS, *supra* note 2, Articles 38 and 42.

19 *Ibid.*, Article 38(2).

20 Virginia Commentary Vol. II (1993), *supra* note 17, at 382–383.

21 See: Shabtai Rosenne and Alexander Yankov (eds.), *United Nations Convention on the Law of the Sea 1982: A Commentary* (Vol. IV) (Virginia Commentary Vol. IV), (Martinus Nijhoff, 1990), 388–390.

22 Interpretation Act (Chapter 1) (Original Enactment: Act 10 of 1965), Article 2(1).

relates to the laws and regulations of merchant shipping that is transposed from the major maritime conventions developed by the IMO. Currently six Acts address maritime issues: the Maritime and Port Authority of Singapore Act; the Merchant Shipping Act; Maritime Labour Convention Act; the Prevention of Pollution of the Sea Act; the Merchant Shipping (Civil Liability and Compensation for Oil Pollution) Act; and the Merchant Shipping (Civil Liability and Compensation for Bunker Oil Pollution) Act.[23] These domestic implementing laws address the rights and obligations of Singapore as a flag State as well as a port State under the relevant international conventions.

III Regulation of Vessels within Waters under Singapore's Sovereignty

1 *Registration of Vessels*

The Singapore Registry of Ships (SRS) is the administration, established in 1966 and currently managed by the MPA, that is responsible for executing the registration of ships sailing under the Singapore flag and ensuring that ships and owners meet the stringent criteria that entitle their ships to obtain Singapore nationality.[24] The SRS has a fleet with more than 4,700 ships of an aggregate over 88 million gross tons (GT), which makes it one of the world's top ten registries with one of the youngest fleets.[25] The Singapore fleet is mainly composed of oil tankers, bulk carriers, general cargo vessels, container ships and other types of ships.[26] The SRS accepts registrations from both newly constructed ships as well as ships previously registered with a foreign flag provided that the ship and its owner meet the legislated criteria and follow the procedures.

Except for fishing vessels, hydrofoils and wooden vessels, the SRS registration is open to all types of ships, including offshore vessels such as oil rigs and floating platforms.[27] In Singapore, there are only two groups qualified to be owners of ships that can register with the SRS, citizens or permanent residents

---

23 MPA, "Maritime Legislation of Singapore," <www.mpa.gov.sg/web/portal/home/port-of-singapore/maritime-legislation-of-singapore>.

24 MPA, "About SRS and What's New: Singapore Registry of Ships," <www.mpa.gov.sg/web/portal/home/singapore-registry-of-ships/about-srs-and-what-new>.

25 *Ibid.*

26 United Nations Conference on Trade and Development (UNCTAD), "Maritime Profile: Singapore," <unctadstat.unctad.org/CountryProfile/MaritimeProfile/en-GB/702/index.html>.

27 MPA, "Pre-Requisites for Ship Registration," <www.mpa.gov.sg/web/portal/home/singapore-registry-of-ships/about-srs-and-what-new/pre-requisites-for-ship-registration>, and Merchant Shipping Act (Chapter 179) (Original Enactment: Act 19 of 1995), Article 7.

of Singapore and companies incorporated in Singapore that are either locally or foreign-owned.[28] For foreign-owned companies to register a vessel, it must meet two further conditions, the company must have a minimum paid-up capital of $50,000 Singapore Dollars, and the vessel must be at least 1,600 GT and be self-propelled.[29]

Once the vessel and the owner meet the pre-requisites for ship registration with the SRS, the registration procedures are straightforward. The owner must obtain approval from the Registrar of Ships for the proposed vessel name, and submit the relevant documents as required for a provisional registry or a permanent registry.[30] A provisional registry is common for ships that were previously registered under a foreign flag. Provisional registration is valid for a maximum period of one year from the date of issue.[31] After paying the initial registration and annual tonnage tax fees, the vessel is successfully registered with the SRS and the owner receives a Certificate of Registry.[32]

2 *Port Regulations and Port State Control*

As Singapore's national port planner, the MPA is responsible for the safe and optimal use of the port and the regulation and control of navigation within the limits of the port and the approaches to the port.[33] The MPA may adopt regulations for the control and management of the port and the approaches thereto and the maintenance of good order therein that apply to all marine activities carried on in the waters within Singapore port.[34] In particular, all vessels arriving to and departing from Singapore are required to make notifications and declarations relating to the vessel, its cargo and the estimated time of entering or leaving the port.[35] The procedure and required information vary depending on the type of the vessel and the cargo it is carrying.[36] For example, ships

28 *Ibid.* and see Merchant Shipping (Registration of Ships) Regulations, Reg 7, Revised Edition 1997, Article 3.

29 *Ibid.*, Articles 5 and 8.

30 *Ibid.*, Articles 9–11.

31 Merchant Shipping Act, *supra* note 27, Article 12.

32 *Ibid.*, Articles 14 and 16.

33 Maritime and Port Authority of Singapore Act (Chapter 170A) (MPA Act) (Original Enactment: Act 7 of 1996), Article 7.

34 *Ibid.*, Article 41.

35 *Ibid.*, Article 44.

36 MPA, "Vessels Arriving in Singapore", <www.mpa.gov.sg/web/portal/home/port-of-singapore/craft-licensing-and-port-clearance/arrival-and-departure-formalities/vessels-arriving-in-singapore>, and MPA, "Vessels Departing from Singapore", <www.mpa.gov.sg/web/portal/home/port-of-singapore/craft-licensing-and-port-clearance/arrival-and-departure-formalities/vessels-departing-from-singapore>.

carrying dangerous goods or intending to load or discharge such cargo from the vessel must give prior notification and obtain permission from the Port Master.[37] While in port, all ships must follow instructions from the Port Master on signals, communication, navigation, loading, berthing and anchoring, and obey the laws and regulations on safety, marine pollution and security.[38] Once a vessel has fulfilled all arrival and departing requirements and paid the port dues, the MPA will issue a Port Clearance Certificate to the vessel, which the vessel needs to leave the port.[39]

The MPA retains the right to deny entry to the port and to detain vessels from proceeding to sea in certain circumstances. For example, if the Port Master has reasonable cause to believe that a foreign vessel that proposes to enter the port has violated Singapore's law on prevention of pollution from vessels, the Master may deny the entry of the vessel to the port.[40] If the Port Master has reasonable cause to believe that a foreign vessel presents an unreasonable threat of harm, or has caused harm to the marine environment, the vessel may be detained.[41] But the reason to detain foreign ships is limited to threats to the marine environment of Singapore which is more limited than the enforcement jurisdiction that exists pursuant to international law. As stated in the UNCLOS, port States have enforcement jurisdiction over a vessel that is voluntarily within its port, where the evidence so warrants, in respect of any discharge from that vessel outside the maritime areas of the port State in violation of applicable international rules and standards.[42]

In addition, the MPA performs Port State Control (PSC) inspections to check and ensure that foreign ships visiting Singapore port are in compliance with international regulations.[43] PSC inspections were developed as a "safety net" to catch substandard ships due to insufficient or irresponsible flag State control.[44] PSC inspection has been widely adopted to ensure that the condition

37 MPA, "Declaring Dangerous Goods," <www.mpa.gov.sg/web/portal/home/port-of-singapore/operations/hazardous-cargo-information/declaring-dangerous-goods>.

38 Maritime and Port Authority of Singapore (Port) Regulations, Reg 7, G.N. No. S 187/1997, Revised Edition 2000.

39 MPA, "Vessels Departing from Singapore: Port Clearance," *supra* note 36 and MPA Act, *supra* note 33, Article 46.

40 Prevention of Pollution of the Sea Act (Chapter 243) (Original Enactment: Act 18 of 1990), Article 23(1).

41 *Ibid.*, Article 23(2).

42 UNCLOS, *supra* note 2, Article 218(1).

43 MPA, "Port State Control," <www.mpa.gov.sg/web/portal/home/port-of-singapore/safety/port-state-control-psc>.

44 International Maritime Organization (IMO), "Port State Control," <www.imo.org/en/OurWork/MSAS/Pages/PortStateControl.aspx>.

of a vessel and its equipment comply with the requirements of international rules and standards, and that the vessel is crewed and operated in compliance with international regulations.[45] As a collective effort to enhance efficient PSC inspections, States have adopted nine regional agreements on PSC to harmonise and coordinate procedures of inspections and to share information and best practice.[46] Singapore is a founding member of the Memorandum of Understanding on Port State Control in the Asia-Pacific Region, known as the Tokyo MOU.[47] According to the 2017 Annual Report, the MPA has inspected 1,027 ships calling at Singapore port that amounts to 3.28% of the total inspections of the participating authorities.[48] PSC inspections ensure that ships leaving the Singapore port meet international safety, security and marine pollution prevention standards. Ships that do not meet these standards due to serious deficiencies may be detained and require a follow-up inspection before they can depart.[49] The master or owner of a detained ship has the right to appeal against detention within 30 days of the date of the detention.[50]

3 *Regulations Relating to Innocent and Transit Passage*

As noted above, Singapore has stated its right to claim a territorial sea and an EEZ but has yet to adopt legislation on maritime zones. As a State party to the UNCLOS, Singapore is bound by the provisions of Part II on the Territorial Sea and Part III on Straits Used for International Navigation that sets out the rights and duties of the coastal State and the rules of the passage regimes for other States. Hence, all foreign ships enjoy the right of innocent passage in the territorial sea of Singapore and the right of transit passage in the part of the territorial sea that forms the Singapore Strait.

Foreign vessels exercising the right of innocent passage must comply with the laws and regulations adopted by the coastal State and all generally accepted international regulations relating to the prevention of collisions at sea.[51] Domestic laws and regulations may relate to all or any of the following

45 *Ibid.*

46 Ibid.

47 Memorandum of Understanding on Port State Control in the Asia-Pacific Region (Tokyo MOU), "Organizational Structure," <www.tokyo-mou.org/organization/organizational_structure.php>.

48 Tokyo MOU, "Annual Report on Port State Control in the Asia-Pacific Region (2017)," 15, <www.tokyo-mou.org/publications/annual_report.php>.

49 MPA, "Applying for Follow-up Inspection," <www.mpa.gov.sg/web/portal/home/port-of-singapore/safety/port-state-control-psc/applying-for-follow-up-inspection>.

50 MPA, "Appealing against Detention," <www.mpa.gov.sg/web/portal/home/port-of-singapore/safety/port-state-control-psc/appealing-against-detention>.

51 UNCLOS, *supra* note 2, Article 21(4).

matters: the safety of navigation; the protection of cables and pipelines; the conservation and management of the living resources; the protection and preservation of the environment; marine scientific research and hydrographic surveys; and the prevention of infringement of the customs, fiscal, immigration or sanitary laws and regulations.[52] The coastal State may, where necessary having regard to the safety of navigation, require foreign ships exercising the right of innocent passage to use designated sea lanes and prescribed traffic separation schemes.[53] The coastal State may exercise enforcement jurisdiction against any foreign vessels that violate its domestic laws and regulations.[54] In addition, the coastal State may take the necessary steps in its territorial sea to prevent passage which is not innocent and to prevent any legal breaches by a foreign ship entering internal waters or calling in at a port facility.[55] Furthermore, the coastal State may, without discrimination in form or in fact among foreign ships, temporarily suspend the innocent passage of foreign ships in specified areas of its territorial sea if such suspension is essential for the protection of coastal State security.[56]

In contrast, States bordering straits used for international navigation have limited legislative and enforcement power over foreign vessels exercising the right of transit passage. The strait state may adopt laws and regulations relating to transit passage with regard to all or any of the following:

(a) the safety of navigation and the regulation of maritime traffic, as provided in article 41;
(b) the prevention, reduction and control of pollution, by giving effect to applicable international regulations regarding the discharge of oil, oily wastes and other noxious substances in the strait;
(c) with respect to fishing vessels, the prevention of fishing, including the stowage of fishing gear; and
(d) the loading or unloading of any commodity, currency or person in contravention of the customs, fiscal, immigration or sanitary laws and regulations of States bordering straits.[57]

Article 41 authorises the State bordering a strait, with the approval and adoption of the competent international organisation, to designate sea lanes and prescribe traffic separation schemes for navigation to promote the safe passage

52 *Ibid.*, Article 21(1).
53 *Ibid.*, Article 22(1).
54 *Ibid.*, Articles 111(1) and 220(1)-(2).
55 *Ibid.*, Article 25(1)-(2).
56 *Ibid.*, Article 25(3).
57 *Ibid.*, Article 42(1).

of ships.[58] The jurisdiction of the States bordering the strait on the safety of navigation and regulation of ship-source pollution is limited to enforcing the international rules and standards. This is consistent with the obligation of foreign ships in transit passage to comply with generally accepted international regulations, procedures and practices for both safety at sea and the prevention, reduction and control of pollution from ships.[59] In the case where a foreign ship has violated the applicable laws and regulations, causing or threatening major damage to the marine environment of the straits, the States bordering the straits may take appropriate enforcement measures.[60]

Under Singapore domestic law, it is the Maritime and Port Authority Act (MPA Act) that specifies the rules and regulations that are applicable in the territorial waters. The domestic legislation addresses the territorial waters as a whole without distinguishing the part that forms the Singapore Strait used for international navigation as it does not affect the legal status of the waters or the exercise of Singapore's sovereignty or jurisdiction over such waters. Overall, the Port Master may regulate, direct and control the use of vessels within the territorial waters of Singapore, including directing where a vessel may be berthed, moored or anchored and the method of anchoring and directing the removal of any vessel within territorial waters.[61] The Port Master's powers mainly relate to the safety of navigation in the territorial waters.

The Port Master may also prohibit vessels from entering territorial waters "if he is of the opinion that it would not be in the public interest for the vessel to enter Singapore."[62] The term "public interest" is undefined in Singapore law and it is in the discretion of the law enforcement agency to decide what may constitute "public interest" under the circumstances. It is unclear whether a violation of public interest would be considered to be prejudicial to the peace, good order or security of Singapore thereby rendering such passage not innocent.[63] It is also not clear whether the Port Master's powers only apply to vessels intended to call at Singapore's port and thereby subject to port clearance requirements, or whether the powers also apply to vessels that merely intend to transit the territorial waters of Singapore. If it were to include the latter, then this provision is, *prima facie*, in breach of Singapore's obligation not to hamper

58 *Ibid.*, Article 41.
59 *Ibid.*, Article 39(2).
60 *Ibid.*, Article 233.
61 MPA Act, *supra* note 33, Articles 41(f) and 43(a)-(b).
62 *Ibid.*, Article 48.
63 UNCLOS, *supra* note 2, Articles 19 and 25(1).

the innocent passage of foreign ships through the territorial sea and more so its obligation not to hamper transit passage in the Singapore Strait.[64]

In addition, the Port Master may direct a vessel to leave the territorial waters "if he is of the opinion that it would not be in the public interest for the vessel to remain within the territorial waters of Singapore."[65] Any person aggrieved by an order for removal by the Port Master may appeal to the Minister of Transportation, whose decision is to be final, within seven days of the receipt of such direction.[66] If the vessel fails to obey the direction to leave the territorial waters within the specified time or where the appeal has been refused, the person is guilty of an offence and liable on conviction to a fine and the vessel will be at the disposal of the MPA.[67] The same uncertainty applies to the interpretation of "public interest" under the Port Master's discretion. However, it is unlikely that this provision would apply to vessels exercising a right of innocent passage or transit passage since most foreign vessels directed to leave the territorial waters of Singapore would be at anchorage or berthed instead of engaging in the continuous and expeditious passage.

All foreign ships are prohibited from engaging in certain activities while in Singapore territorial waters. For example, foreign ships that are exercising the right of innocent passage are not to carry out any hydrographic or hydrologic surveying or other study of the waters and seabed within the territorial waters of Singapore.[68] Moreover, special works and operations, as well as salvage services, are considered to be activities not "having a direct bearing on passage" and hence may only be carried out within Singapore territorial waters with the authorisation from the MPA.[69]

Foreign vessels are subject to Singapore's laws and regulations in respect to the prevention, reduction and control of ship-source pollution. The Prevention of Pollution of the Sea Act[70], enacted in 1991 and amended subsequently, gives

64 *Ibid.*, Articles 24(1) and 44.

65 MPA Act, *supra* note 33, Article 49(1).

66 *Ibid.*, Article 49(2).

67 *Ibid.*, Articles 49(3) and 50. "Person" is not defined under the MPA Act, in contrast to "body of persons" which refer to a company, firm, society or other body of persons, person used in singular refers to natural person such as master, owner or person in charge of vessel.

68 UNCLOS, *supra* note 2, Articles 19(2)(j) and 40 MPA Act, and *supra* note 33, Articles 78 (1)-(2).

69 UNCLOS, *supra* note 2, Article 19(2)(l) and MPA Act, *supra* note 33, Articles 79–80 and Second Schedule Power of Authority, paras. 6 and 8.

70 Prevention of Pollution of the Sea Act, *supra* note 40. There are 12 Subsidiary Legislation under the Act covering issues on: Air, Ballast Water Management, Composition of Offences, Garbage, Harmful Anti-Fouling Systems, Hazardous and Noxious Substances Pollution Preparedness, Response and Co-operation, Noxious Liquid Substances in Bulk, Oil

effect to the International Convention for the Prevention of Pollution from Ships 1973 as modified and added to by the Protocol of 1978 (MARPOL)[71], and to other international agreements relating to the prevention, reduction and control of pollution of the sea and pollution from ships. By definition, "Singapore waters" includes the whole of the sea within the seaward limits of the territorial waters of Singapore.[72] All ships are prohibited from disposing or discharging any refuse, garbage, waste matter, trade effluents, plastics or marine pollutant in packaged form; oil and oily mixtures; noxious liquid substances or any dangerous pollutants into Singapore waters.[73] In the case of a violation of these obligations, the master, the owner and the agent of the ship are each guilty of an offence and liable on conviction to a fine and/or imprisonment.[74] Under the UNCLOS, States bordering straits used for international navigation may adopt laws and regulations in respect of "the prevention, reduction and control of pollution, by giving effect to applicable international regulations regarding the discharge of oil, oily wastes and other noxious substances in the strait."[75] Although ships in transit passage are required to "comply with generally accepted international regulations, procedures and practices for the prevention, reduction and control of pollution from ships,"[76] the obligation on foreign ships has a broader scope than the jurisdiction of the States bordering the straits. It is the flag State that has the primary jurisdiction to ensure that ships flying its flag comply with all international rules and standards relating to the ship-source pollution, i.e. MARPOL as a whole including all the Annexes. The States bordering the straits, *prima facie*, may only adopt laws and regulations giving effect to MARPOL and the two mandatory Annexes, Annex I (Oil) and Annex II (Noxious Liquid Substances). Given that part of Singapore's territorial waters forms the Singapore Strait, it arguably would be exercising excessive jurisdiction over foreign vessels in transit passage if it enforced its domestic laws regulating the discharge of other forms of pollutants other than oil, oily wastes and noxious substances.

Pollution Preparedness, Response and Co-operation, Oil, Reception Facilities and Garbage Facilities, Reporting of Pollution Incidents, and Sewage.

71 International Convention for the Prevention of Pollution from Ships 1973, as modified by the 1978 Protocol (MARPOL), (1978), 17 *I.L.M.* 546.

72 Prevention of Pollution of the Sea Act, *supra* note 40, Article 2.

73 *Ibid.*, Articles 6(1), 7(1) and 10(1).

74 Ibid.

75 UNCLOS, *supra* note 2, Arctic 42(1)(b).

76 *Ibid.*, Article 39(2)(b).

4 *Trilateral Cooperation*

Indonesia, Malaysia, and Singapore have been cooperating to promote the safety of navigation and the prevention of ship-source pollution in the SOMS since the 1970s despite their differences on the legal status and the issue of internationalisation of the SOMS.[77] In 1971, the three States signed a Joint Statement on the Straits of Malacca (1971 Joint Statement) with a view to adopting a common position on matters relating to the SOMS.[78] The 1971 Joint Statement acknowledged that the safety of navigation in the SOMS should be the responsibility of the littoral States concerned and that issues concerning the safety of navigation could be separated from the issue of internationalisation of the straits.

In 1977, the littoral States established the Tripartite Technical Expert Group on Safety of Navigation in the Straits of Malacca and Singapore (TTEG) to set guidelines for senior officials and technical experts to further their cooperation in managing the SOMS.[79] The TTEG is comprised of experts from the maritime administrations of the three littoral States and meets annually to discuss and collaborate on issues of enhancing the safety of navigation and promoting cooperation and coordination on anti-pollution policies and measures in the SOMS. Through the TTEG the three littoral States have worked with the IMO to adopt routeing measures, navigational rules and a ship reporting system for ships transiting the SOMS.

In 2007, after three years of discussions and negotiation, the three littoral States, with the assistance from the IMO, formally launched the Cooperative Mechanism on Safety of Navigation and Environment Protection in the Straits of Malacca and Singapore (Cooperative Mechanism).[80] The Cooperative Mechanism is the first international effort to implement Article 43 of UNCLOS which enables user States and other stakeholders to cooperate with the littoral States by sharing the responsibility of maintaining and enhancing navigational safety and protecting the marine environment in the SOMS from the impacts of international shipping. The Cooperative Mechanism has three components, the Cooperation Forum – the main avenue for the States, the shipping industry and other stakeholders to discuss and exchange views on issues of common

---

77 See: Leifer, *supra* note 4 at 31–35.

78 Joint Statement of Indonesia, Malaysia and Singapore on the Straits of Malacca, announced on 16 November 1971 (1971 Joint Statement), in (1972) 5 *New York University Journal of International Law and Politics* 425 at 425–426.

79 Cooperative Mechanism on Safety of Navigation and Environment Protection in the Straits of Malacca and Singapore (Cooperative Mechanism), Tripartite Technical Experts Group (TTEG), <www.cm-soms.com/index.php?p=component-info&id=1>.

80 "Cooperative Mechanism, Establishment," <www.cm-soms.com/index.php?p=td&id=6>.

interests in the SOMS; the Project Coordination Committee – comprised of the littoral States and sponsors of the projects, oversees the implementation of projects to promote safety of navigation and environmental protection; and the Aids To Navigation Fund – administrated by a Fund Committee comprising representatives from the littoral States and invited contributors, collects voluntary contributions and distributes the fund to littoral States for maintenance of critical aids to navigation in SOMS.

IV IMO Measures in the Singapore Strait

As detailed above, under the UNCLOS, Singapore, as a State bordering a strait used for international navigation, may designate sea lanes and prescribe traffic separation schemes to promote the safety of navigation in the strait.[81] Before designating sea lanes or prescribing traffic separation schemes (TSS), Singapore must submit such proposals to the IMO, the competent international organisation responsible for establishing and adopting international measures concerning ships' routeing systems.[82] The IMO may adopt only such sea lanes and TSS as may be agreed with Singapore.[83] Given that the Singapore Strait and the Malacca Strait have historically been treated as a single strait, the three littoral States – Indonesia, Malaysia and Singapore – have been cooperating in formulating joint proposals to be submitted to the IMO.[84]

1 *Ships' Routeing Measures*

The three littoral States submitted a joint proposal to the IMO (then Intergovernmental Maritime Consultative Organization (IMCO)) to establish a TSS and standards for under-keel clearance in the SOMS, which were adopted in

81 UNCLOS, *supra* note 2, Article 41(1).

82 International Convention for the Safety of Life At Sea (SOLAS), adopted 1 November 1974, entry into force 25 May 1980, 1184 *U.N.T.S.* 278, Chapter V Safety of Navigation, Regulation 10 – Ships' Routeing, para. 2.

83 UNCLOS, *supra* note 2, Article 41(4).

84 *Ibid.*, Article 41(5). See also IMO, MSC/Circ.1060, 6 January 2003, "Guidance Note on the Preparation of Proposals on Ships' Routeing Systems and Ship Reporting Systems for Submission to the Sub-Committee on Safety of Navigation," <www.imo.org/en/OurWork/Safety/Navigation/Documents/Ships'%20routeing/MSC.1-Circ.1060-asAmended-consolidated-Guidance%20Note%20on%20the%20Preparation%20of%20Proposals%20onShipsRouteingReporting.pdf>.

1977 by Resolution A.375(X) on Navigation through the Straits of Malacca and Singapore.[85]

In 1998, the three littoral States proposed to the IMO that the TSS for the SOMS should be amended to facilitate the safe and efficient flow of traffic. The IMO approved the proposal to amend the TSS so that the operational areas extended for more than 260 M, from One Fathom Bank through the southern half of the Malacca Strait and the entire Singapore Strait, to the Horsburgh Lighthouse area in the South China Sea.[86] Along with these new and amended TSS and deep water routes, eleven precautionary areas, area to be avoided and inshore traffic zones have been approved for vessels navigating through the SOMS. These measures have subsequently been amended to further enhance the safety of navigation in the SOMS.[87]

The Singapore Strait is covered by a TSS, a routeing measure that separates opposing streams of traffic by the establishment of traffic lanes (see Figure 8.2 in the Annex).[88] From the west end of the Singapore Strait, that is east of the Sultan Shoal Lighthouse, a separation zone exists that embraces an anchorage area within it. The westbound traffic uses the traffic lane on the northern side of the separation zone, and the eastbound traffic uses the traffic lane on the southern side. A deep-water route exists in the eastbound traffic lane for deep-drafted vessels. Two precautionary areas exist west and east of the line connecting St. John's Island on the Singapore side and Pulau Belakang Padang on the Indonesia side to accommodate vessels crossing the TSS. East of the Singapore Island, another precautionary area is established between Tanjung Stapa on Malaysia side and Pulau Bintan on Indonesia side. The TSS ends on the east of the Horsburgh Lighthouse area.[89]

Under SOLAS, the general provisions on regulations apply to ships engaged on international voyages, and each Chapter defines precisely the classes of ships to which it applies.[90] Chapter V specifies it applies to all ships, meaning

85 The Inter-Governmental Maritime Consultative Organization (IMCO), Res.A.375(X), "Navigation through the Straits of Malacca and Singapore," adopted 14 November 1977, <www.imo.org/blast/blastDataHelper.asp?data_id=26756&filename=A375(X).pdf>.

86 "Report of the Maritime Safety Committee on Its Sixty-Ninth Session, Annex 6, 'New and Amended Existing Traffic Separation Schemes'," IMO, MSC.69/22/Add.1, 1 June 1998 (available at IMODOCS at <webaccounts.imo.org>, registration is required).

87 IMO, *Ships' Routeing* (IMO Publication Sales Number: IE927E, 12th edition, 2015), Part B – Traffic Separation Schemes and Inshore Traffic Zones, Section V – South-East Asia, V1-V9.

88 "General Provisions on Ships' Routeing," IMO Res.A.572(14), adopted 20 November 1985, Annex, para. 2.1.2, <www.imo.org/blast/blastDataHelper.asp?data_id=22369&filename=A572(14).pdf>.

89 IMO, *Ships' Routeing* (2015), *supra* note 87, Session V, V6-9.

90 SOLAS, *supra* note 82, Chapter I – General Provisions, Regulation 1 – Application.

"any ship, vessel or craft irrespective of type and purpose" on all voyages except warships and ships solely navigating the Great Lakes of North America.[91] This scope of application means that the ships' routeing measures adopted for the SOMS apply to all ships navigating within these operational areas.[92] Vessels transiting the Singapore Strait are to enter and exit the TSS system at designated locations and proceed in the appropriate traffic lane in the general direction of traffic flow for that lane and keep clear of, so far as practicable, the traffic separation line.[93] In addition, the vessel should avoid crossing traffic lanes if practicable and cross on a heading at right angles to the general direction of traffic flow if obliged to leave the traffic lane.[94]

One of the contributing factors to incidents in the Singapore Strait has been that vessels transiting in the Strait were unable to distinguish whether a vessel arriving or departing from the port of Singapore would be crossing the TSS, especially during hours of darkness.[95] In order to address the issue of identifying crossing vessels, the three littoral States proposed to the IMO in 2010 an interim recommendatory measure for the Singapore Strait that crossing vessels display special night signals. The interim measure was adopted as a recommendatory measure with effect from 1 June 2013.[96] Vessels of 300 GT and above or 50 metres or more in length and vessels engaged in towing or pushing with a combined 300 GT and above or with a combined length of 50 metres or more are expected to display the recommended night signals.[97]

---

91 *Ibid.*, Chapter V – Safety of Navigation, Regulation 1 – Application and Regulation 2 – Definitions.

92 *Ibid.*, Chapter V – Safety of Navigation, Regulation 10 – Ships' Routeing.

93 International Regulations for Preventing Collisions at Sea (COLREGS), 1050 *U.N.T.S.* 16, adopted 20 October 1972, entry into force 15 July 1977, Rule 10 – Traffic Separation Schemes, para. (b).

94 *Ibid.*, Rule 10 – Traffic Separation Schemes, para. (c).

95 MPA, Port Marine Circular, No. 02 of 2011, 30 May 2011, To: Shipping Community, Night Signals for Vessels Crossing the Traffic Separation Scheme (TSS) and Precautionary Areas in the Singapore Strait During the Hours of Darkness, MPA, Port Marine Circular, No. 04 of 2013, 07 May 2013, Recommendatory Measure for Vessels Crossing the Traffic Separation Scheme (TSS) and Precautionary Areas in the Singapore Strait During the Hours of Darkness, <www.mpa.gov.sg/web/wcm/connect/www/529dd2d3-49b4-4c58-8ab0-040d1bc93dac/pc13-04.pdf?MOD=AJPERES>.

96 IMO, MSC 91/22, 17 December 2012, Report of the Maritime Safety Committee on Its Ninety-First Session, para. 12.4.8 (available at IMODOCS at <webaccounts.imo.org>, registration is required).

97 IMO, MSC 91/22/Add.2, 20 December 2012, Report of the Maritime Safety Committee on Its Ninety-First Session Annex 26 "Routeing Measures other than Traffic Separation Schemes," "Recommendatory Measures for Vessels Crossing the Traffic Separation

2 *STRAITREP*

The ship reporting system is another measure under Chapter V of SOLAS that contributes to the safety of life at sea, safety and the efficiency of navigation, and the protection of the marine environment.[98] The procedures to adopt ship reporting systems are similar to those for ships' routeing systems. The IMO is recognised as the competent international organisation for developing international guidelines, criteria and regulations for ship reporting systems.[99] It is the States concerned that are responsible for planning and proposing to the IMO the adoption of ship reporting systems as well as implementing the systems.[100]

In order to improve the communication capability and streamline the monitoring systems to enhance the safety of navigation in the SOMS, the littoral States proposed to the IMO that a mandatory ship reporting system is established. The ship reporting system was adopted by Resolution MSC.73(69) that entered into force on 1 December 1998.[101] It is known as STRAITREP. The operational area of STRAITREP overlaps with the TSS from One Fathom Bank in the west to the Horsburgh Lighthouse area in the east.[102] In contrast to the TSS that applies to all ships navigating in the operational areas, the mandatory reporting system applies to:

1. vessels of 300 GT and above;
2. vessels of 50 metres or more in length;
3. vessels engaged in towing or pushing with a combined GT of 300 and above, or with a combined length of 50 metres or more;
4. vessels of any tonnage carrying hazardous cargo;
5. all passenger vessels that are fitted with VHF, regardless of length or GT; and
6. any category of vessels fitted with VHF that uses the appropriate traffic lane or separation zone in an emergency situation to avoid immediate danger.[103]

Scheme (TSS) and Precautionary Areas in the Singapore Strait during Hours of Darkness," para. 2 (available at IMODOCS at <webaccounts.imo.org>, registration is required).

98 SOLAS, *supra* note 82, Chapter V – Safety of Navigation, Regulation 11 – Ship Reporting Systems, para. 1.

99 *Ibid.*, para. 2.

100 IMO, MSC/Circ.1060, *supra* note 84, Annex, para.6.1.

101 IMO, Res. MSC.73(69), adopted on 19 May 1998, Mandatory Ship Reporting Systems, <www.imo.org/blast/blastDataHelper.asp?data_id=15439&filename=73(69).pdf>.

102 IMO, *Ships' Routeing* (2015), *supra* note 87, Session G – Mandatory Ship Reporting Systems, Mandatory Routeing System and Mandatory No Anchoring Areas, I/16-1, para.2.

103 *Ibid.*, para.1.1.

The operational area for STRAITREP is divided into nine sectors each with a VHF channel for communicating with the vessel traffic service (VTS) authorities in Malaysia and Singapore.[104] The Singapore VTS covers sector seven to nine corresponding with the Singapore Strait (see Figure 8.2 in the Annex).[105] The ship report needs to be by the prescribed reporting format and required content, be submitted to the correct VTS at a required time and geographical position.[106] Only information that is essential to meet the objectives of the STRAITREP is required including: the name of ship, call sign, IMO identification number (if available); position of ship; hazardous cargo, class (if applicable); any breakdown, damage and/or deficiencies affecting the structure, cargo or equipment of the ship; any circumstances affecting normal navigation defined according to SOLAS and MARPOL; and the course and speed of ship when requested by the specific VTS authority.[107]

Traffic in the Singapore Strait and Singapore waters are monitored and regulated by Singapore's Vessel Traffic Information System (VTIS), operated by the MPA.[108] The VTIS can track up to 10,000 vessels at any one time. The VTIS can pull together information from various sources including radar, Automatic Identification Systems (AIS), Harbour Craft Transponder Systems (HARTS), Closed Circuit Television Systems (CCTV) and ship databases to present a comprehensive picture of the monitored sections of the Strait. Enhanced monitoring functions also assist VTIS operators in detecting potential collisions and grounding situations, thus facilitate timely warnings to ships.[109] At the Port Operations Control Centre (POCC), each VTIS operator is assigned one particular area in the TSS or the Singapore waters. With information from the available sources, the VTIS assigns each category of ship a symbol for easy identification, such as passenger ship, bunkering vessel, bulk carrier, oil tankers, cargo ship, ships carrying chemicals, liquefied natural gas (LNG) carriers, special service ships, and very large crude carrier (VLCC). Under normal circumstance, after receiving the report from the ship that has entered the STRAITREP operational area, the VTIS operators will track and monitor the movement of the ship and communicate with the ship operators about the traffic situation and any potentially dangerous situation in the Strait. Whenever a ship is in breach

104 *Ibid.*, para.2.1, and I/16-2, para.3.4.

105 *Ibid.*, I/16-2, para.3.4, and I/16-7, Appendix 3.

106 *Ibid.*, para.3.

107 *Ibid.*, para.3.2, and I/16-7, Appendix 4.

108 MPA, "Port of Singapore: Vessel Traffic Information System," <www.mpa.gov.sg/web/portal/home/port-of-singapore/operations/vessel-traffic-information-system-vtis>.

109 MPA, "A Vessel Traffic Information System for the Future," 25 July 2011, <www.mpa.gov.sg/web/portal/home/media-centre/news-releases/detail/52cd3a9f-3dcd-4e29-9376-6ec4cb496537>.

of navigation rules, such as not following the TSS, causing or threatening to cause a collision, the VTIS operator will warn the ship, notify the flag State if the circumstance warrants, and record such violations in the database for further investigation if the ship calls in at a Singapore port.[110]

3 *Enforcement Jurisdiction*

Under the law of the sea, the flag State has primary responsibility to ensure compliance by vessels flying its flag with the applicable international rules and standards for safety of navigation and the prevention, reduction and control of pollution from vessels, including for ships exercising the right of transit passage in the straits used for international navigation.[111] The States bordering the straits may exercise a limited prescriptive jurisdiction over specific issues relating to transit passage.[112] Such laws and regulations of the States bordering the straits must not "discriminate in form or in fact among foreign ships or in their application have the practical effect of denying, hampering or impairing the right of transit passage."[113]

States bordering the straits do not have explicit enforcement jurisdiction over violations by foreign ships in transit passage under Part III of UNCLOS. Nonetheless, within the territorial sea, the coastal State may take the steps necessary to prevent passage which is not innocent under the rights of protection.[114] For straits used for international navigation, "any activity which is not an exercise of the right of transit passage through a strait remains subject to the other applicable provisions of this Convention."[115] Hence, for ships that are not exercising the navigational freedom "solely for the purpose of continuous and expeditious transit of the strait" will be subject to coastal State jurisdiction over the territorial sea.[116] The unclear question is whether a foreign ship that violates the laws and regulations on the safety of navigation or the control of marine pollution would be considered not to have been exercising the right of transit passage.

In UNCLOS Part XII, Protection and Preservation of the Marine Environment, a safeguard provision concerning straits used for international navigation protects the interests of the States bordering the straits.[117] Article 233

110 Information gathered during a visit at the Port Operations Control Centre (POCC-Vista) hosted by the Singapore MPA.

111 UNCLOS, *supra* note 2, Articles 21(4), 39(2), 94, and 217.

112 *Ibid.*, Article 42(1).

113 *Ibid.*, Article 42(2).

114 *Ibid.*, Article 25(1).

115 *Ibid.*, Article 38(3).

116 *Ibid.*, Article 38(2).

117 *Virginia Commentary*, Vol. IV (1990), *supra* note 21, at 383.

provides that if a foreign ship has violated the laws and regulations on the safety of navigation or the control of marine pollution adopted by the States bordering the strait, "causing or threatening major damage to the marine environment of the straits, the States bordering the straits may take appropriate enforcement measures."[118]

Malaysia, Indonesia and Singapore have, as noted above, through the adoption of the IMO (then IMCO) Resolution A.375(X) in 1977, designated a number of TSS and adopted rules of navigation for ships using the SOMS. The three littoral States, in consultation with the major users of the SOMS, submitted a critical interpretation respecting the enforcement jurisdiction regarding foreign ships exercising the right of transit passage in the SOMS in relation to the draft Article 233.[119] It was the understanding among these States that a violation of the provision of IMO Resolution A.375(X) would be deemed to be a violation within the meaning of Article 233, and therefore the littoral States may take appropriate enforcement measures for such violation, including preventing a vessel violating the required under keel clearance from proceeding.[120] Consequently, a breach of any IMO measures for improving the safety of navigation and enhancing the prevention, reduction and control of vessel-source pollution in the SOMS would fall under the enforcement jurisdiction of the littoral States.

V Conclusions

Singapore's geography limits its right to regulate foreign ships. The Singapore government has stated its right to claim a territorial sea up to 12 M and an EEZ subject to delimitation with its neighbouring States but has not yet adopted legislation to clarify its maritime claims. All the relevant Singaporean domestic laws apply to its territorial waters, but no legislation mentions the application of these laws in the EEZ. As an important international maritime centre, much

118 See: J. Ashley Roach and Robert W. Smith, *Excessive Maritime Claims* (3rd Edition, Martinus Nijhoff, 2012) at 305–306.

119 See: *Virginia Commentary*, Vol. IV (1990), *supra* note 21, at 388–389 and John G. Butcher and R.E. Elson, *Sovereignty and the Sea: How Indonesia Became an Archipelagic State* (NUS Press, 2017), at 404 and 415-416.

120 *Virginia Commentary*, Vol. IV (1990), *supra* note 21, at 388–389 and United Nations *"Third United Nations Conference on the Law of the Sea,"* Volume XVI, A/CONF.62/L.145 (the consulted users States of the SOMS were Australia, Federal Republic of Germany, France, Japan, United Kingdom and the United States), <www.legal.un.org/diplomaticconferences/1973_los/vol16.shtml>.

of Singapore's legislation relating to maritime matters is transposed from the IMO conventions to ensure consistency with international rules and standards.

Foreign vessels navigating through the territorial waters of Singapore must obey its applicable laws and regulations. In addition, vessels exercising the right of transit passage must comply with the measures adopted by the IMO for improving the safety of navigation and enhancing the prevention, reduction and control of vessel-source pollution in the Singapore Strait, including the ships' routeing measures, mandatory ship reporting system and rules of navigation.

Moving forward, Singapore has an important task to finalise the scope of its maritime jurisdiction. There are three elements to this task. First, Singapore must clarify its position on the legal status of Pedra Branca, most importantly whether it will claim an EEZ from it. Second, Singapore needs to announce and give due publicity of the precise geographical coordinates of its territorial sea and EEZ. Third, Singapore needs to work with both Malaysia and Indonesia to finalise the maritime boundaries at both ends of the Singapore Strait. The certainty in maritime jurisdiction is a crucial factor in establishing stability and good order in the Singapore Strait.

VI Annex

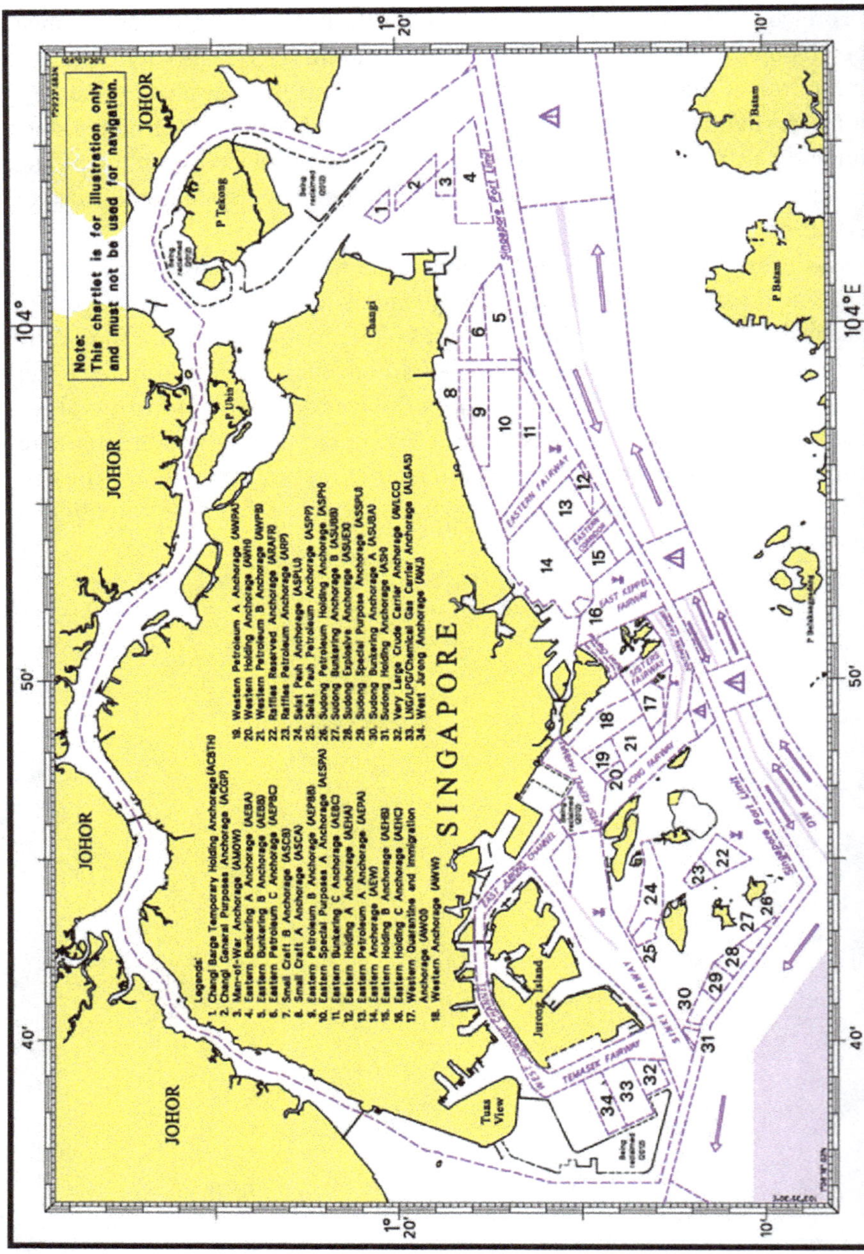

FIGURE 8.1 Port of Singapore – Anchorages Chartlet.
Note: See *supra* note 5.

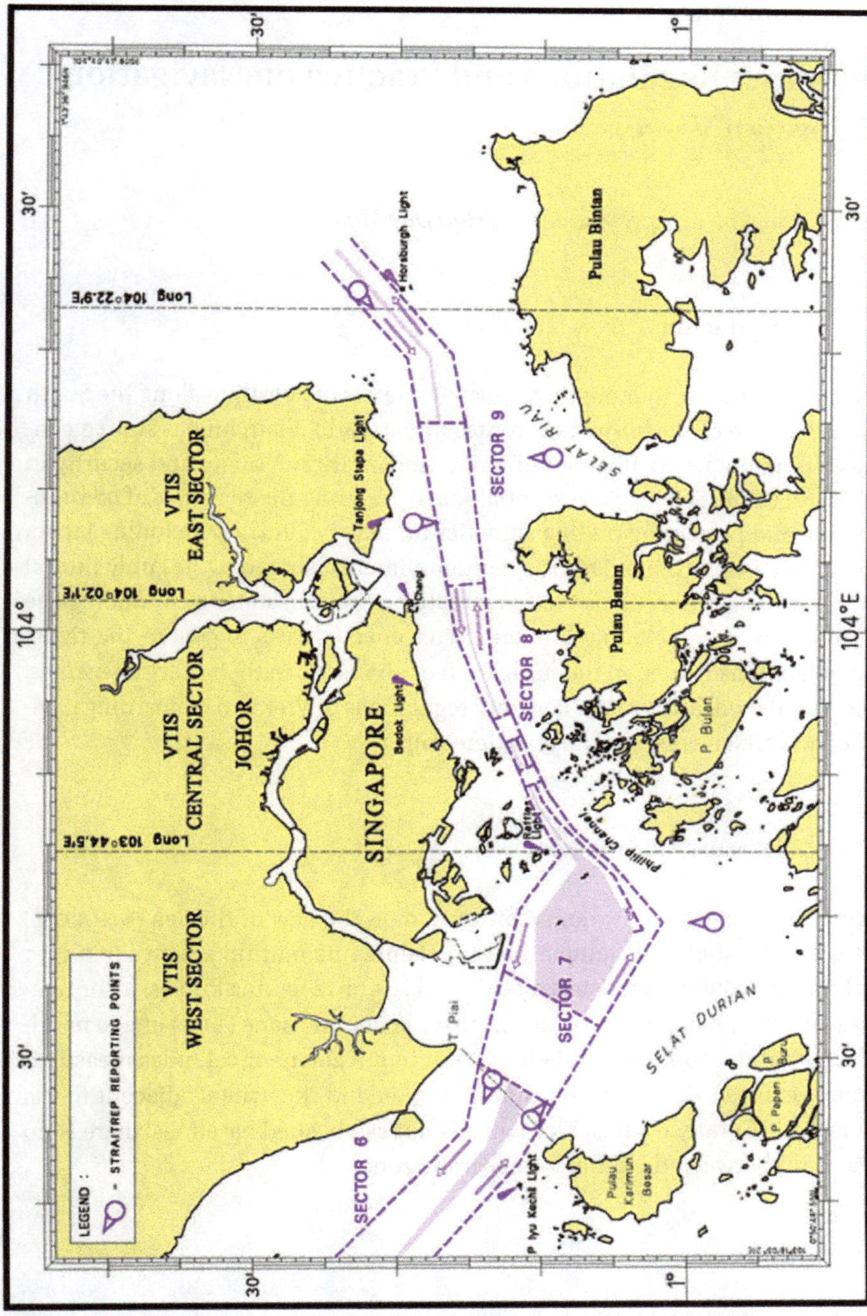

FIGURE 8.2 STRAITREP Operational Areas from Sector 7 to Sector 9 (with TSS).
SOURCE: MPA, MAPS OF THE STRAITREP OPERATIONAL AREAS, <WWW.MPA.GOV.SG/WEB/PORTAL/HOME/PORT-OF-SINGAPORE/OPERATIONS/VESSEL-TRAFFIC-INFORMATION-SYSTEM-VTIS/OPERATIONAL-AREAS>

CHAPTER 9

Vietnam's Regulations and Practice on Navigation of Foreign Vessels

Lan-Anh T. Nguyen and Tran Huu Duy Minh

I Introduction

As a coastal state with more than 3200 kilometers of coastline along the South China Sea, one of the busiest sea routes in the world, Vietnam has strategic interests in maintaining freedom of navigation. Maritime safety and security in the South China Sea play an essential role in securing the sea lanes of communication and protecting trading activities for many countries, including Japan, South Korea, and China. This is a common interest shared by not only littoral states, but also other sea users. To regulate navigation, states surrounding the South China Sea, including Vietnam, have enacted laws to govern the rights and obligations related to the navigation of all vessels in their maritime zones. This chapter will analyze the laws and regulations of Vietnam concerning navigation of foreign vessels in its maritime zones.

II Vietnam's Maritime Zones

Before the 1982 United Nations Convention on the Law of the Sea (UNCLOS)[1] came into legal effect, Vietnam had proclaimed its maritime zones in a 1977 declaration, which establishes a territorial sea of 12 nautical miles, a contiguous zone of 24 nautical miles, an exclusive economic zone (EEZ) of 200 nautical miles, and a continental shelf of a minimum 200 nautical miles measured from baselines.[2] As within the Gulf of Tonkin and the waters adjacent to the Paracel and Spratly Islands, Vietnam has not established baselines, there is no clear limit between the different maritime zones.

---

1 U.N. Convention on the Law of the Sea, 1833 *U.N.T.S.* 397.

2 Declaration on Territorial Sea, Contiguous Zone, Exclusive Economic Zone and Continental Shelf of Vietnam, 12 May 1977.

 | DOI:10.1163/9789004396272_010

III Laws and Regulations concerning Navigation

The navigation of foreign vessels in the maritime zones under the jurisdiction of Vietnam is governed mainly by two laws: the Law of the Sea of Vietnam, adopted on 21 June 2012, which entered into force on 1 January 2013,[3] (referred to in this chapter as "Law of the Sea"), and the newly adopted Maritime Law of 2015 that entered into force on 1 July 2017.[4] There are also specific regulations adopted by the Government, Prime Minister and specialized agencies. Generally, in these laws and regulations, the right of innocent passage and freedom of navigation in respective Vietnam's maritime zones are recognized and protected in accordance with the UNCLOS.

1 *The Prevailing Effects of Treaties over the National Laws*

The Vietnam Constitution of 2013 for the first time provides that Vietnam is to comply with the United Nations Charter and all treaties to which Vietnam is a party.[5] This constitutional requirement has been inserted as a common provision into a number of laws and regulations. Paragraph 1 of Article 6 of the Law of Treaties 2016 provides that "in case of conflicts between Vietnamese legal normative documents with a treaty to which Vietnam is a party, the treaty will prevail, except the Constitution."[6] This common provision also appears in the Law of the Sea of Vietnam.[7] In the context of this chapter, the principle allows foreign vessels to claim the application of the UNCLOS or other treaties to which Vietnam is a party as having priority over Vietnamese laws and regulations that are not in accordance with these treaties.

The Constitution, which has the highest legal effect in Vietnam, takes priority over the application of a treaty that is contrary to the Constitution, even if this may trigger a claim of State responsibility. Until now there have been no cases where the application of a treaty obligation has conflicted with the Constitution.

Possible conflicts between a treaty and national laws are considered when adopting a new law. When a central government organ drafts a law, regulation or any other legally normative document, the drafters must consider the compatibility between the draft document and any treaties in force for Vietnam.[8] This applies to documents adopted by the National Assembly and

3 *Law of the Sea of Vietnam* (2012).
4 *Maritime Law* (2015).
5 *The Constitution of Vietnam* (2013), Article 12.
6 *Law of Treaties of Vietnam* (2016), Article 6(1).
7 *Law of the Sea* (2012), Article 2(2).
8 *Law on Promulgation of Legislative Documents* (2015), Article 5(5).

Government or issued by the Prime Minister and Ministers. In sum, the Vietnamese legal system places a great emphasis on ensuring compliance with treaties to which Vietnam is a party, including those concerning navigation e.g. the UNCLOS and those adopted by the International Maritime Organization (IMO).[9] Vietnam guarantees the implementation of navigational rights under UNCLOS. Other party states and their vessels will be accorded navigational rights in accordance with UNCLOS, even when there is a conflict between the laws of Vietnam and UNCLOS.

In the maritime zones of Vietnam, the navigation of foreign vessels is generally governed by the Law of the Sea of Vietnam and the Maritime Law. The Law of the Sea applies to matters relating to sovereignty and the legal regimes of maritime zones; whereas the Maritime Law applies to matters relating to vessels and navigational activities. The navigational regime is covered generally by the provisions on the legal regime of maritime zones in the Law of the Sea, while some specifics of the regime are governed by the Maritime Law. If a conflict arises between these two laws, as the later law, the Maritime Law is to apply.[10]

2 *General Rules concerning Navigation*

In general, the laws and regulations of Vietnam simply repeat the rules in the UNCLOS. Foreign vessels are assured the right of innocent passage in Vietnam's territorial sea, and freedom of navigation in its exclusive economic zone.[11] Article 12 of the Law of the Sea specifically states that "vessels of all states enjoy the right of innocent passage in the territorial sea of Vietnam." Article 16 provides that "The Government [of Vietnam] respects the freedom of navigation [...] of other states in the exclusive economic zone of Vietnam."

While operating in Vietnamese maritime zones, foreign vessels are required not to interfere with and to "respect the sovereignty, territorial integrity, sovereign rights, the jurisdiction and national interests of Vietnam in accordance with Vietnamese laws and international agreements to which Vietnam is a member, including the UNCLOS."[12] Specifically, foreign vessels are prohibited from: human trafficking; unlawful trafficking, transportation or stockpiling of narcotic drugs;[13] and illegal broadcasting.[14] These rules are consistent with

9 Vietnam has ratified 24 IMO conventions of which the Convention on Control and Management of Ship Ballast Waters and Sediments, 30 *I.L.M.* 1455 is the latest.

10 *Law on Promulgation of Legislative Documents,* Article 156(3).

11 *Law of the Sea* (2012), Articles 12 and 16.

12 *Ibid.*, Article 16(2) and 22(1).

13 *Ibid.*, Article 39.

14 *Ibid.*, Article 40.

Articles 99, 108 and 109 of the UNCLOS. Moreover, Article 38 of the Law of the Sea also prohibits vessels engaging in illicit stockpiling, use or trafficking of weapons, explosive and toxic substances while operating in Vietnam's maritime zones.[15] As these activities are not regulated expressly in the UNCLOS, they may fall within the unallocated jurisdiction under Article 59 of the UNCLOS. In practice, it would be doubtful that Vietnam would take enforcement actions against vessels carrying weapons and explosives which sail through its EEZ without entering internal waters.

To operate in port waters or in other Vietnamese maritime zones, foreign vessels must have a certificate of tonnage.[16] Certificates may be issued by Vietnamese authorities or authorities of a flag state but the certificates must be in accordance with Vietnamese laws or the relevant treaties. Vietnamese authorities may request a re-checking of tonnage capacity where they have reasonable doubts.

The Maritime Law provides for institutional administration of navigation and other related activities in Vietnam's maritime zones. The Minister of Transport is responsible for the management of maritime shipping and navigation,[17] including, *inter alia,* designating agencies in charge of ship registration, ship inspection, and adopting regulations on standards for maritime safety and security, labour safety and pollution prevention.[18] The Vietnam Maritime Administration (VINAMARINE) within the Ministry of Transport is the specialized agency primarily dealing with implementation of the Maritime Law. Each port is managed by a Port Authority established by the Minister of Transport on the basis of the recommendation of the Director General of the VINAMARINE and under the direct supervision of the VINAMARINE.[19] Directors of port authorities have the responsibility to enforce laws and regulations, inspect and monitor maritime activities of individuals and organizations within their ports, grant permits and monitor the arrival, departure, or activities of vessels in port, execute vessel arrest decisions issued by competent state agencies, temporarily detain vessels, organize search and rescue in port waters, and sanction administrative violations in the maritime domain within their competence, etc.[20]

15 *Ibid.*, Article 38.
16 *Maritime Law* (2015), Article 35.
17 *Ibid.*, Article 10(2).
18 *Ibid.*, Article 28.
19 Circular of the Minister of Transport No. 31/2016/TT-BGTVT, 31 Oct 2016, enter into force on 1st July 2017, Article 2–3.
20 *Maritime Law* (2015), Articles 91 and 92.

3 *Rules Applicable to Port Waters and Internal Waters*

In accordance with the regime of internal waters under the UNCLOS, Vietnam's ports are subject to the sovereignty of Vietnam as internal waters. Foreign vessels of all nationalities, both commercial and military, are required to obtain permission to enter and leave Vietnamese ports. Vessels are only permitted to approach Vietnamese ports if they satisfy all the requirements of maritime safety and security, maritime labour, environmental protection laws and other requirement in accordance with Vietnamese laws.[21]

Commercial vessels may apply for permission after anchoring in the port.[22] However, they are required to submit to port authorities in advance a ship's security notification and a general declaration detailing the vessel's identification, list of crew, voyage details, purpose of the visit, type of cargo, list of passengers, etc.[23] Vessels are only allowed to proceed to Vietnamese ports if the port authorities approve.[24] They are not required to request for new permission if they travel to another port in Vietnam.[25] To depart ports, foreign vessels are required to submit in advance a request indicating the time and date of leaving.[26]

For military vessels to enter into Vietnam's internal water or to proceed to Vietnamese ports, it is required that the vessels obtain permissions in advance through diplomatic channels, including the permission for anchoring in ports and/or for crew to travel on land.[27] Foreign military vessels are required to operate according to the agreed plans and any changes must be submitted and approved by Vietnamese authorities.[28] Before the adoption of the Law of the Sea of Vietnam, the regulations were much stricter due to the influence of the Cold War. Foreign military vessels were required to apply for permission 30 days before visiting Vietnam, and to notify the Ministry of Defence 48 hours before entering the territorial sea.[29] No more than three military vessels of a

21 *Ibid.*, Article 94.

22 *Ibid.*, Article 96.

23 Government Decree No. 58/2017/ND-CP on Specifying certain provisions of the Maritime Law of Vietnam on Management of Navigation Activities, adopted on 10 May 2017, enforce on 1 July 2017, Article 87, (hereafter Government Decree No. 58/2017/ND-CP).

24 *Ibid.*, Article 89.

25 *Maritime Law* (2015), Article 6(3).

26 Government Decree No. 58/2017/ND-CP, Article 87.

27 *Law of the Sea* (2012), Article 27; *Maritime Law* (2015), Article 95; and Government Decree No. 104/2012/ND-CP on Regulations on the Visit of Foreign Military Vessels to Vietnam, adopted 05 December 2012, entered into force 20 January 2013, Article 4.

28 *Maritime Law* (2015), Article 95(3) and Government Decree No. 104/2012/ND-CP, Article 4(3).

29 Government Decree No. 55/CP (1996), Article 6. This Decree was replaced by Government Decree No. 104/2012/ND-CP (2012).

foreign state could be in the same port at the same time, and military vessels could not be anchored in the port for more than seven days, except if otherwise agreed by Vietnam.[30]

For foreign nuclear-powered vessels and radioactive substance carrying vessels require the permission from the Prime Minister to enter and operate in port waters, the internal waters and territorial sea of Vietnam.[31] Requests must be sent to the Ministry of Transport to report to the Prime Minister.[32] Within 10 days of reviewing the request and all the required documents the Ministry of Transport must answer whether the permission is to be granted by the Prime Minister.[33] As there is no express exception, arguably this regulation does apply to those vessels entering into the territorial sea of Vietnam to exercise solely the right of innocent passage.

For foreign vessels conducting activities concerning marine scientific research, fisheries, search and rescue, recovery of sunken properties, assisting towage in seaport waters, repairing or building services of vessels, training, culture, sport, construction of maritime or submerged installations and structures, services supporting resource surveys, exploration, exploitation activities, environment-related activities, etc., they are required to submit a request to VINAMARINE for permission.[34]

Port authorities have the responsibility to monitor the activities of foreign vessels beyond port waters to ensure that the vessel do not endanger navigation safety, maritime security and coastal pollution prevention efforts.[35] Thus, foreign vessels are required to register with the port authorities in charge of the areas where they operate.[36] This requirement is the same as requesting permission to enter and leave ports. It is expected that all vessels conducting activities beyond port waters shall observe the same requirements as those within port waters.

4 *Innocent Passage in the Territorial Sea*

The Law of the Sea of Vietnam affirms the right of innocent passage for all vessels. Articles 18, 19, 20 and 21 of the UNCLOS are restated as Articles 23 and 29 in the Law of the Sea. In addition to the list of non-innocent activities in Article

30 *Ibid.*, Article 10.
31 *Maritime Law* (2015), Article 105(5).
32 Government Decree No. 58/2017/ND-CP, Article 75(2).
33 *Ibid.*
34 *Ibid.*, Article 75(3).
35 *Maritime Law* (2015), Article 94(3).
36 *Ibid.*

19 of the UNCLOS, Article 23 of the Law of the Sea provides one additional activity that Vietnam does not regard as innocent—foreign vessels must not use or threaten to use force against the sovereignty, independence or territorial integrity of other states while exercising innocent passage. This reaffirms Vietnam's neutral foreign policy not to let other states use its territory to threaten other states. In sum, the rules of innocent passage in Vietnam's territorial sea are the same as those of the UNCLOS, and thus ensure that all foreign vessels can navigate freely within the territorial sea of Vietnam.

Pursuant to the Maritime Law,[37] Vietnam may designate sea lanes in its territorial sea for the purposes of innocent passage or safety of navigation. The establishment of any sea lanes will be notified to the competent international organizations and given due publicity. In practice, no sea lane in the territorial sea is known to be established.

Vietnam may impose temporary no-entry zones or suspension of navigation in its territorial sea for the purpose of "safeguarding the sovereignty, national defence, national security and interests or securing safety of navigation, protecting marine resources and marine ecology, combatting pollution, tackling maritime accidents or marine environmental disasters, preventing the spread of epidemics,"[38] which is in line with Articles 21 and 25 of the UNCLOS. In practice, the suspensions are usually due to military exercises.[39] There is no provision to allow for the establishment of a permanent non-entry zone, and Vietnam has not designated any such area in its territorial sea. Indeed, it may not necessary to establish such a non-entry zone in the territorial sea for defence or security purposes as the internal waters of Vietnam are broad enough to cover all areas near its military bases.

Concerning the exercise of criminal and civil jurisdiction, Vietnam's regulations are generally in conformity with Articles 27 and 28 of the UNCLOS. In order to clarify Article 27(5), the Law of the Sea of Vietnam provides that it may exercise criminal jurisdiction over foreign vessels as necessary to prevent or restrict marine pollution or to exercise its jurisdiction in the EEZ.[40]

37 *Ibid.*, Articles 109–112. For detailed regulations, see Government Decree No. 16/2018/ND-CP on the Publication of sea lanes and navigation in the territorial sea of Vietnam, adopted on 2 February 2018, entered into force 01 April 2018.

38 *Law of the Sea* (2012), Article 26.

39 For example, on 16 March 2015, a suspension was announced on the area adjacent to Khanh Hoa province due to a live fire exercise on 22 March 2015, see Marine Notice No. KHA – 04 – 2015 (16 March 2015), available at <www.vms-south.vn/thong-bao-hang-hai/thong-bao/ban-dan-that-phong-tha-bom-nem-bom-chong-ngam-tren-bien-cua-quan-chung-hai-quan-tai-vung-bien-tinh-khanh-hoa>.

40 *Law of the Sea* (2012), Article 30.

Under the current Law of the Sea, most foreign vessels are not required to obtain prior permission to undertake innocent passage, however, prior notification is required for military vessels. Before the adoption of the 2012 Law, foreign military vessels were required to request prior permission when they intend to navigate in the contiguous zone, territorial sea or internal waters of Vietnam.[41] This requirement adopted in 1980 was justified on the basis of national security and defence and the capacity to control the sea.[42] It was argued that the UNCLOS did not have any express provision concerning the right of innocent passage by military vessels, and thus the requirement of prior permission was not contrary to the UNCLOS.[43] Moreover, Vietnam was not the only state to have this requirement.[44] The changes in the Law of the Sea of 2012 can be considered as to expand the right of innocent passage rather than to bring Vietnamese law into a closer accordance with the UNCLOS. The removal of the requirement of prior permission is to facilitate and make the exercise of the right of innocent passage for foreign military vessels more convenient.

Although providing for the requirement of prior notification, the Law of the Sea neither imposes any punishment or rejects innocent passage of those who fail to comply with the requirement. The application of prior notification is further illustrated in the context of the recent U.S. Freedom of Navigation Program (FONOP) in the South China Sea. According to a report by Lynn Kuok citing a letter from the U.S. Secretary of Defense Carter, U.S. military vessels navigated within 12 nautical miles of several of the Spratly Islands without prior notice to any states, including Vietnam.[45] In response to the U.S. FONOP through the territorial sea of some high tide features in the Spratlys in 2015 and 2016, Vietnam did not protest on the basis that the United States had failed to provide prior notification. In a statement, the Spokesman of the Ministry of Foreign Affairs of Vietnam had no words of protest but simply reaffirmed that "Vietnam respects the right to innocent passage in the territorial

---

41 Government Decree No. 30-CP (1980) on the Regime of Foreign vessels operating in Vietnamese waters provides that foreign military vessels must obtain permission before entering the territorial sea and contiguous zone of Vietnam.

42 Nguyen Ba Dien, Nguyen Hung Cuong, "Right to innocent passage of foreign military vessels in the territorial sea under international law and Vietnamese law," 28 *Journal of Jurisprudence, Journal of Science of the National University of Hanoi*, 2012, 8–16 (in Vietnamese).

43 *Ibid.*

44 *Ibid.*

45 Lynn Kuok, "The U.S. FON Program in the South China Sea: A lawful and necessary response to China's strategic ambiguity," (June 2016), p. 15, available at <www.brookings.edu/~/media/research/files/papers/2016/06/07-kuok-fon-south-china-sea/the-us-fon-program-in-the-south-china-sea.pdf>

sea in accordance with relevant rules of international law, in particular the [UNCLOS] (Article 17)."[46]

Regarding the innocent passage of foreign nuclear-powered vessels or foreign vessels carrying radioactive, noxious or dangerous substances, the Law of the Sea requires them to carry sufficient technical documents related to the vessels and goods on board and documents of mandatory civil insurance, to provide these documents to competent Vietnamese authorities if requested, to fully implement the special precautionary measures required by Vietnamese laws and treaties to which Vietnam is a party, to observe decisions made by competent Vietnamese authorities on the application of the special precautionary measures, including the ban of passage through Vietnam's territorial sea and the demand to leave immediately Vietnam's territorial sea in case there are clear signs or evidence of possible leakage or environmental pollutions.[47] Such vessels may be required to use the sea lanes specifically designated on a case by case basis.[48] The vessels are prohibited from discharging or dumping industrial waste, nuclear waste or other toxic waste in the maritime zones of Vietnam.[49]

5 *Navigation in the Exclusive Economic Zone*

In the EEZ, foreign vessels enjoy the freedom of navigation.[50] While exercising the freedom of navigation, they are prohibited from conducting any activities violating the sovereign rights and jurisdiction of Vietnam over its EEZ, such as exploitation of living and non-living resources, generation of energy from currents and winds, marine scientific research, construction and operation of artificial installations, drilling, causing marine pollution, etc.[51] These activities may only be conducted on basis of a treaty, a contract or a permission from the Vietnamese government.[52]

The establishment of safety zones around artificial installations and structures is regulated by the Law of the Sea of Vietnam, the Law on Petroleum and its guiding documents. The current regulations originated from Government Decree No. 30-CP (1980), the first Law of Petroleum (1993), and Government Decree No. 84/CP (1996), which have since all been terminated. The 1980

46 "Statement by the Spokesman of the Ministry of Foreign Affairs of Vietnam", 31 January 2016, available at <www.mofa.gov.vn/vi/tt_baochi/pbnfn/ns160131112114> [in Vietnamese].

47 *Law of the Sea* (2012), Article 24(2).

48 *Ibid.*, Article 25(2).

49 *Ibid.*, Article 35(3).

50 *Ibid., Article 16(2).*

51 *Ibid., Article 37.*

52 *Ibid.*, Article 16(3).

Decree provided for a 500 meter zone from the outermost points of the installations and structures. The 1996 Decree added a provision on establishing a non-anchoring zone of two nautical miles around artificial installations and structures. The requirement of a safety zone and non-anchoring mentioned above are reaffirmed in the Law of the Sea of Vietnam, Article 34(3) which provides that: "Artificial islands, installations and structures at sea and supporting facilities have a safety zone of 500 meters from the furthest point of those artificial islands, installations and structures at sea, but do not have the territorial sea or other maritime zones of their own." Government Decree No. 95/2015/ND-CP (2015) elaborates on the extent of safety zones around petroleum-related structures and installations, providing that:

> the minimum distance from the safety zones for offshore oil and gas works is five hundred-meter (500 m) outwards from the outermost edge of the works to all directions or from the anchoring position of floating means, mobile works, except for the special cases decided by the Prime Minister.[53]

No one except authorized persons may enter safety zone.[54] In practice, the VINAMARINE occasionally has instructed vessels not to navigate in a broader zone ranging from one to two nautical miles. The distance varies depending on the nature of the operations. It should be noted that in its Marine Notices, the word "instruct" is used, not "prohibit." Such instructions are designed to secure the safety for both the structures and installations in an area, and vessels navigating through the areas. No arrest or other enforcement measures against vessels navigating within the instructed areas has been recorded.

Vietnamese law offers an additional protection for installations and structures at sea, including that no vessel may anchor or conduct underwater activities within a distance of two nautical miles from offshore installations or structures.[55] For pipelines, which transfer oil and gas, vessels are also prohibited from anchoring within two nautical miles from the pipelines.[56]

Along with regulations on protecting artificial installations and structures, Vietnam has limited its authority to establish safety zones. In accordance with Article 60(7) of the UNCLOS, building permanent or floating installations or

53 Government Decree No. 95/2015/ND-CP on guiding the application of certain provisions of the Law on Petroleum, 16 Oct 2015, Article 47(1).

54 *Ibid.*

55 *Ibid.*

56 Prime Minister Decision No. 04/2015/QD-TTg on Safety Management on Petroleum-related activities, 20 Jan 2015, Article 31(4).

establishing safety zones in areas recognized as essential for international navigation if there is risk of interfering with freedom of navigation on the seas is prohibited.[57]

Concerning military activities in the EEZ, the debate is ongoing internationally. The UNCLOS has one provision concerning military activities in the territorial sea.[58] The absence of similar provisions within the legal regime of EEZ has led to conflicting views among states. One of the examples of this conflict is between China and the United States. China protests all military activities by foreign warships in its EEZ based on security reasons, while the United States insists that such activities are not within the sovereign rights and jurisdiction of coastal states under the UNCLOS.

The Law of the Sea of Vietnam and other laws and regulations have no express provisions on this matter. However, the Law of the Sea contains several provisions that may be relevant. Article 37(1) generally prohibits all acts "threatening sovereignty, defence and security of Vietnam". The phrase is ambiguous and subject to interpretation by Vietnamese authorities on a case-by-case basis. It may be interpreted as having a broader meaning than merely the use or threat of force. Article 38 prohibits the illegal use of weapons or explosives in all maritime zones of Vietnam including the EEZ. In the ordinary meaning of these provisions, a military activity by foreign vessels such as a live-fire exercise is generally not permitted.

Under the Decree of Government No. 30-CP (1980), the prohibition on certain military activities expands beyond the territorial sea to the contiguous zone. Although some parts of this Decree have been replaced by the Law of the Sea, the Decree has not been publicly terminated. Thus, it is not clear whether the prohibition on certain military activities by foreign vessels in the contiguous zone has been lifted. In practice, it seems that the Vietnamese authorities would require foreign military vessels conducting activities in its EEZ, other than navigation, for example, search and rescue activities to obtain prior permission.[59] However, as there is no express provision, a definite conclusion may not be reached.

---

57 *Law of the Sea* (2012), Article 34(4) and Government Decree No. 95/2015/ND-CP on guiding the application of certain provisions of the Law on Petroleum, 16 Oct 2015, Article 47(2).

58 UNCLOS, *supra* 1, Article 19(2).

59 In 2014 when searching for flight MH370 in the Gulf of Thailand, military vessels from China, the United States and Singapore were permitted by Vietnam to enter Vietnamese maritime zones to search. See: Tien Phong, "Stop searching for MH370, request foreign vessels to leave", 16 March 2014, available at <www.tienphong.vn/xa-hoi/dung-tim-kiem-mh370-yeu-cau-nuoc-ngoai-rut-khoi-viet-nam-686752.tpo> [in Vietnamese].

Within the Gulf of Tonkin, a semi-closed bay surrounded by Vietnam and China, Vietnam has not yet drawn baselines. Vietnam and China have delimited the maritime boundary in this area.[60] The boundary is composed of lines connecting 21 points. The lines from point 1 to point 9 are the boundary of territorial sea and the lines from point 10 to point 21 are boundaries for the EEZ and continental shelf. However, due to the absence of baselines, it is uncertain where the outer limits of internal waters and the territorial sea of Vietnam in the Gulf is located exactly. To avoid possible trespass into the internal waters of Vietnam, vessels should navigate in areas beyond 12 nautical miles from the coast of Vietnam and follow the normal routes or practices of navigation within the Gulf.

IV Conclusion

Vietnam, as a coastal state and a party to the UNCLOS and other navigation-related treaties, has enacted laws and regulations to govern navigational activities in its maritime zones. Generally, the law and regulations are in accordance with the UNCLOS and the other treaties to which Vietnam is a party. Vietnam recognizes and protects the right of innocent passage of all vessels in its territorial sea, and the freedom of navigation in its EEZ. All vessels have the right to navigate peacefully in Vietnam's maritime zones without prejudice to Vietnam's rights and interests as provided by the UNCLOS and other treaties. Although there may be some confusion and inconsistency in the laws and regulations, Vietnam resolutely assures the right of navigation of foreign vessels, and is gradually reviewing its national laws and regulations to create a clearer legal framework in order to facilitate navigation in its maritime zones.

60 Agreement on Delimitation of Territorial Sea, Exclusive Economic Zone and Continental Shelf in the Gulf of Tonkin between Vietnam and China (2000).

PART 3

North America

CHAPTER 10

Regulation of Foreign Commercial Vessel Navigation in Canadian Waters: Issues of International Law

Ted L. McDorman

1 Introduction

Canada has coasts on three oceans – the Atlantic, the Pacific and the Arctic. In general terms, on the Atlantic coast there is significant foreign vessel commercial traffic to and from Canadian ports as well as traffic that does not visit Canada but travels through Canada's exclusive economic zone (EEZ) between the United States and Europe. On the Pacific coast there is significant foreign vessel traffic to and from Vancouver and the Seattle area that travel through Canadian waters in the Juan de Fuca Strait that separates Canada and the United States. Unlike on the Atlantic, there is little foreign commercial traffic along the Canadian coast that does not go to the Vancouver-Seattle area. In the Arctic there is little foreign commercial traffic of any kind within Canadian waters with what little there is involving vessels destined for Canadian stops.

Canada is a significant trading State with cargoes going to and from Canada predominantly carried by foreign flag vessels. In addition, Canada is a member of the North Atlantic Treaty Organization (NATO) and has close neighbourly relations on naval matters with the United States. These factors indicate that Canada supports the package of international legal rights associated with freedom of navigation: freedom of navigation on the high seas (waters beyond 200 nm); navigational freedoms within the 200 nm EEZ; innocent passage rights in the territorial sea of States; and transit passage rights for vessels within "straits used for international navigation" as set out in the 1982 U.N. Convention on the Law of the Sea.[1] While Canadian statements on the freedoms of navigation are rare, the July 2016 "Canadian Statement on South China Sea Arbitration," asserted that: "Actions that could jeopardize freedom of navigation and overflight exercised in accordance with international law, maritime security and international trade must ... be avoided."[2]

1 U.N. Convention on the Law of the Sea, 1833 *U.N.T.S.* 397.

2 Global Affairs Minister Dion, "Canadian Statement on the South China Sea Arbitration," 21 July 2016, at <news.gc.ca/web/article-en.do?nid=1102379>.

DOI:10.1163/9789004396272_011

The other side of this coin, and the principal subject matter of this contribution, are the international legal disputes that exists regarding Canada's regulation of and assertions respecting the non-existence of international navigational rights for commercial vessels within certain Canadian waters. Most of these disputes involve or are directly with the United States. The best known of these disputes concerns the Northwest Passage. Much like the debate as regards the Northwest Passage, there is the curious situation as regards Head Harbour Passage on the Atlantic coast where the major navigable channel to Eastport, Maine requires vessel passage through Canadian waters. The core of these two disputes is not a rejection of navigational rights by Canada *per se*, rather it is the Canadian view that these waterways are of an international legal status, internal waters, within which no international navigational rights exist. As will be explained below, through these waterways the United States asserts that there exists a navigational passage right. The Juan de Fuca Strait on the Pacific coast also deserves commentary, though as a result of an accord between the two States, there is no operational dispute. In addition to these waterway-navigation issues, and also to be discussed below, is the difference of view between Canada and the United States regarding the nature of the national laws that have been adopted by Canada to protect and preserve the marine environment from vessel-source pollution within Canada's Arctic Ocean 200 nm EEZ. The dispute here is not about the legal status of the waters but rather the interpretation and application of the "Arctic provision" (Article 234) in the LOS Convention.

II The Principal Canadian Legislation

It is not the intention here to review in detail Canada's legislation relevant to the commercial vessel navigation in Canadian waters. Nevertheless, a brief discussion is warranted.

First, the Oceans Act sets out Canada's various offshore areas, which includes: a 12 nm territorial sea; a 12 nm contiguous zone adjacent to the territorial sea; a 200 nm EEZ; and rights over the continental shelf within and beyond 200 nm.[3] Canada has straight baselines along the coasts of Nova Scotia, Newfoundland and Labrador and both Vancouver Island and Queen Charlotte Islands of British Columbia which results in the waters landward of these baselines being internal waters.[4] Canada has claimed that Hudson Bay, both

---

3 Oceans Act, *Statutes of Canada 1996*, Ch. 31, as amended.

4 Territorial Sea Geographical Coordinates Order, *Consolidated Regulations of Canada*, (1978), Vol. XVIII, Chapter 1550, at pp. 13751–13758.

the Gulf of St. Lawrence and the Bay of Fundy on the Atlantic coast, and Dixon Entrance, Hecate Strait, the Queen Charlotte Sound and the Strait of Juan de Fuca on the Pacific coast are the internal waters of Canada as a result of historic claims.[5] While Canada had claimed the waters within the Arctic archipelago, including the Northwest Passage, as historic internal waters, in 1985 baselines were constructed around the Arctic archipelago delineating the precise location of the claimed Arctic historic internal waters.[6] Of note is that in Canadian legislation references to law applying in Canada or in Canadian waters, unless expressly defined differently, refers to the internal waters and territorial sea of Canada.[7]

With one exception to be noted below, there is no reference in Canadian legislation to the right of innocent passage or any other international navigational right within ocean areas under Canadian jurisdiction. The territorial sea is spatially defined without indication of the international legal rights or obligations that Canada has or does not have respecting the territorial sea.[8] Most foreign commercial vessels enter Canada's territorial sea on their way to or from a Canadian port, which despite innocent passage attaching to a foreign vessel "proceeding to or from internal waters,"[9] gives to the port State significant authority over a visiting vessel. There are few instances where a foreign commercial vessel exercises a right of innocent passage in Canada's territorial sea without entering or having entered a Canadian port.

The one place where innocent passage is specifically mentioned in Canadian legislation is Section 27(3) of the Nuclear Liability and Compensation Act.[10] This provision, which follows the wording of Article 6(3) of the Annex to the Convention on Supplementary Compensation for Nuclear Damage,[11] exempts foreign vessels transporting nuclear material that are exercising the right of innocent passage in Canadian waters from complying with Canadian requirements to demonstrate that they have financial security to compensate for a nuclear incident. It has been noted that "the capacity of coastal states to

5 Canada, Department of External Affairs, Letter, 17 December 1973 in (1974) 12 *Canadian Yearbook of International Law* 277, at p. 279. See generally: T.L. McDorman, *Salt Water Neighbors: International Ocean Law relations between the United States and Canada* (New York: Oxford University Press, 2009), at pp. 207–280.

6 Territorial Sea Geographical Coordinates (Area 7) Order, *Canada Gazette Part II*, Vol. 119, SOR/85-872, 10 September 1985, at pp. 3996–4002.

7 Interpretation Act, Revised *Statutes of Canada, 1985*, Ch. I-21, as amended, s. 35(1) and Oceans Act, *supra* note 3, s. 7.

8 Oceans Act, *supra* note 3, s. 4.

9 LOS Convention, *supra* note 1, Article 18(1)(b).

10 Nuclear Liability and Compensation Act, *Statutes of Canada, 2015*, Ch. 4.

11 Convention on Supplementary Compensation for Nuclear Damage, see the website of the International Atomic Energy Agency at <www.iaea.org>.

impair freedom of navigation [innocent passage] of vessels carrying inherently dangerous cargoes has been a matter of debate since the 1990s."[12] Canada is clearly not in favour of such impairment. A 1980 Canadian Government memorandum commented that within the LOS Convention: "the right of innocent passage has been defined in detail and strengthened by a new explicit limitation on certain coastal state powers of environmental regulation."[13]

Canada's EEZ spatial definition and the nature of the rights exercisable by Canada, which tracks Article 56 of the LOS Convention, are set out in the Oceans Act.[14] Article 58(2) of the LOS Convention, a key provision that makes it clear that high seas navigational rights apply within the EEZ, is not explicitly reproduced in form or substance in Canadian legislation. A 1980 Canadian Government memorandum commented that the EEZ regime "may place some very limited restrictions on rights of passage, but in principle the high-seas freedom of navigation and overflight will apply."[15]

Like other States Canada has detailed legislation that covers vessel-source pollution,[16] ocean dumping[17] and fishing[18] within Canadian waters including the EEZ. Of note is that foreign fishing vessels require a licence for entry into Canada's EEZ.[19] As regards vessels in Canada's Arctic waters there is the Arctic Waters Pollution Prevention Act, first enacted in 1970 as applying within a 100 nm zone, now extended to the 200 nm EEZ.[20] The Arctic waters legislation, which predates the idea of a 200 nm zone, was originally strongly contested by the United States.[21]

Also, like many other States, Canada has a system of vessel traffic management that has two principal components: mandatory ship reporting/authorization within designated vessel traffic service (VTS) zones; and vessel traffic

12 Donald R. Rothwell and Tim Stephens, *The International Law of the Sea*, (Oxford/Portland, Hart Publishing, 2nd ed., 2016), at p. 239.
13 Canada, Department of External Affairs, Memorandum, 15 July 1980, in (1981) 19 *Canadian Yearbook of International Law* 328.
14 Oceans Act, *supra* note 3, ss. 12–14.
15 Canada, Memorandum, 15 July 1980, *supra* note 13, at p. 328.
16 See: Canada Shipping Act, *Statutes of Canada, 2001*, Ch. 26, as amended, Parts 8 and 9.
17 See: Canadian Environmental Protection Act, *Statutes of Canada, 1999*, Ch. 33, Part 7, Division 2.
18 Coastal Fisheries Protection Act, *Revised Statutes of Canada, 1985*, Ch. C-33, as amended.
19 *Ibid.*, Section 3: "No foreign fishing vessel shall enter Canadian fisheries waters for any purpose unless authorized by this Act or the regulations, any other law of Canada or a treaty" and s. 17(1) "Every person is guilty of an offence who (a) being master or in command of a fishing vessel, (i) enters Canadian fisheries waters contrary to this Act."
20 Arctic Waters Pollution Prevention Act, *Revised Statutes of Canada, 1985*, Ch. A-12, as amended. This legislation will be discussed in further detail below.
21 See: McDorman, *supra* note 5, at pp. 67–74 and see further below Section VI.

separation schemes, some of which are mandatory and others of which are voluntary.[22] The Canada Shipping Act provides that mandatory reporting and obtaining of clearance is required for vessels to enter, leave or proceed within a designated VTS Zone.[23] Canada's traffic separation schemes are created and communicated through Notices to Mariners issued and maintained by the Canadian Coast Guard.[24] The Canada-United States vessel traffic system applicable to the Juan de Fuca Strait will be discussed below.

Outside the disputes in the Arctic and the noted waterways, there have been no major or high profile international disputes respecting the application of Canadian law to foreign commercial or fishing vessels navigating within Canadian waters including Canada's EEZ.

III The Northwest Passage (Arctic Coast)[25]

Much has been written about the Northwest Passage legal dispute. All that is provided here is a brief summary. The international legal issue as regards the Northwest Passage, which dates back to the 1970s, is the extent of control that Canada can exercise respecting foreign vessels navigating through the Passage. There is no question that the waters of the Passage are under the jurisdiction of Canada such that Canada has exclusive authority as regards all living and non-living resources within the Passage. It is the Canadian view that all the waters within the Arctic archipelago, including the Northwest Passage, are historic internal waters with the result that Canada has absolute jurisdiction over all foreign vessels (commercial and military) within the Northwest Passage and, in particular, that foreign vessels can be required to request and receive the permission of Canada to utilize the Passage.

---

22 For a detailed review, see: T.L. McDorman, "Canada's Vessel Traffic Management Regime: An Overview in the Context of International Law" in Aldo Chircop, et al., *The Regulation of International Shipping: International and Comparative Perspectives* (Leiden/Boston: Martinus Nijhoff, 2012), pp. 509–524.

23 Canada Shipping Act, *supra* note 16, s. 126(1)(a).

24 See generally: Canadian Coast Guard, website for "Notice to Mariners" available at www.notmar.gc.ca.

25 This section is drawn with modification from T.L. McDorman, "Old Issues and New Developments Respecting International Navigational Rights and Obligations in Arctic Waters" a paper presented at the Fifth ZJU Annual Ocean Law and Governance Symposium, "The Belt and Road Initiative and the Law of the Sea," Zhejiang University Ocean College, Centre for Ocean Law and Governance and Guanghua Law School, Zhoushan, China, to be published in the proceedings. For a more fulsome discussion, see: Ted L. McDorman, *supra* note 5, at pp. 225–245.

The U.S. view is that the waters within Canada's Arctic archipelago do not meet the requirements of historic waters and, moreover, that the Northwest Passage is a strait used for international navigation. As a result, the U.S. view is that all foreign-flagged vessels engaged in thru-traffic of the Northwest Passage, while subject to Canadian laws, are not required to request and receive the permission of Canada to utilize the Passage.

Regardless of the divergent positions, the two States have had significant success in managing their legal differences. A testament to this is the 1988 Arctic Cooperation Agreement that deals with U.S. Coast Guard ice-breaker traffic in the Northwest Passage.[26] The Agreement provides that Canada will consent to voyages of U.S. Coast Guard ice-breakers through Canadian Arctic waters (the Northwest Passage) where the United States requests permission for such a voyage. The wrinkle is that the U.S. Coast Guard vessels are deemed by the Agreement to be carrying out marine scientific research such that, from the U.S. perspective, what is being requested is consent to undertake marine scientific research in Canadian waters.[27] Essentially, the 1988 accord is an "agreement-to-disagree" and, while operationally and politically important, does not resolve the underlying differences held by the two States regarding the existence of a navigational right in or the international legal status of the Northwest Passage as the Agreement is expressly without prejudice to the legal posture of the two States.

IV Head Harbour Passage (Atlantic Coast)[28]

A less well-known navigational dispute between Canada and the United States concerns Head Harbour Passage. Head Harbour Passage, on the Atlantic coast, engages the state of Maine and the province of New Brunswick as the Passage runs between the islands south of Deer Island and Campobello Island (both of which are Canadian) before reaching U.S. waters east of Eastport, Maine which is located on Moose Island (United States). At its narrowest, Head Harbour Passage is less than one nautical mile wide. It is approximately

26 Agreement between Canada and the United States on Arctic Cooperation, 11 January 1988, *Canada Treaty Series* 1988/29 and *T.I.A.S.* 1565.

27 See: McDorman, *supra* note 5, at pp. 248–251.

28 See generally: McDorman, *supra* note 5, pp. 254–269. See also: Jon Van Dyke, "Canada's Authority to Prohibit LNG Vessels From Passing Through Head Harbor Passage To U.S. Ports," (2008), 14 *Ocean and Coastal Law Journal* 45–72 and James Kraska, "Law of the Seas and LNG: Cross-Border Law and Politics over Head Harbor Passage" (2012), 37 *Canada-United States Law Journal* 131–170.

four nautical miles in length. Head Harbour Passage is the principal navigation route to Eastport. There is no question that the waters of Head Harbour Passage are Canadian.

The U.S. view is that Head Harbour Passage meets the wording of Article 45(1)(b) of the LOS Convention as connecting "a part of the high seas or an economic zone and the territorial sea of a foreign State," which gives rise to a right of non-suspendable innocent passage.[29] Article 45(1)(b) creates what is known as a "dead-end" international strait and replicates Article 16(4) of the 1958 Territorial Sea and Contiguous Zone Convention,[30] which was adopted primarily to deal with the Strait of Tiran which connects the Red Sea with the Gulf of Aqaba.[31]

Canada's legal view of Head Harbour Passage was not until 2013 fully clear.[32] In a May 2013 letter from the Canadian Ambassador in Washington to the U.S. Federal Energy Regulatory Commission it was asserted that "the waters of Head Harbour Passage are internal waters of Canada by virtue of historic title and are therefore subject to the control and regulation of the Government of Canada."[33]

The Canada – U.S. dispute regarding Head Harbour Passage arose first in the mid-1970s as a result of proposal to locate an oil refinery near Eastport and more recently a decade ago as a result of a proposal for LNG facilities near Eastport. Both of these proposals would have necessitated tanker traffic through the Passage. Smaller commercial vessels have long utilized Head Harbour Passage to go both to Eastport and a small Canadian port.

---

29 United States, "Commentary – The 1982 United Nations Convention on the Law of the Sea and the Agreement on Implementation of Part XI" attached to "Message from the President of the United States transmitting United Nations Convention on the Law of the Sea, with Annexes, done at Montego Bay, December 10, 1982 (the Convention) and the Agreement Relating to the Implementation of Part XI of the United Nations Convention on the Law of the Sea of 10 December 1982, adopted at New York, July 28, 1994 (the Agreement) and signed by the United States, subject to ratification, on July 29, 1994," Senate, Treaty Document 39, 103d Congress, 2d Session IV (1994), at p. 19, reprinted in (1995), 34 *International Legal Materials* 1393–1447.

30 Territorial Sea and Contiguous Zone Convention, 516 *U.N.T.S.* 205.

31 Four States share the Gulf of Aqaba – Egypt, Saudi Arabia, Israel and Jordan – with the latter two having coastal areas (ports) only at farthest reaches of the Gulf and Egypt and Saudi Arabia dominating the entrance of the Gulf of Aqaba and the Strait of Tiran. See: Leo Gross, "The Geneva Conference on the Law of the Sea and the Right of Innocent Passage Through the Gulf of Aqaba" (1959), 53 *American Journal of International Law* 564, at p. 593.

32 See: McDorman, *supra* note 5, pp. 261–264.

33 Canada, Letter of 17 May 2013 from Canadian Ambassador to the United States Gary Doer to the Chair of the U.S. Federal Energy Regulatory Commission, 17 May 2013, in the possession of the author.

Interestingly, and little noted, in 1982, Canada adopted a regulation which restricted the amount of oil that could be carried by an oil tanker through Head Harbour Passage.[34] The regulation was carefully crafted to deal specifically with the proposed tanker traffic and not that of the perceived oil needs of the Eastport population. The United States publicly protested Canada's regulation and announced that an official protest would be delivered to Canada, taking the view that the regulation exceeded Canada's jurisdictional authority.[35] In 1983 the proponent decided not to proceed with the proposed Eastport refinery and the Canadian regulation was subsequently revoked.[36] Regarding the LNG proposal, in August 2016 the U.S. Federal Energy Regulatory Commission terminated the application made for permits to construct the LNG facilities.[37] Hence, there is no longer an active international legal issue.

The positions of Canada and the United States regarding the Head Harbour Passage and the Northwest Passage disputes involve virtually the same international legal issues – historic internal waters and rights of passage through an international strait. A major difference, however, is that unlike within the Northwest Passage, there has long been regular commercial small-scale marine traffic through Head Harbour Passage to both U.S. and Canadian ports. Moreover, for the United States the geography and politics of the disputes are different. The U.S. concern in the Northwest Passage is principally one of global precedent; not so as regards Head Harbour Passage. Canadian action could result in preventing marine transportation into a U.S. port and this makes the issue simultaneously local, northeastern Maine, and one of national concern, protection of U.S. citizens' rights. For Canada, Head Harbour Passage has yet to, and may never, generate the national sovereignty response that has accompanied the Northwest Passage issue, though the proposed tanker traffic generated intense local interest.

---

34 Canada, Oil Carriage Limitation Regulations, *Canada Gazette Part II*, Vol. 116, SOR/82-244, 11 February 1982, at pp. 892–893.

35 See: John E. Carroll, *Environmental Diplomacy: An Examination and a Prospective of Canadian-U.S. Transboundary Environmental Relations* (Ann Arbor: University of Michigan Press, 1983), at p. 71.

36 The Regulation was revoked in May 1987 on the grounds that it was *ultra vires* the enabling legislation. Note was made that there was no longer need for the Regulation since the plans to build the facility in Eastport had been abandoned. See: Canada, Oil Carriage Limitation Regulations, revocation, *Canada Gazette Part II*, Vol. 121, SOR/87-268, 7 May 1987, at pp. 2077–2078.

37 U.S. Federal Regulatory Commission, "Order Dismissing Dockets and Terminating Proceedings," 17 August 2016, at <www.ferc.gov/CalendarFiles/20160817113357-PF14-19-000.pdf>.

V Strait of Juan de Fuca (Pacific Coast)[38]

The Juan de Fuca Strait between Vancouver Island and the U.S. state of Washington is not an area of significant bilateral dispute. What had arisen occasionally were Canadian complaints about attempts or actual U.S. regulation of vessels in the Juan de Fuca Strait heading to or from Canadian ports such as Vancouver. The maritime boundary in the Strait has existed since 1846 with that Treaty providing that "the navigation of the whole of the said channel and Straits south of the forty ninth parallel of north latitude remain free and open to both Parties."[39] Thus, within the Juan de Fuca Strait and adjacent areas covered by Article I of the 1846 Treaty, a navigational right exercisable by both Canada and the United States exists as a matter of treaty law. The precise legal nature of the navigational right and the international legal status of the waters within the Strait are not clear. A recent article has argued that the U.S. waters are not historic internal waters.[40] This same author also summarized that:

> The U.S. and Canadian governments appear to be content with the ambiguous status quo, with neither nation publicly asserting historic title to the boundary straits as internal waters, denying access to foreign vessels, or imposing a regulatory burden on foreign vessels passing through the straits en route to or departing from a port in the other state that would rise to the level of "hampering" or, as a practical matter, denying or impairing the vessels' right of innocent passage.[41]

Consistent with the above, for the most part, questions about the international legal status of the waters and the legal nature of the navigation right within the Juan de Fuca Strait have largely been made moot by the bilateral 1979 Vessel Traffic Management Agreement for the Juan de Fuca Region.[42]

---

38 This section is drawn, with modification, from McDorman, *supra* note 5, at pp. 276–278 and McDorman, *supra* note 22, at pp. 520–521.

39 Treaty Establishing the Boundary in the Territory on the Northwest Coast of America Lying Westward of the Rocky Mountains, done at Washington, 15 June 1846, entered into force 5 August 1846 (The Oregon Treaty), 100 *Consolidated Treaty Series* (C. Parry, ed.,), pp. 39–42, Article I.

40 Craig H. Allen, "The Salish Sea Boundary Straits: 'Historical Internal Waters' or Territorial Sea?," (2017), 48 *Ocean Development and International Law* 81–127.

41 *Ibid.*, at p. 109.

42 The Canada – United States Cooperative Traffic Management System (CVTMS) arises from the 1979 Exchange of Notes constituting and Agreement on Vessel Traffic Management for the Juan de Fuca Region, 19 December 1979, entered into force 19 December 1979, 1221 *U.N.T.S.* 67.

The 1979 Agreement states that it is "without prejudice to position of the … United States and Canada with respect to the character of, and the nature and extent of coastal state jurisdiction over the applicable and adjacent waters."[43]

The purpose of the 1979 Agreement was to create "a cooperative system of vessel traffic management" throughout the Juan de Fuca Strait.[44] Under the traffic separation scheme, inbound vessels use the U.S. side of the Strait and outbound vessels use the Canadian side. A key legal matter in the 1979 Agreement is the application and enforcement of laws respecting vessels navigating on the U.S. side of the Juan de Fuca Strait headed for Canadian ports and vice-a-versa. The Agreement provides that each State in applying its laws to vessels in its waters "will consider compliance with the requirements of the other Party to be effectively equivalent to material compliance with its own requirements,"[45] but that this does not prevent a State from taking action in regard to a vessel in its waters where "the condition or activities" of a vessel "may pose an actual threat to marine safety or the marine environment."[46]

VI Canadian Arctic Waters[47]

From a Canadian perspective one of the major accomplishments of the Third United Nations Conference on the Law of the Sea was the inclusion in the LOS Convention of Article 234 titled "Ice-covered Areas." Article 234 was negotiated primarily between Canada and the United States with consultation with the Soviet Union. Canada's objective was international legal support for its 1970 Arctic Waters legislation that allowed national action to be taken against foreign-flagged vessels in Canadian Arctic waters to protect the Arctic marine and terrestrial environment from vessel-source pollution.

Article 234 recognizes that vessel traffic in Arctic waters may encounter conditions and risks that are not experienced elsewhere and, therefore, the balance of legal rights and obligations in these areas favours vessel safety and environmental protection (coastal State concerns) rather than freedom of navigation.

43 *Ibid.*, Annex, para. 205.1.

44 *Ibid.*, Annex, para 100.1. See generally: U.S. Coast Guard, "Canada /U.S Cooperative Vessel Traffic Service (CVTS)," available at <www.uscg.mil/d13/cvts/>.

45 *Ibid.*, Annex, para. 204.2.

46 *Ibid.*, Annex, para. 204.3.

47 This section is drawn with modification from McDorman, "Old Issues and New Developments Respecting International Navigational Rights and Obligations in Arctic Waters," *supra* note 25.

The United States has explicitly accepted that Article 234 is part of customary international law[48] and has noted that:

> The purpose of article 234 ... is to provide the basis for implementing the provisions applicable to commercial and private vessels found in the 1970 Canadian Arctic Waters Pollution Prevention Act ..., while protecting fundamental U.S. security interests in the exercise of navigational rights and freedom throughout the Arctic.[49]

There are a number of elements of Article 234:
- a coastal State can adopt and enforce within its 200-n. mile zone laws containing more stringent standards than the internationally accepted rules;
- this is a unilateral right of the coastal State and not subject to pre-approval or review by the IMO or any other international body;[50]
- warships and other government vessels are exempted from the laws;[51]
- the laws are to be non-discriminatory;
- the laws are to be for "the prevention, reduction and control of marine pollution from vessels in ice-covered areas ..., where particularly severe climatic conditions and the presence of ice covering ... create obstructions or exceptional hazards to navigation ...";[52]
- the laws are to be "based on the best available scientific evidence;" and
- the laws "shall have due regard to navigation."[53]

Canadian regulations adopted in 2010[54] led to questions and concerns raised by the United States and several other States about whether the new regulations were consistent with the rights afforded to Arctic States under Article 234. The regulations adopted by Canada made mandatory what had long been voluntary that most non-government vessels entering into the Canada's

48 Brian Hoyle, "The United States Government Perspective," in Lawrence Juda (ed.) *The United States without the Law of the Sea Treaty: Opportunities and Costs* (Times Press, Wakefield, R.I., 1983), at p. 135.

49 United States, "Commentary," *supra* note 29, at p. 40.

50 See: Kristin Bartenstein, "The 'Arctic Exception' in the Law of the Sea Convention: A Contribution to Safer Navigation in the Northwest Passage?" (2011) 42 *Ocean Development and International Law* 22, at p. 37 who comments that: "The absence of an international review process is one of the few certitudes in Article 234."

51 LOS Convention, *supra* note 1, Article 236.

52 *Ibid.*, Article 234.

53 *Id.*

54 Northern Canada Vessel Traffic Services Zone Regulations and Order Amending the Shipping Safety Control Zones Order, *Canada Gazette Part II*, Vol. 144, No. 13, 23 June 2010.

Northern Canada Vessel Traffic Services Zone (NORDREG),[55] which covers Canada's Arctic 200 nm zone, are to report to and receive clearance from Canadian authorities.

The United States expressed the view that it "did not believe that the new Canadian northern zone regulations were consistent with key law of the sea principles related to freedom of navigation, including the right of innocent passage and the right of transit passage through straits used for navigation."[56] More specifically, the United States argued that the requirement for permission to enter and transit Canada's waters was not supported by Article 234.[57] Canada asserted that Article 234 provided "a complete legal justification in international law for NORDREG."[58]

The Canadian position that the NORDREG is supported by Article 234 is premised on the value of the measure for environmental protection; whereas the U.S. view of Article 234 is primarily that the NORDREG law and requirements does not have "due regard for navigation."[59]

VII Conclusion

Three of the four international legal disputes that have arisen as a result of Canada's regulation of foreign commercial vessels in its waters discussed above are long-standing and explained primarily by three considerations.

First is national politics. The Northwest Passage and Arctic marine environmental protection (Article 234) have been and remain issues that attract

55 Since 1977 Canada had a voluntary ship reporting system in place for Canada's Arctic waters up to 100-n. miles.

56 International Maritime Organization (IMO), Sub-Committee on Safety of Navigation, "Report to the Maritime Safety Committee," Doc. NAV/56/20, 31 August 2010 (Report of the 56th session of the Sub-Committee), para. 19.21.

57 United States, *Diplomatic Note*, 18 August 2010, para. 4 and United States Embassy, "Letter to Canadian Department of Transport," 19 March 2010, at para. 4, in *Digest of United States Practice in International Law, 2010*, (Oxford University Press), at pp. 515–518.

58 Canada, "Comments on Document MSC 88/11/2," IMO Doc. MSC/88/11/3, 5 October 2010, para. 5.

59 See generally: T.L. McDorman, "National Measures for the Safety of Navigation in Arctic Waters: NORDREG, Article 234 and Canada," in Myron H. Nordquist, John Norton Moore, A.H.A. Soons and Kak-so Kim (eds.), *The Law of the Sea Convention: US Accession and Globalization* (Martinus Nijhoff: Leiden, 2012), at pp. 409–424; James Kraska, "The Northern Canada Vessel Traffic Services Zone Regulations (Nordreg) and the Law of the Sea," (2015), 30 *International Journal of Marine and Coastal Law* 225–254; and James Kraska, "Governance of Ice-Covered Areas: Rule Construction and the Arctic Ocean" (2014), 45 *Ocean Development and International Law* 260–271.

wide-spread cross-country public interest such that a sitting national government would face a firestorm should Canada's marine Arctic interest not be protected and, as feasible, expanded. While Head Harbour Passage is not part of the national consciousness, the issues involved have a striking similarity to the Northwest Passage issues such that linkage is a concern.

Second, Canada has been and still is primarily a State with coastal State interests as oppose to a State, like the United States, which carefully balances its coastal State interests with strong navigational interests. Canada's "aggressive coastal state,"[60] policies were prominent in the UNCLOS III era and continued into the 1990's with such actions as the 1995 arrest of the Spanish vessel *Estai* engaged in fishing on high seas adjacent to Canada. All of the disputes discussed above continue to reflect a policy of the protection of national and coastal State interests.

Third, as regards the Northwest Passage and the interpretation of Article 234, the United States interest has been as much about the possible precedent value rather than a direct national interest at stake. A recent article has suggested that the United States should embrace the Canadian (and Russian) view of Article 234.[61] In the 1980s, U.S. President Reagan made clear the primary U.S. concern of the precedential value of the Northwest Passage.[62] As noted above the Head Harbour Passage dispute has the potential to be of direct interest to the United States and thus, should it arise again, requires nuanced and careful handling by Canada.

Overall, Canada has comfortably supported global freedom of navigation rights while asserting that there are no international straits through which navigational rights exist in Canada and that Article 234 allows for a purposive approach that favours the protection of the marine environment.

---

60 Douglas M. Johnston, *Canada and the New International Law of the Sea* (Toronto: University of Toronto Press, 1985), at p. 65.

61 Stanley P. Fields, "Article 234 of the United Nations Convention on the Law of the Sea: The Overlooked Linchpin for Achieving Safety and Security in the U.S. Arctic?" (2016), 7 *Harvard National Security Journal* 55.

62 Brian Mulroney, *Memoirs* (Toronto: McClelland and Stewart, 2007), at p. 495 quotes President Reagan stating in a private letter to the Prime Minister: "I have to say in all candor that we cannot agree to an arrangement that obliges us to seek permission for our vessels to navigate through the Northwest Passage. To do so would adversely affect our legitimate right to transit other important areas globally."

CHAPTER 11

United States Practice regarding Innocent Passage and Navigational Transit

Anastasia Telesetsky

1 Introduction

In May 2016, the United States (U.S.) military vessel USS *William P. Lawrence* operated within the 12 nm limit of Yongshu Jiao in the Nansha archipelago as a demonstration of the U.S.' right to freedom of navigation.[1] When the Peoples' Republic of China protested the incident because it involved a U.S. military vessel operating in waters over which China asserted maritime jurisdiction, the United States countered that it was exercising its customary rights of innocent passage as codified by the UN Convention on the Law of the Sea (UNCLOS).[2] Protecting freedom of navigation is a hallmark of U.S. maritime policy. In spite of the disapproval of some States, the United States has been engaged proactively since 1979 in promoting and protecting global navigational freedoms both within its own maritime jurisdiction and abroad.

The U.S. freedom of navigation policy is based on comity. The policy is best summarized in the 1983 Statement on U.S. Oceans Policy whereby "the United States will recognize the rights of other states in the waters off their coasts, as reflected in the Convention, so long as the rights and freedoms of the United States and others under international law are recognized by such coastal states."[3] This chapter summarizes contemporary U.S. legal practice on the treatment of foreign vessels operating within U.S. territorial waters/ exclusive economic zones (EEZs) and on expectations for how U.S. flagged vessels will be treated in foreign territorial waters/EEZs.

1 Sam LaGrone, "U.S. Destroyer Passes Near Chinese Artificial Island in South China Sea Freedom of Navigation Operation," *USNI News* (May 10, 2016). *See also* "China Opposes US Distortion of Navigation Freedom," <europe.chinadaily.com.cn/world/2016-05/12/content_25223459.htm>.

2 U.N. Convention on the Law of the Sea, 1833 *U.N.T.S.* 396.

3 "Statement on United States Ocean Policy," President Ronald Reagan (March 10, 1983) 22 *I.L.M.* 464 (1983).

 | DOI:10.1163/9789004396272_012

II Innocent Passage for Foreign Vessels Operating in U.S. Territorial Waters

The United States from its earliest post-colonial history has been a supporter of the principle of *mare liberum* to ensure the security of essential trade channels to connect the fledgling nation to the European mainland. As John Adams remarked in 1783 when he served as the first Vice-President of the United States:

> The United States of America have propagated far and wide in Europe the ideas of the liberty of navigation and commerce. The powers of Europe, however, cannot agree as yet, in adopting them to their full extent.... For my own part, I think nature wiser than all the courts and estates of the world, and, therefore, I wish all her seas and rivers upon the whole globe free.[4]

This concept of free seas continued as a central part of U.S. foreign policy in the 18th and 19th centuries as the United States extended its globalizing reach west to the Pacific to take advantage of abundant whaling, sealing, and fishing opportunities. The United States entered the War of 1812 with Britain with the objective of protecting the freedom of the high seas.[5] The growing success of U.S. entrepreneurialism depended on maintaining open access to the oceans and particularly on protecting the freedom of navigation and the right of innocent passage.

At the conclusion of World War I with the recognition that freedom of the seas could become a foundation for peace, President Woodrow Wilson provided in his "Fourteen Point Peace Plan" a call for the "absolute freedom of navigation upon the seas, outside territorial waters, alike in peace and in war, except as the seas may be closed in whole or in part by international action for the enforcement of international covenants."[6] The geopolitical significance of the seas continued to be reinforced by the United States as its naval capabilities

4 John Adams to Robert R. Livingston, 14 July 1783, in Founding Families: Digital Editions of the Papers of the Winthrops and the Adamses, ed., C. James Taylor (Boston: Massachusetts Historical Society, 2015), <ift.tt/1XI8Lvj>.

5 J.S. Reeves, "Two Conceptions of the Freedom of the Seas," *American Historical Review* (1917): 540; at 543 (Criticizing the U.S. concept of the freedom of the seas as focused on a "challenge to British sea power" and "the development of large navy to contest the balance of naval power.").

6 U.S. National Archives, "President Woodrow Wilson's 14 Points (1918)," <www.ourdocuments.gov/doc.php?flash=true&doc=62>.

grew and during the negotiation of the UNCLOS, the United States specifically called for the preservation of navigational freedoms to include the innocent passage of warships. This was an important negotiation position because the United States regards all of the oceans as "maneuver space."[7] This space is critical for the Navy to do its job "to maintain, train and equip combat-ready Naval forces capable of winning wars, deterring aggression and maintaining freedom of the seas."[8]

In the 21st century, the United States understands the freedom of navigation to encompass both the rights of innocent passage within U.S. territorial seas and transit rights within straits used for international navigation. This subsection will discuss the provision for innocent passage within U.S. waters. For the United States the right of innocent passage is the right of every State to navigate its flagged vessels continuously, expeditiously, and in an unobstructed fashion as long as such passage "is not prejudicial to the peace, good order or security" of the United States.[9] The United States understands as provided in UNCLOS Article 17, that the right of innocent passage applies to "ships of all States" with no distinction made between civilian ships or military ships. The government has summarized U.S. policy on warships and innocent passage in the "Commander's Handbook on the Law of Naval Operations":

> All warships enjoy the right of innocent passage on an unimpeded and unannounced basis. If a warship does not comply with coastal national regulations that conform to established principles of international law and disregards a request for compliance that is made to it, the coastal nation may require the warship immediately to leave the territorial sea in which case the warship shall do so immediately.[10]

The United States permits innocent passage of all vessels within its territorial sea as long as there is no threat or use of force directed at the United States, no exercise or practice with weapons, no collection of information prejudicial to U.S. security, no propaganda acts aimed at U.S. defense or security, no illegal use of aircraft or military devices, no unlawful immigration activity, no unlawful smuggling, no unlawful pollution, no illegal fishing activity, no illegal

7 U.S. Navy, "Naval Operations Concept 2010" (2010) at p. 14.

8 U.S. Navy, "Mission of the Navy," <www.navy.mil/navydata/organization/org-top.as>.

9 UNCLOS, supra note 2, Article 19.

10 "The Commander's Handbook on the Law of Naval Operations," U.S. Navy, U.S. Marine Corps, U.S. Coast Guard, Naval Warfare Publication 1-14M/MCWP5-2.1/COMDTPUB P5800.1 (July 2007): Section 2.5.2.4, <www.jag.navy.mil/documents/NWP_1-14M_Commanders_Handbook.pdf> ("Commander's Handbook").

engagement in research or survey activities, and no act aimed at interfering with communications, facilities or other installations of the United States.[11]

Notably, innocent passage only applies to vessels and does not include a right of overflight within the zone of the territorial seas.[12] Where a vessel enters into the U.S. territorial sea with the intent of a "non-innocent passage" such as overflight or submerged transit in the case of a submarine, then the United States approach is to inform the vessel or aircraft that they are presumed not to be exercising a right of innocent passage and to allow the vessel an opportunity to clarify its intentions or correct its conduct within "a reasonably short period of time."[13]

The United States does not discriminate among vessels in extending the rights of innocent passage based on "size, purpose, or type of cargo."[14] The United States extends navigational rights under the regimes of innocent passage to unmanned surface vessels and unmanned underwater vessels.[15] For example, in 2015, the United States did not challenge the entry of Chinese naval ships into U.S. territorial waters in the Bering Sea off the coast of Alaska as the ships were operating consistent with international law.[16] In this case, there had been no expectation of prior notification being provided by the warships. In fact, the U.S. Northern Command issued a press release reporting that "The five PLAN [People's Liberation Army Navy] ships transited expeditiously and continuously through the Aleutian Island chain in a manner consistent with international law."[17] Likewise, the United States has never protested the entry of Russian warships into U.S. territorial waters as long as they are complying with innocent passage. The United States does not challenge ships executing an innocent passage that is consistent with international law so that the United States has a secure legal position to challenge the limitations that other nations have placed on freedom of navigation that exceed international law.

As per the UNCLOS, the United States has the right to adopt rules involving safety, maritime traffic (including the imposition of the use of sealanes or traffic separation schemes), protection of navigation aids, protection of cables,

11 These exceptions to innocent passage are outlined in UNCLOS, supra note 2, Article 19. The United States accepts Article 19 as customary international law. See also "Commander's Handbook," supra note 10 at Section 2.5.2.1.

12 "Commander's Handbook," supra note 10 at Sections 1.3.2 and 2.5.2.1.

13 *Ibid.*, at Section 2.5.2.1.

14 *Ibid.*, at Section 2.5.2.5.

15 *Id.*

16 Jim Sciutto, "Chinese Navy Ships Entered U.S. Waters off Alaska," CNN (September 4, 2015) <www.cnn.com/2015/09/04/politics/china-ships-alaska-us-waters/>.

17 Sam LaGrone, "Chinese Warships Made 'Innocent Passage' Through U.S. Territorial Waters off Alaska," USNI News (September 3, 2015).

conservation of living resources, fishing, environmental protection, marine scientific research, and the enforcement of customs, fiscal, immigration, or sanitary laws.[18] For example, the United States has adopted and enforced rules against foreign vessels for the illicit trafficking of drugs in U.S. territorial waters.[19] The right of innocent passage set out in U.S. regulations, in some instances, imposes less onerous burdens on vessels undertaking an innocent passage than on domestic vessels plying U.S. waters. For example, in the U.S. Code on Shipping that regulates the transport of hazardous cargo by requiring certain design measures, the Code in keeping with the UNCLOS provides that the chapter "does not apply to a foreign vessel on innocent passage on the navigable waters of the United States."[20] In the chapter on navigation in the U.S. Code, specific vessel operating requirements including some vessel traffic rules are not applied "except pursuant to international treaty, convention, or agreement to which the U.S. is a party" if the foreign vessel is "not destined for, or departing from, a port or place subject to the jurisdiction of the United State" and the vessel is either in "innocent passage through the territorial sea of the United State" or in "transit through navigable waters of the United States which form a part of an international strait."[21] Identical language appears in regulations on maritime security[22] and navigational safety guidelines.[23] For example, foreign tank barges are not required to implement certain emergency control systems to prevent oil pollution if they are transiting Admiralty Inlet off the coast of Washington State and are "engaged in innocent passage (i.e. not entering or leaving a U.S. port)."[24] Likewise, foreign vessels are not required to implement ballast water management requirements if the vessel "is merely traversing the territorial sea of the United States."[25]

The U.S Code recognizes an exception from the preservation of innocent passage rights when there is a treaty-regime to which the United States is a party. In such cases, the United States may still impose certain conditions on foreign vessels in innocent passage depending on specific treaty obligations under related treaty agreements such as the International Convention for the Prevention of Marine Pollution and the 1978 Amendment[26] or the London

18 UNCLOS, supra note 2, Article 21(1) and Article 22(1).
19 "Commander's Handbook," supra note 10 at Section 3.11.2.2 and 3.11.4.1.
20 46 U.S.C. 3702.
21 33 USC 1223(d).
22 33 CFR 104.105(f).
23 33 CFR 164.02.
24 33 CFR 155.230(a)(5).
25 33 CFR 151.2020.
26 MARPOL 73/78, 12 I.L.M. 1319 (1973) and 17 I.L.M. 546 (1978).

Convention on Dumping.[27] The United States understands that domestic sanctions for international violations must not interfere with a vessel's innocent passage unless permitted under international law.[28]

In a few cases, the U.S. Code extends specific obligations to foreign vessels engaged in innocent passage or exercising navigational rights but these are stated implicitly. For example, the Shipping Code provides that vessels involved in a marine accident must make a report of the accident even if the vessel was exercising innocent passage at the time of the accident. The Code states simply that the requirement to report certain types of marine casualties "applies to a foreign vessel when involved in a marine casualty on the navigable waters of the United States."[29] The understanding that this applies to all foreign vessels follows from reading the historical notes in the Annotated Code that state unequivocally that "the reporting requirements...are applicable to foreign vessels...whether in innocent passage or not."[30] The U.S. Coast Guard expects all foreign vessels to report marine casualties.

While the United States may under Article 25 of the UNCLOS impose temporary restrictions on the innocent passage of foreign vessels "if such suspension is essential for the protection of its security," the United States has been reluctant to do so. For example, in 1998, the United States declared a national emergency that included a security zone adjacent to the coastal waters of Southern Florida due to tensions between the United States and Cuba, but specifically provided that foreign flagged vessels in innocent passage would be exempt from the security zone control regulations.[31] After the terrorist attacks on September 11, 2001, the United States provided for naval vessel protection zones to regulate vessel traffic in the vicinity of U.S. naval vessels including any vessel owned, operated, chartered, or leased by the U.S. Navy as well as any vessel under the operational control of the U.S. Navy.[32]

Other laws which deal with the territorial sea apply equally to all vessels operating within the U.S. territorial sea regardless of whether a vessel is transiting in innocent passage. A number of U.S. publishers regularly release a volume of "Foreign Vessel Rules" that compiles the rules and regulations for foreign vessels operating in U.S. waters regarding navigation and shipping.[33]

27 London Convention, 11 I.L.M. 1294 (1972).

28 R. Wolfrum, "Freedom of Navigation: New Challenges," <www.itlos.org/fileadmin/itlos/documents/statements_of_president/wolfrum/freedom_navigation_080108_eng.pdf>.

29 46 USC 6101.

30 *Id.*

31 33 CFR 165.1313.

32 14 USC 91.

33 See e.g. American Nautical Services, "Rules and Regulations for Foreign Vessels Operating in the Navigable Waters of United States" (A compilation of Applicable CFR 33 & 46

III Rights for Foreign Vessels in the U.S. EEZ

The United States respects the rights of foreign vessels to operate within the U.S. EEZ and does not require notification from vessels that are operating in compliance with the navigational freedoms secured under the UNCLOS Article 58(1). Unlike in the territorial sea, aircraft have a right of overflight in the EEZ.[34] Moreover, the United States does not require foreign vessels to obtain the permission of the United States when conducting marine scientific research in the U.S. EEZ.[35]

One U.S. Navy commander explained in 1995 that navigational rights in the EEZ are akin to high seas navigational freedoms. He wrote that the EEZ regime:

> does not permit the coastal state to limit traditional non-resource related high seas activities in this EEZ, such as task force manoeuvers, flight operations, military exercises, telecommunications and space activities, intelligence and surveillance activities, marine data collecting and weapons testing and firing.[36]

The United States takes this perspective because the UNCLOS is not explicit about whether military activities are included in EEZ navigational freedoms. The United States presumes that military activities that do not interfere with EEZ resource uses are permissible.[37] The United States accepts that military surveys where marine data (oceanographic, geophysical, chemical, biological, acoustic data) is collected exclusively for military purposes are part of the freedom of navigation and do not require permission under marine scientific research regimes.[38]

While the United States takes the perspective that foreign vessels in the EEZ have a relatively wide latitude for "non-resource related" activities, the United States asserts that it has the right to regulate navigation that may impact resources within the EEZ by, for example, requiring vessels to use certain anchoring zones, avoiding particularly sensitive sea areas, and requiring ship reporting

regulations) <www.amnautical.com/products/pub-515-u-s-coast-guard-515-rules-regulations-for-foreign-vessels-operating-in-us-waters-including-cd-2015-2016#.WSmy9-n9Gyc>.

34 Commander's Handbook, *supra* note 10, at Section 1.3.4.

35 *Ibid.*, at Section 2.6.2.1.

36 W. Doran, "An Operational Commander's Perspective on the 1982 LOS Convention" *International Journal of Marine and Coastal Law*, Vol. 10 (1995): 341.

37 Commander's Handbook, *supra* note 10, at Section 2.6.2.

38 *Ibid.*, at Section 2.6.2.2.

systems in certain areas. For example, in July 1999, with the endorsement of the International Maritime Organization (IMO), the United States implemented a mandatory ship reporting system in two regions where right whales congregate to protect Atlantic right whales from ship collisions.[39] More recently, the United States has required all ships to reduce their speed to 10 knots if crossing areas where right whales are breeding or feeding.[40]

The U.S. *Oil Protection Act* imposes certain design standards for all oil tankers operating in U.S. waters. All tankers, as of January 1, 2015 are to be double-hulled.[41] Typically a State does not impose laws and regulations that apply to the design, construction, manning or equipment of foreign ships unless they are giving effect to generally accepted international rules or standards.[42] While the United States imposed these laws before the IMO adopted standards, the IMO has subsequently adopted design standards requiring double-hulling.[43]

IV The U.S. Freedom of Navigation Program

In protecting innocent passage within U.S. waters, the United States has established a "bright line" rule which permits all passage unless the passage is not innocent based on UNCLOS Article 19 or the activities of the vessel interfere with resource uses in the EEZ. The United States expects other States to apply the same rules to U.S. vessels. Concerned that States were asserting maritime jurisdictional claims beyond the areas to which they might be entitled under customary international law or treaties, the United States launched a program during President Jimmy Carter's Administration to protect the "rights and freedoms of navigation" for all nations.[44] The "U.S. Freedom of Navigation Program" is "designed to be politically neutral as well as nonprovocative" and to "encourage nations to amend their claims and bring their practices into conformity with the Convention."[45] Specifically, the United States began to regularly deploy Navy ships and Air Force patrols to assert the right of innocent passage and navigation rights across the globe. The motivation was to ensure that

39 US Coast Guard (2001), Mandatory ship reporting system off the Northeast and the Southeast Coasts of the United States, Final Rule, 66 FR 58066-580704.

40 50 CFR 224.

41 46 USC 3703a, introduced in 1990.

42 UNCLOS, supra note 2, Article 21(2).

43 MARPOL Convention, supra note 26, Regulation 13 F of Annex 1.

44 W.J. Aceves, "Diplomacy at Sea: U.S. Freedom of Navigation Operations in the Black Sea," *Naval War College Review* 46(2) 59, 60 (1993) 68.

45 "Commander's Handbook," supra note 10, at Section 2.8.

maritime nations do not acquiesce to excessive claims and thereby relinquish their rights. The United States has been keenly aware that its security strategies including the delivery of disaster relief and humanitarian assistance, depend on the ability of the United States to transit the archipelagic waters of Asian states and the Straits of Malacca, Gilbraltar, Torres, Hormuz, and Bab el Mandeb without the advance permission of the coastal States. The U.S. government has focused its attention on "excessive maritime claims" that include:

- "territorial sea claims that impose impermissible restrictions on the innocent passage of military and commercial vessels, of ships owned or operated by a state and used only on government non-commercial service, and of nuclear-powered warships or warships and naval auxiliaries carrying nuclear weapons or specific cargoes";
- "claims requiring advance notification or authorization for innocent passage of warships and naval auxiliaries through the territorial sea or EEZ or applying discriminatory requirements to such vessels";
- "territorial sea claims not exceeding 12 miles that overlap straits used for international navigation and do not permit transit passage, including submerged transit of submarines, overflight of military aircraft, and surface transit of warships and naval auxiliaries…without prior notification of authorization";
- "archipelagic claims that do not permit archipelagic sea lanes passage, including submerged passage of submarines, overflight of military aircraft, and surface transit of warships and naval auxiliaries…without prior notice of authorization."[46]

This early effort by the United States to protect its right and the rights of other States began while States were negotiating the UNCLOS and continues today. In support of the objectives of this program, the United States engages in bilateral consultations with States and may issue diplomatic protests. From 1979 to 1992, the United States sent or conveyed 110 formal diplomatic protests regarding excessive maritime claims that violate international customary law.[47] There have been a few high profile incidents that have illustrated the extent to which the United States will go to protect innocent passage. For example, in 1986, the United States patrolled in the Gulf of Sidra in protest of Libya's claim that the Gulf of Sidra was a historic inland sea.[48]

46 See: United States Department of State, Bureau of Oceans and International Environmental and Scientific Affairs, *Limits in the Sea: United States Responses to Excessive National Maritime Claims*, No. 112 (1992): 7–8 <www.state.gov/documents/organization/58381.pdf>.

47 *Ibid.* at p. 6.

48 *Id.*

The U.S. position on the freedom of navigation was further crystallized in February 1988. In a global jockeying of Cold War powers, the Soviet frigate *Bezzavetny* operating in U.S.S.R. territorial waters in the Black Sea intentionally pushed the U.S. cruiser *USS Yorktown* towards international waters. At the same time, the Soviet Mirka Class frigate hull number 824 pushed the U.S. destroyer *USS Caron* towards international waters. The Soviet Union defended its actions arguing that the U.S. vessels at the time of the incident were not operating within designating sea lanes.[49]

Subsequent to this event, the United States and U.S.S.R. concluded the "Uniform Interpretation of Norms of International Law Governing Innocent Passage."[50] The Joint Statement with its uniform interpretation was not just the product of the diplomatic aftermath of the Black Sea incident but was also based on other communications that have taken place since 1986 between the two States. The Statement was designed to resolve legal differences in order to avoid further provocations and confrontations over the interpretations of innocent passage sea rights. The two parties agreed that for purposes of their own territorial seas:

> All ships, including warships, regardless of cargo, armament or means of propulsion, enjoy the right of innocent passage through the territorial sea in accordance with international law, for which neither prior notification nor authorization is required.[51]

The two States further agreed that the UNCLOS provides an "exhaustive list of activities that would render passage not innocent" and that any vessel undertaking activity that is not listed in Article 19 "is in innocent passage."[52] The United States and the U.S.S.R. agreed that each State could question whether "the particular passage of a ship through its territorial sea is innocent" as long as it informs the ship of the reasons that it "questions the innocence of the passage and provides the ship an opportunity to clarify its intentions or corrects its conduct in a reasonably short period of time."[53] Foreign vessels must still

49 Soviet Council of Ministers, The Rules of Navigation and Sojourn of Foreign Warships in the Territorial Waters and Internal Waters and Ports of the USSR (1983) (Restricting warships to parts of the Baltic Sea, Sea of Okhotsk, and Sea of Japan).

50 Joint Statement by the United States and the Union of Soviet Socialist Republics on the Uniform Interpretation of Norms of International Law Governing Innocent Passage (September 23, 1989), *Law of the Sea Bulletin* 14 (December 1989) pp. 12–13.

51 *Ibid.* at p. 13, para 2.

52 *Ibid.* at p. 13, para 3.

53 *Ibid.* at p. 13, para. 4.

comply with coastal State rules on safety, environmental law, marine scientific work, and other matters that are "inextricably linked with the protection and promotion of societal values ashore."[54] The two States agreed that the existence of a sea lane or a traffic separation scheme is not necessary for the exercise of the right of innocent passage.[55] As a reminder that warships are permitted to engage in "innocent passage", the final paragraph of the Joint Statement provided that a warship which violates coastal State laws or regulations or is not in innocent passage based on UNCLOS Article 19 should "take corrective action upon request." Where a warship does not take the appropriate corrective action, "the coastal State may require it to leave the territorial sea" and the warship "shall do so immediately."[56] Any differences over "a particular case of passage of ships" must be settled by diplomatic means.[57] While not a source of law for any other State, the Joint Statement has been instructive in articulating the expectations that both the United States and the U.S.S.R. have for how foreign vessels will conduct innocent passage in United States and Soviet territorial waters.

The right to exercise innocent passage and freedom of navigation, which has been at the core of U.S. military policy, is likely to remain so because it is not perceived as a partisan political issue. The U.S. "National Security Strategy" in 2010 provided that the United States must focus on "keeping strategic straits and vital sea lanes open."[58] In 2015, the National Security Strategy emphasized that the "United States has an enduring interest in freedom of navigation and overflight."[59] The Freedom of Navigation Program, initiated under President Carter's Administration, has been actively supported by the Administrations of President Reagan, President George H. Bush, President Clinton, President George W. Bush, President Obama, and President Trump.[60]

---

54 W.L. Schacte, "History of the Territorial Sea from a National Security Perspective," *Territorial Sea Journal*, l, (1990) 143, 147.

55 Joint Statement U.S./U.S.S.R., supra note 50, at p. 13, para. 5.

56 *Ibid.* at p. 13, para. 7.

57 *Ibid.*, at p. 14, para. 8.

58 President Barack Obama, "National Security Strategy of the United States of America" (May 2010): 50, available at <nssarchive.us/NSSR/2010.pdf>.

59 President Barack Obama, "National Security Strategy of the United States of America" (February 2015): 13, available at <nssarchive.us/wp-content/uploads/2015/02/2015.pdf>.

60 President Reagan announced in 1982 that the United States would

> exercise and assert its navigation and overflight rights and freedoms on a worldwide basis in a manner that is consistent with the balance of interests reflected in the convention. The United States will not, however, acquiesce in unilateral acts of other States designed to restrict the rights and freedoms of the international community in navigation and overflight and other related high seas uses.

President Ronald Reagan, "Statement of United States Ocean Policy" (March 10, 1983) www.jag.navy.mil/organization/documents/Reagan%20Ocean%20Policy%20Statement

The United States does not, in general, recognize any peacetime right of a state to restrict navigation and overflight of foreign warships or military aircraft beyond the territorial sea through the declaration of security or defense zones.[61] The United States has produced an annual freedom of navigation report articulating its concerns about excessive maritime claims. An example of the types of concerns publicly raised in these reports is provided in Appendix 1 from the 2017 official "Freedom of Navigation Report".

Regarding the use of submarines, the United States endeavors to comply with the terms of the UNCLOS on transit passage. For example, the United States interprets its global right of transit passage as a right to be exercised on the basis of the normal mode of operation of a vessel. In practice, this means that a submarine transiting an international strait between one EEZ and another EEZ or between one EEZ and the high seas that would ordinarily transit below the water may transit submerged.[62] The U.S. submarine fleet does not travel submerged within the territorial sea of another country or outside of archipelagic sea lanes.[63] The United States also takes the position that transit passage does not cover just the waters within an international strait, but also the approaches to a strait.[64]

Finally, the United States expects that when its ships are in the territorial waters of another State that the coastal State will provide some protection of U.S. flagged vessels.[65] The United States is responsible for protecting its own vessels and citizens beyond the territorial sea.[66] If a coastal state is "unable or unwilling" to extend protection, then the United States asserts that "international law recognizes the right of another nation to direct its warships and military aircraft to use proportionate force in or over those waters to protect its flag vessels, its flag aircraft, and its nationals."[67]

.pdf. Secretary of Defense William Cohen under President William Clinton noted that "despite positive developments in the law of the sea, it remains necessary for maritime nations, like the United States, to protest excessive claims…[the] Freedom of Navigation Program has challenged excessive claims to counter any argument that such claims are valid due to acquiescence over time." William Cohen, Secretary of Defense, "Annual Report to the President and the Congress," (1997) at H-1; Geoff Ziezulewicz, "New in 2018: Showdown in the South China Sea?" (January 2, 2018) available at www.navytimes.com/news/your-navy/2018/01/02/new-in-2018-showdown-in-the-south-china-sea/ (Noting that the number of Freedom of Navigation operations have increased under President Trump).

61 "Commander's Handbook," supra note 10, at Section 2.6.4.

62 *Ibid.* at Section 2.5.3.1.

63 *Ibid.* at Section 2.5.4.2.

64 *Ibid.* at Section 2.5.3.1.

65 *Ibid.* at Section 3.10.1.1.

66 *Ibid.* at Section 3.10.1.2.

67 *Id.*

V Other States' Perspectives on the U.S. Freedom of Navigation Policies

The United States has been a champion of the freedom of navigation for decades. In many aspects, the United States is in conformity with the shared expectations of other States regarding innocent passage and transit rights. The United States disagrees strongly with others States about the need to request permission before engaging in innocent passage of a coastal State's territorial waters. In the South China Sea and waters within Southeast Asia, the U.S. freedom of navigation operations have received criticism and in some cases have provoked conflicts.[68] A number of States including China, India, Pakistan, Sri Lanka, and Malaysia insist on prior authorization before a warship qualifies for innocent passage through their territorial seas and protest U.S. military activities in the waters of their EEZ.[69] The U.S. claims because it is not involved in "use of force" or "militarization" when it undertakes its freedom of navigation operations that it is entitled to innocent passage with no pre-notification required. Other States are less trusting of U.S. intentions. As one Chinese diplomat has commented:

> We are very clear that we support freedom of navigation in accordance in accordance with international law, not only in the South China Sea, but also other parts of the world. The difference is that we think the United States takes freedom of navigation as an excuse. What their ships and planes have been doing is actually a close surveillance of China's coastlines and islands and reefs.[70]

States requiring preauthorization before innocent passage or the undertaking of military activities in the EEZ express concern that the United States is

---

68 See e.g., USS *Impeccable*, Testimony of Deputy Assistant Secretary, Bureau of East Asian and Pacific Affairs, Scot Marciel, "Maritime issues and sovereignty disputes in East Asia," statement before the Subcommittee on East Asian and Pacific Affairs, Senate Foreign Relations Committee, Washington, DC, July 15, 2009, <www.state.gov/p/eap/rls/rm/2009/07/126076.htm> (Describing interference by Chinese fishing vessels with U.S. Navy vessel navigation).

69 U.S. Department of Defense, Freedom of Navigation Report for Fiscal Year 2017, p 3 available at policy, <defense.gov/Portals/11/FY17%20DOD%20FON%20Report.pdf?ver=2018-01-19-163418-053. 3>.

70 Lynn Kuok, "U.S. FON Program in the South China Sea: A lawful and Necessary Response to China's Strategic Ambiguity" (July 2016), U.S. Brookings Institute Center for East Asian Policy Studies, <www.brookings.edu/wp-content/uploads/2016/07/The-US-FON-Program-in-the-South-China-Sea.pdf> (Quoting from interview with Chinese diplomat).

interfering with their national security prerogatives and the ability of States to exercise sovereignty over maritime resources. Depending on the State, different reasons are proffered for restricting military activities. China claims interference with "historical rights."[71] Thailand expresses concerns about military activities that affect the rights or interests of the coastal State.[72] India protests the use of weapons and explosives in the EEZ and asserts "exclusive rights" over non-resource activities.[73]

VI Conclusion

In spite of not being a party to the UNCLOS, the United States has been active in protecting both its navigational rights and the navigational rights of others that arise from customary international law and are codified in the UNCLOS. While the United States takes the position that it does not need to notify States when it is engaged in innocent passage or transit, it must take care not to confuse its related but different rights and obligations. As the rights associated with innocent passage are not identical to those available for navigation in the EEZ, the United States must be clear in its own implementation about what rights it is seeking to assert. In October 2015, the United States navigated within 12 miles of a man-made island in the South China Sea. In announcements about the exercise, the United States originally stated that it was an exercise of innocent passage and then within a few hours retracted that characterization.[74] Ultimately, the Defense Secretary wrote that: "The FONOP (Freedom of Navigation Operation) involved a continuous and expeditious transit that is consistent with both the right of innocent passage, which only applies in a territorial sea, and with the high seas freedom of navigation that applies beyond any territorial sea."[75] Freedom of navigation operations require the United States to

71 *Ibid.* at p. 8.

72 Thailand, declaration upon ratification of UNCLOS, May 15, 2011, paragraph 4, <www.un.org/Depts/los/convention_agreements/conven-tion_declarations.htm-Thailand Upon ratification>.

73 United Nations General Assembly (1992), Law of the Sea: Report of the Secretary-General: Progress made in the implementation of the comprehensive legal regime embodied in the United Nations Convention on the Law of the Sea, A47/512, November 5, 47th session, agenda item 32, p. 10, para. 33.

74 Joseph Bosco, "Start 2016 by Ending U.S. Ambiguity in East Asia," *The National Interest* (January 10, 2016) available at <nationalinterest.org/feature/start-2016-by-ending-us-ambiguity-east-asia-14860>.

75 *Ibid.*, (Quoting from a December 2015 letter from Secretary of Defense Carter to Senate Armed Services Chairman John McCain).

be clear about its understanding of the extent of a given excessive maritime claim. Otherwise, any operation designed to protect navigational freedom may fail to persuade another State to change its maritime actions to conform with U.S. expectations of navigational freedoms. Freedom of navigation operations will continue for the foreseeable future in the global oceans and particularly in the area of the South China Sea and the Indian Ocean. It remains to be seen whether differences in legal opinions about the extent of the freedom of navigation will generate future volatile geopolitical controversies.[76]

76 See: Ben Westcott and Barbara Starr, "South China Sea: U.S. Warship Challenges China's Claims with First Operation under Trump" CNN (May 25, 2017), <www.cnn.com/2017/05/24/politics/south-china-sea-us-mischief-reef/index.html>, (noting that when a U.S. Destroyer sailed within 12 miles of Chinese-controlled Mischief Reef that China sent two Chinese frigates to warn the U.S. that the vessel had entered Chinese-controlled waters "without permission").

APPENDIX 11.1 Examples of "excessive maritime claims" in Asia from U.S. Department of Defense Freedom of Navigation Report for Fiscal Year 2017 related to innocent passage and transit passage

Country	Excessive Maritime Claim
Cambodia	Excessive straight baselines.
China	Jurisdiction over airspace above the Exclusive Economic Zone (EEZ); restriction on foreign aircraft flying through an Air Defense Identification Zone (ADIZ) without the intent to enter national airspace; domestic law criminalizing survey activity by foreign entities in the EEZ; prior permission required for innocent passage of foreign military ships through the TTS.
India	Prior consent required for military exercises or manoeuvres in the EEZ.
Indonesia	Limits on archipelagic sea lane passage through normal routes used for international navigation.
Malaysia	Prior authorization required for nuclear-powered ships to enter the territorial sea; consent required for military exercises or manoeuvres in the EEZ.
Maldives	Prior permission required for foreign vessels to enter the EEZ.
Philippines	Claims archipelagic waters as internal waters.
Sri Lanka	Prior consent required for foreign warship to enter or pass through the territorial sea; claims a security jurisdiction in the contiguous zone.
Taiwan	Prior notification required for foreign military or government vessels to enter the territorial sea.
Vietnam	Prior notification required for foreign warships to enter the territorial sea; excessive straight baselines.

PART 4

Australasia

CHAPTER 12

Regulation of Navigation of Foreign Vessels in Australia

Warwick Gullett

1 Introduction

The freedom of navigation is an important principle that underpins much of Australia's approach to the law of the sea. Australia has been a strong advocate of navigational freedoms, especially through nearby regional seas and archipelagos. It has been prepared to assert navigational freedom, most notably in 2001 when three Royal Australian Navy ships transited the Taiwan Strait, and contemplated freedom of navigation exercises in the South China Sea in the wake of heightened State assertiveness[1] during the 2013–2016 proceedings of the *Philippines v China South China Sea Arbitration*.[2] Australia's advocacy for freedom of navigation is tempered by concern about environmental and security risks within its jurisdiction.[3] Australia has introduced environmental measures to manage the passage of vessels through particularly sensitive and vulnerable marine ecosystems in the Torres Strait and the Great Barrier Reef and has enhanced notification requirements for foreign ships heading to Australian ports.

Australia's approach to foreign vessel navigation owes much to the location, size and characteristics of its maritime jurisdiction which makes it critically reliant on seaborne trade and vulnerable to ship groundings and collisions, as well as customs, quarantine and immigration threats. As such, it is in Australia's interests that international shipping is safe and efficient and that all efforts

1 "Government reportedly planning 'freedom of navigation' exercise in South China Sea," ABC – *RN Breakfast*, 2 June 2015, <www.abc.net.au/radionational/programs/breakfast/government-reportedly-planning-freedom-of/6513778> [Accessed 30 March 2017].

2 *Arbitration between the Philippines and China, Award on Jurisdiction and Admissibility* (29 October 2015) and *Award* (12 July 2016) on the Permanent Court of Arbitration website at <www.pca-cpa.org>.

3 Bateman argued that Australia's interest in freedoms of navigation can sometimes conflict with its interests as a coastal State and in maintaining a stable neighbourhood. See Sam Bateman, "Some thoughts on Australia and the freedoms of navigation" (2015) 11 *Security Challenges* 57–66, 57.

 | DOI:10.1163/9789004396272_013

are made to minimise threats posed by items or personnel aboard ships, such as contaminated or illicit cargo, and criminals or undocumented migrants. Australia has the third largest maritime jurisdiction in the world, with a total marine area of approximately 10 million square km, which is larger than its 7.69 million square km mainland.[4] Approximately two million square km of the exclusive economic zone (EEZ) surrounds the Australian Antarctic Territory. Australia has a total coastline of 59,736 km, 40 per cent of which comprises island coastlines. Australia's location far from major world suppliers and markets explains why 99.5 per cent of the international trade in terms of volume is transported by ship.[5] Ten per cent of the world's sea trade is managed by Australian ports.[6] The growth in shipping activity has increased significantly since 2000.[7] In 2017, there were 28,502 port visits by 5,873 foreign flagged vessels.[8] In that year, bulk carriers accounted for 50 per cent of the ships that visited Australia, followed by container ships, vehicle carriers, chemical carriers, general cargo vessels, oil tankers, gas carriers and passenger ships.[9] Offshore oil and gas is also an emerging source of energy, with Australia being the ninth largest energy producer.[10]

Marine pollution, especially from oil and hazardous and noxious substances, is one of the significant threats to the Australian marine environment from shipping. Australia's experience of pollution incidents, especially from groundings, has led to the development of navigation regulations, increased financial liability, and the development of contingency response plans.[11] Since 1970, Australia has recorded 26 major oil spills and smaller offshore spills from ships that were considered significant either because of their resulting legal

4 Australian Government, Geoscience Australia, Oceans and Seas, <www.ga.gov.au>. See also Warwick Gullett, Clive Schofield and Joanna Vince, "Girt by sea: The challenge of managing Australia's marine resources," in Warwick Gullett, Clive Schofield and Joanna Vince (eds.) *Marine Resources Management* (LexisNexis 2011) 3–8, 4.

5 Australian Government, *Options Paper: Approaches to Regulating Coastal Shipping in Australia* (Commonwealth of Australia, 2014), p. 6.

6 *Ibid.*

7 Australian Maritime Safety Authority (AMSA), *Navigational Services in Australian Waters 2010–2025* (AMSA, 2009), p. 19.

8 AMSA, *Port State Control 2017 Report Australia* (AMSA, 2018), p. 4.

9 *Ibid.*, p. 12.

10 Australian Government, Department of Infrastructure and Transport, Office of the Inspector of Transport Security, *Offshore Oil and Gas Resources Sector Security Inquiry*, (Commonwealth of Australia, 2012), p. 1.

11 Warwick Gullett, "Marine contingency planning in Australia," in Anastasia Telesetsky, Warwick Gullett and Seokwoo Lee (eds.) *Marine Pollution Contingency Planning in the Asia-Pacific* (Brill, 2017), pp. 13–40.

action or that they required a substantial coordinated response between the Commonwealth and state governments and stakeholders.[12] One of the higher profile incidents was the grounding of the *Oceanic Grandeur* in 1970, in which the Liberian-flagged tanker carrying 55,000 tonnes of crude oil struck an unchartered rock in the Torres Strait. Such incidents highlight risk factors, such as proximity to critical marine habitat (in this case the Great Barrier Reef), potential effects on beaches and fisheries habitats, and the impact of chemical dispersants on marine resources. The 270 tonnes of oil spilled off southern Queensland from the Hong Kong-registered *Pacific Adventurer* in 2009 required the rehabilitation of birds, turtles and sea snakes, removal of 3,000 tonnes of contaminated sand, and deployment of 2,500 personnel for a two-month clean-up operation.[13] In 2010, the Chinese-flagged *Shen Neng 1*, a 230-metre long bulk carrier, left the Port of Gladstone for China carrying 68,000 tonnes of coal. It ran aground on a reef outside the shipping lane for the Great Barrier Reef, releasing four tonnes of fuel oil into the water. The *Shen Neng 1* was successfully refloated within 10 days with no further loss of oil. The incident resulted in changes in legislative requirements for vessels traversing the area. The ship's master and officer-on-watch were prosecuted.[14] After the incident the maximum fine for shipping companies that cause damage to the Reef was increased under Queensland legislation. Similarly, the vessel tracking system known as REEFVTS was extended to the entire length of the Great Barrier Reef (see below).

This chapter outlines the main measures Australia has taken to regulate passage of foreign vessels within its jurisdiction, reflecting the concerns outlined above about Australia's interest in free navigation, environmental protection, effective safety measures and minimising customs, quarantine and immigration risks. Australia does not have specific regulations on innocent passage in the territorial sea or freedom of navigation in the EEZ. Nevertheless, it has introduced a number of measures that restrict navigation in certain identified areas.

---

12 For details of each incident, see "Major Historical Incidents" on the AMSA Website at <www.amsa.gov.au>.

13 See, e.g., Michael White, "Pacific Adventurer oil spill 2009: Lessons past and future," (2013) 87 *Australian Law Journal* 320–330.

14 The officer-on-watch pleaded guilty to controlling the vessel when it damaged the reef in the Marine Park and served three months in prison. The ship's master was also convicted and fined $25,000.

II Regulatory Structure and Strategic Priorities for Navigation in Australia

The Australian Maritime Safety Authority (AMSA) is the federal government entity responsible for ensuring safe navigation in Australian waters. Its jurisdiction under the Navigation Act[15] includes foreign-flagged commercial vessels in Australian waters, including vessels solely engaged in intra-state operations. AMSA identifies areas for improved safety and environmental protection where there is projected increase in shipping activity, such as in waters off the northwest coast of Australia, and in the Great Barrier Reef and Torres Strait. This includes implementing an under-keel-clearance management system in the Torres Strait whereby deep draught vessels are monitored in real time together with bathymetry and environmental data from tide, stream, wind and wave sensors to enable the planning and monitoring of safe passage through shallow, reef-strewn waters which are navigationally challenging.[16] AMSA administers the marine navigation levy which is a "user pays" mechanism designed to recover from the commercial shipping industry the cost of operating and maintaining coastal marine aids to navigation. The fee is payable by overseas commercial trading vessels with a length of 24 metres or greater upon arrival at Australian ports and is based on net vessel tonnage.[17]

Australia's approach to management of international shipping is informed by a number of issues, including:[18]

- an increase in the size, speed and draughts of container vessels;
- a reduction in crew levels and declining crew competencies;
- the need to manage the movement of shipping in certain areas and the community's zero tolerance for shipping accidents and ship-sourced marine pollution;
- the continuing trend of introducing electronic aids to navigation;
- the proliferation of offshore oil and gas production and loading facilities; and
- the increase in number of offshore aquaculture and renewable energy installations.

---

15 *Navigation Act 2012 (Cth)*.

16 AMSA, supra note 7, and AMSA, *Under keel clearance management (UKCM) in Torres Strait*, Marine Notice 3/2016.

17 See Marine Navigation Levy Collection Regulations 1990 (Cth).

18 AMSA, supra note 7.

Priorities for AMSA include enhancing maritime safety and environment protection in the waters off the northwest coast of Australia and in the Great Barrier Reef and Torres Strait (in response to projected increase in shipping).[19]

III Registration of Foreign Vessels in Australia

Australia only commenced registration of ships in 1982 when it established the Australian Register of Ships. Before this, Australian-owned ships were listed in the British Register pursuant to the U.K. Merchant Shipping Act 1894.[20] Australia's requirements for the registration of vessels, which include Australian ship ownership or operation and certain protections for seafarers, ensure that it cannot be considered as a "flag of convenience" State. All Australian owned ships of 24 metres or greater length (other than government ships, fishing vessels and pleasure craft) and which are capable of navigating the high seas must be registered under the Shipping Registration Act 1981, as well as all Australian-owned ships, regardless of size (including fishing vessels) undertaking overseas voyages.[21]

Australia faces the challenge of supporting employment and the development of skills in the Australian maritime industry while also enabling trading vessels operating in the large intra-state market to be competitive. In 2012 the Australian Government instituted significant changes to cabotage aimed at facilitating the use of Australian rather than foreign registered vessels for domestic intra-state trade[22] and relaxed requirements for Australian vessel registration to make it a more attractive option for ship owners.[23]

Australia replaced the 1982 Registry in 2012 and now operates two vessel registries. The Australian General Register is primarily for domestic vessels and pleasure craft that travel to overseas ports.[24] The Australian International Shipping Register is for international trading ships that meet specific criteria, including ownership or operation by Australians, but without a number of the previous requirements regarding labour standards. The International Register is intended to be internationally competitive while facilitating Australian

19 *Ibid.*

20 *Merchant Shipping Act 1894* (Imp), Sections 88–90. See also *Foreign Jurisdiction Act 1890* (Imp) and Michael White, *Australian Offshore Laws* (Federation Press, 2009), 329.

21 *Shipping Registration Act* 1981 (Cth), ss. 3, 12(2), 68.

22 *Coastal Trading (Revitalising Australian Shipping) Act* 2012 (Cth).

23 *Shipping Registration Act* 1981 (Cth), as amended.

24 *Ibid.*, s. 14.

participation in international trade, supporting Australian maritime skills and employment and the Australian shipping industry more broadly.[25] The Registrar of Ships has the discretion not to register a ship, based on matters such as its age and record of compliance with regulations (such as its detention history), and "any matter that the Registrar considers relevant."[26] Mixed nationality crews are permitted, thus there is no longer a requirement that the majority of the officers and crew be Australian citizens or residents. However, it is a condition of registration of a ship in the International Register that there be an Australian master or chief mate and chief or first engineer.[27] Ship operators do not need to apply Australian labour laws. For example, the Fair Work Act 2009 (Cth) does not apply to ships on international voyages.[28] However, various seafarer rights are provided for, such as protection against victimisation,[29] compulsory insurance for death or long-term disability,[30] and specified liability for wages of sick or injured seafarers.[31]

The success of the 2012 reform of Australian vessel registration is disputed. While maritime unions support protection of employment and working conditions of Australian and foreign seafarers, companies that rely on intra-state trade have been critical of significantly increased shipping costs. An attempt by the Australian Government in 2015 to revise shipping registration laws was unsuccessful with its proposed legislative provisions failing to be approved by Parliament.[32] Despite more than five years of operation, no ships are presently registered on the Australian International Shipping Register.

IV Regulation of the Navigation of Foreign Vessels in Australian Waters

Australia has introduced measures to regulate or restrict the navigation of foreign vessels within some parts of its jurisdiction, comprising the maritime zones of the territorial sea, EEZ, and straits used for international navigation. Various restrictions of foreign vessel navigation are permitted under the

25 *Ibid.*, s. 15A.
26 *Ibid.*, s 15F(2).
27 *Ibid.*, s. 33A.
28 *Ibid.*, s. 61AA.
29 *Ibid.*, s. 61AL.
30 *Ibid.*, s. 61AM.
31 *Ibid.*, s. 61AO.
32 Shipping Legislation Amendment Bill 2015 (Cth).

United Nations Law of the Sea Convention (LOSC),[33] such as regulating innocent passage through the territorial sea for the safety of navigation and the regulation of maritime traffic, the protection of navigational aids, the protection of submarine cables and the conservation of living marine resources,[34] and the broader freedom of navigation within the EEZ especially with respect to fishing vessels.[35] The controls Australia has imposed cover various fields, such as physical restrictions around submarine pipelines, requests for information from ships intending to visit Australian ports, and the exercise of criminal enforcement jurisdiction. Australia exercises prescriptive and enforcement port State jurisdiction across fields such as pollution prevention, safety of navigation, maritime security and crimes, and fisheries. Various pieces of legislation provide Australian agencies with authority over foreign vessels suspected of breaching legislated standards, such as, inspection, detention, removal from port and initiation of enforcement proceedings.[36] Australia is a participant in the 1993 Memoranda of Understanding on Port State Control in the Asia Pacific Region (Tokyo MOU).[37]

1 *Protection Areas for Cables and Offshore Facilities*

Legislation is in place to protect offshore infrastructure from risks posed by approaching foreign vessels. Submarine cables are protected from risk of interference by the establishment of protected areas in Australian waters by the Australian Communications Management Authority.[38] Protected areas are established 1,852 metres either side of a cable, extending from the sea surface to the seabed.[39] A range of activities may be prohibited in a protected area including fishing involving the use of seabed trawl gear or lines designed to

33 United Nations Convention on the Law of the Sea (LOSC), Montego Bay, 10 December 1982 (in force 16 November 1994), 1833 *U.N.T.S.* 396.

34 *Ibid.*, art 21.

35 *Ibid.*, arts 58, 62.

36 See e.g., *Protection of the Sea (Prevention of Pollution from Ships) Act 1983* (Cth); Australian Marine Orders (oil, noxious liquid substances, harmful substances in packaged forms, garbage, sewage, air pollution); *Protection of the Sea (Civil Liability) Act 1981* (Cth); *Marine Pollution Act 2012* (NSW); *Navigation Act 2012* (Cth); *Maritime Transportation and Offshore Facilities Security Act 2003* (Cth); *Crimes at Sea Act 2000* (Cth); *Customs Act 1901* (Cth); *Fisheries Management Act 1991* (Cth); and *Fish Resources Management Act 1994* (WA).

37 See <www.tokyo-mou.org>.

38 *Telecommunications Act 1997* (Cth), sch 3A, cl 4(1).

39 *Ibid.*, cl 9(2).

catch fish at or near the seabed, anchoring, and seabed mining.[40] Other activities may be restricted, such as the use of pelagic fishing gear.[41]

Safety zones of 500 metres can be proclaimed around offshore petroleum and greenhouse gas facilities. Vessels, including foreign vessels, may be prohibited from entering or being present in a "petroleum safety zone"[42] surrounding a petroleum well, structure, or equipment, or in a "greenhouse gas safety zone"[43] surrounding a greenhouse gas well, structure, or equipment. A 5,362 square kilometre "area to be avoided"[44] has been established off the coast of Victoria in the Bass Strait in which unauthorised vessels (intended to be those in excess of 200 gross tonnage) may not enter due to the high concentration of offshore infrastructure which makes navigation particularly hazardous. An owner or master of an unauthorised vessel which enters or remains in a safety area or the area to be avoided commits an offence which carries the risk of a significant term of imprisonment.[45]

2 *Security Areas*

Australian legislation empowers the Defence Minister to proclaim an "offshore general security area" for defence training and responding to security threats.[46] Such areas may be specified to surround vessels or aircraft. This means that the boundaries of a security area may change as the protected craft moves location.[47] The Minister has a broad discretion regarding the size and boundaries of such security areas and even whether to notify affected persons of the existence of such areas.[48] The Australian Defence Force enjoys extensive powers within offshore security areas, such as to search and move ships including with the aid of reasonable force.[49] The potential ambit of activities or actions that might be taken by members of the Australian Defence Force under these broad powers could conceivably be inconsistent with rights under LOSC enjoyed by foreign vessels while traversing Australian waters, most notably when they exercise the freedom of navigation in the Australian EEZ.[50] Nevertheless, under Australian

40 *Ibid.*, cl 10.

41 *Ibid.*, cl 11.

42 *Offshore Petroleum and Greenhouse Gas Storage Act 2006* (Cth), s. 616.

43 *Ibid.*, s. 617.

44 *Ibid.*, s. 613.

45 *Ibid.*, ss. 616, 617, 619.

46 *Defence Act 1903* (Cth), s. 51SF(1).

47 *Ibid.*, s. 51SF(2)(a).

48 *Ibid.*, s. 51SF(3)-(6).

49 *Ibid.*, ss. 51SJ(1), 51SP(1).

50 Stuart Kaye, "Security and defence in Australia's marine domain", in Gullett, Schofield and Vince, supra note 4, 133–144, 138.

law, actions authorised by the Defence Act 1903 (Cth) are lawful because the legislation is validly made under the Australian Parliament's legislative powers for "external affairs" contained in the Constitution, and Australian courts only consider a domestic law's constitutional legitimacy rather than its consistency with international conventions when determining its lawfulness.[51]

3 *Vessel Security and Information Requirements*

Australia has adopted measures requiring foreign vessels intending to call at an Australian port or otherwise enter Australia's territorial sea to meet international security standards. Foreign ships are required to have aboard an international ship security certificate[52] within the meaning of the International Ship and Port Facility Security Code.[53] A more controversial aspect of Australia's enhanced security requirements for incoming foreign passenger ships and large commercial vessels is that a range of pre-arrival information must be provided to Australian Customs before vessels enter Australia's territorial sea.[54] The information required includes the security level at which the ship is operating, its last 10 ports of call, and the next four if known.[55] These requirements were introduced in the Maritime Transportation and Offshore Facilities Security Act 2003 (Cth) in addition to pre-arrival information requirements that already existed in the Customs Act 1901 (Cth) regarding cargo, passengers and crew (including for pleasure craft).[56] The pre-arrival reporting must be completed for commercial ships and pleasure craft at least 96 hours before the estimated time of arrival of the vessel.[57] Shorter reporting periods apply where the duration of the voyage from the previous port is less than 96 hours.[58] Vessel

---

51 See *ibid.*; Warwick Gullett and Gregory Rose, "Australia's marine jurisdictions under international and domestic law," in Gullett, Schofield and Vince, supra note 4, 25–40, 38; and *Polyukhovich v Commonwealth* (1991) 172 C.L.R. 501, 632 (Dawson J). See also *Horta v Commonwealth* (1994) 181 C.L.R. 183 and *XYZ v Commonwealth* (2006) 227 C.L.R. 532.

52 *Maritime Transportation and Offshore Facilities Security Act 2003* (Cth) s. 91.

53 International Convention for the Safety of Life at Sea (SOLAS), 1974 1184 *U.N.T.S.* 278, amendments contained in Resolutions 1, 2, 6 and 7 of the Conference of the Contracting Governments and Including the Ship and Port Facility Security (ISPS) Code, see [2004] *A.T.S.* No 29.

54 *Maritime Transport and Offshore Facilities Security Act*, supra note 52, ss, 17, 92.

55 Maritime Transport and Offshore Facilities Security Regulations 2003, reg 5.10.

56 See *Customs Act 1901* (Cth), ss. 64, 64AB, 64ACA, 64ACB.

57 Maritime Transport and Offshore Facilities Security Regulations, supra note 55, reg. 5.10(1), read with *Customs Act 1901*, supra note 56, s. 64(5)(b)(i), 5A)(b)(i) and Customs Regulations 2015, reg. 15.

58 Customs Regulations 2015, reg. 16.

operators who do not provide such reports either commit an offence[59] or expose themselves to the prospect of being issued a "control direction" requiring them to take or refrain from taking specified action in relation to their vessel, such as removing it from Australia's territorial sea or holding it in a particular position.[60]

The introduction of the requirement for vessels to provide additional pre-arrival information, including for vessels merely passing through Australian waters, generated international controversy when it was announced by the Australian Prime Minister in 2004. This is largely because the announcement characterised the changes as being part of a new maritime identification "zone" that would extend 1,000 nautical miles offshore and thereby overlap the jurisdiction of Papua New Guinea, Indonesia, Timor Leste and Indonesia.[61] The initiative was soon relabelled as the Australian Maritime Identification System and explained as forming part of a larger cooperative approach of States to enhance maritime domain awareness.[62] Enforcement actions can be taken by Australia against vessels that do not comply with the pre-arrival notification requirements under domestic law, nevertheless, it can be assumed that it is in the interests of operators of foreign vessels to provide the requested information "in order that their subsequent visits to Australia are trouble-free."[63]

4 *Fishing*

Foreign fishing vessels have freedom of navigation in Australia's EEZ although pursuant to the LOSC they must have "due regard" to the rights and duties of Australia and comply with Australian laws, including those concerning the conservation and management of living resources.[64] A coastal State may prohibit foreign fishing vessels from fishing in its EEZ or allow fishing in accordance with access agreements.[65] In Australia, this takes the form of a number of offences, including a strict liability offence of using a foreign boat for commercial fishing without authorisation.[66] To respect the freedom of navigation

59 See e.g., *Customs Act 1901*, supra note 56, s. 64(13).

60 *Maritime Transportation and Offshore Facilities Security Act*, supra note 52, ss. 92(5), 99.

61 See Natalie Klein, "Legal implications of Australia's Maritime Identification System," (2006) 55 *International and Comparative Law Quarterly* 337–368, 337, 345. See also IMO 2004 circular, "Guidance to Masters, Companies and Duly Authorized Officers on the Requirements Relating to the Submission of Security-Related Information Prior to the Entry of a Ship into Port," which permits the collection of security information from foreign vessels prior to them arriving in port.

62 *Ibid.*, 339.

63 Kaye, supra note 50, 135.

64 LOSC, supra note 33, art. 58.

65 *Ibid.*, art. 62.

66 *Fisheries Management Act 1991* (Cth), s. 100.

of foreign fishing vessels within Australia's EEZ, the offence of having a foreign boat equipped with nets, traps or other equipment for fishing at a place inside the Australian fishing zone (AFZ) without authorisation does not apply if the fishing equipment is stored and secured "and the boat was traveling through the AFZ from a point outside the AFZ to another point outside the AFZ by the shortest practicable route."[67]

Foreign fishing vessels may traverse another State's territorial sea in accordance with the requirements of innocent passage.[68] A foreign vessel will not be engaging in innocent passage if it conducts fishing activities in the territorial sea of another State.[69] The LOSC also provides that coastal States may regulate innocent passage through the territorial sea in respect of a number of matters, including the conservation of living resources and the prevention of infringement of domestic fisheries laws.[70] It is an offence to use a foreign boat for fishing within Australia's territorial sea without authorisation as well as to have a foreign boat equipped for fishing in the territorial sea without authorisation.[71]

Australia has developed cooperative surveillance and enforcement arrangements with other States. For example, two bilateral treaties have been concluded with France which apply to Australia and France's adjacent areas of marine jurisdiction in the Southern Ocean.[72] The treaties enable surveillance and joint patrols of the other party's maritime zones, the exchange of information about the location, movements and other details of vessels suspected of fishing illegally, provision of logistical support in the conduct of hot pursuits, and cooperative enforcement action including boarding, inspection, apprehension, seizure and investigation of fishing vessels suspected of operating illegally. Most notably, there is provision in the agreements for Australia and France to conduct hot pursuits of foreign fishing vessels through each other's territorial sea.

---

67 *Ibid.*, ss. 101(1)(d), 101A(4)(d).

68 LOSC, supra note 33, arts. 17, 18.

69 *Ibid.*, art. 19(2)(i).

70 *Ibid.*, art. 21.

71 *Fisheries Management Act*, supra note 66, ss. 100B, 101AA.

72 Treaty between Australia and France on Cooperation in the Maritime Areas adjacent to the French Southern and Antarctic Territories (TAAF), Heard Island and the McDonald Islands, Canberra, 24 November 2003, [2005] *A.T.S.* 6 and Agreement on Cooperative Enforcement of Fisheries Laws between Australia and France in the Maritime Areas Adjacent to the French Southern and Antarctic Territories, Heard Island and the McDonald Islands, Paris, 8 January 2007, [2007] *ATNIF 1*. See Warwick Gullett and Clive Schofield, "Pushing the limits of the Law of the Sea Convention: Australian and French cooperative surveillance and enforcement in the Southern Ocean," (2007) 22 *International Journal of Marine and Coastal Law* 545–583.

5 *Australia's EEZ Adjacent to Antarctica*

Arguably the most contentious area in which Australia could purport to limit foreign vessel activities is in its EEZ surrounding parts of Antarctica. Australia claims sovereignty over a large proportion of Antarctica although few States recognise the claim. Waters adjacent to Australia's Antarctic territory are included in Australia's EEZ. However, for reasons of international diplomacy, these waters are not included in the AFZ and thus Australian fisheries regulations do not apply to foreign vessels.[73] Nonetheless, the provisions of the Environment Protection and Biodiversity Conservation Act 1999 (Cth) which protect cetaceans by the establishment of an Australian Whale Sanctuary in all Commonwealth waters inside the EEZ apply to foreigners in the waters adjacent to Australia's Antarctic Territory.[74] This is an ongoing issue with respect to Japan and its Southern Ocean whaling program. Australia has exercised restraint in not seeking to conduct enforcement operations against foreign whaling vessels in the Antarctic EEZ because such actions would be premised on disputed Australian sovereignty over relevant portions of Antarctica. In light of the likelihood that any foreign whaling vessel arrested in the Antarctic EEZ would protest the legality of Australia's exercise of enforcement jurisdiction, Australia has taken the approach of monitoring the activities of such vessels rather than conducting arrests.[75] In 1994, the United States formally protested Australia's assertion of an EEZ adjacent to Antarctica.[76]

---

73 Ruth Davis, "Enforcing Australian law in Antarctica: The HSI litigation," (2007) 8 *Melbourne Journal of International Law* 142–158. Another example of the diplomatic treatment of Antarctica is found in the *Biosecurity Act 2015* (Cth). Section 261 provides that ballast water discharge regulations do not apply to foreign vessels in Australia's territorial sea adjacent to Antarctica. Notwithstanding that Australia's principal fisheries legislation, the *Fisheries Management Act*, supra note 66, does not apply to Australian waters adjacent to Antarctica due to such waters being "excepted waters" and not part of the AFZ (ss. 4, 11; Commonwealth of Australia Gazette, No. S 52, 14 February 1992), some provisions of the Act apply to Australians in these waters. Further, additional regulations applicable to Australians in these waters have been established under the *Antarctic Marine Living Resources Conservation Act 1981* (Cth).

74 Warwick Gullett, *Fisheries Law in Australia* (LexisNexis, 2008) 211–212.

75 See e.g., "Australia completes first flyover mission monitoring Japanese whaling fleet," *ABC News*, 13 January 2014, <www.abc.net.au/news/2014-01-13/customs-charters-plane-for-first-monitoring-mission-of-japanese/5196972> [Accessed 30 March 2017].

76 US Navy Judge Advocate General's Corps, *Maritime Claims Reference Manual*, "Australia" <www.jag.navy.mil/organization/code_10_mcrm.htm> [Accessed 30 March 2017].

6 *Historic Bays in South Australia*

In 1987, Australia proclaimed four small bays in South Australia (Anxious Bay, Encounter Bay, Lacepede Bay and Rivoli Bay) as "historic" bays.[77] This had the effect of enclosing their waters within the territorial sea baseline, although there is doubt as to whether the bays qualify for historic status.[78] The United States protested the claim in 1991.[79] Nevertheless, the United States has not conducted freedom of navigation operations in these areas, despite doing so with regard to other claimed historic bays by other States,[80] possibly due in part to the remote location and modest size of the four South Australian bays.

7 *Compulsory Pilotage: Great Barrier Reef and Torres Strait*

The waters adjacent to north-eastern Australia are crucial areas for foreign vessels to access Australian eastern shore ports,[81] yet are notoriously treacherous for navigation. Numerous groundings have occurred, including Lieutenant James Cook's HMS *Endeavour* in 1770 and the *Shen Neng 1* (noted above) in 2010 in the Great Barrier Reef and the *Oceanic Grandeur* (also noted above) in 1970 in the Torres Strait. The Great Barrier Reef is the world's largest reef system. It extends over 2,600 kilometres and is around 15 to 150 kilometres offshore, in some parts about 65 kilometres wide. It is strewn with more than 900 islands and other navigational hazards. It is a major tourist destination and has numerous species including cetaceans and turtles. It attained World Heritage status in 1981. The adjacent Torres Strait separates northern Queensland from Papua New Guinea. It is 200 kilometres long and about 150 kilometres wide with many islands, small islets, reefs and shoals, shallow water, strong currents and variable tides.[82] Despite its width, there are a limited number of routes available for large vessels, including the Prince of Wales Channel which

---

77 Stuart Kaye, "The South Australian historic bays: An Assessment," (1995) 17 *Adelaide Law Review* 269, 270.

78 *Ibid.*, 282. The 1987 proclamation was replaced in 2006 by the *Seas and Submerged Lands (Historic Bays) Proclamation 2006* (Cth) which revised the limits of the bays and the location of the baseline.

79 United States Navy, *Maritime Claims Reference Manual*, "Australia", supra note 76, <www.jag.navy.mil/organization/code_10_mcrm.htm> [Accessed 30 March 2017].

80 Bateman, supra note 3, 63.

81 Especially the major Queensland ports of Cairns, Townsville, Gladstone and Mackay, and the coal ports of Abbott Point and Hay Point.

82 For interesting accounts of the earliest passages through the Torres Strait, see Kenneth Morgan, "From Cook to Flinders: The navigation of Torres Strait," (2015) *International Journal of Maritime History* 27: 41–60.

narrows to 800 metres.[83] The majority of the ships that utilize the Torres Strait each year are engaged in trade between ports in southern Asia, Australia, New Zealand, South America, Papua New Guinea and in Pacific Island States.[84]

Australia has taken innovative measures to reduce the risk of ship accidents in the navigationally hazardous waters of the Great Barrier Reef and Torres Strait by extending pilotage to large vessels in transit in the busy shipping lanes. The use of pilots – who are experienced mariners with extensive navigational skills and detailed knowledge of a particular body of water[85] – has been common place in many areas around the world for centuries to assist ships in entering and exiting ports where ship navigation is especially difficult.[86] Many of the world's ports have made use of pilots compulsory for large vessels seeking to enter. Australia has been a pioneer in extending the use of pilots outside ports in waters which are highly challenging for navigation, experience high rates of ship movements (including dangerous goods such as crude oil, petroleum products, bulk fertilizer and mineral concentrates),[87] and encompass areas that are highly valued for their environmental features.

Voluntary pilotage regimes in the Great Barrier Reef and Torres Strait have existed under Queensland regulations since 1884.[88] In 1991, Australia introduced compulsory pilotage in the Great Barrier Reef in the Inner Route (from Cape York to Cairns through Australia's territorial sea)[89] in order to reduce the risk of collisions and groundings posed by vessels transiting without pilots. The compulsory pilotage regime applies in any prescribed waters within Australia's

83 Stuart Kaye, "Regulation of navigation in the Torres Strait: Law of the Sea issues," in Don Rothwell and Sam Bateman (eds.) *Navigational Rights and Freedoms and the New Law of the Sea* (Martinus Nijhoff, 2000) 119–135, 119.

84 Julian Roberts, "Balancing Australia's rights and obligations to protect the marine environment: The Torres Strait Particularly Sensitive Sea Area," in Gullett, Schofield and Vince, supra note 4, 279–296, 280.

85 Craig Forrest, "Shipping and the marine environment in Australia," in Gullett, Schofield and Vince, supra note 4, 123–132, 128.

86 See Donald K. Anton, "Making or breaking the international law of transit passage? Meeting environmental and safety challenges in the Torres Strait with compulsory pilotage," in David D. Caron and Nilufer Oral (eds.) *Navigating Straights: Challenges for International Law* (Brill, 2014) 49–86, 55.

87 Sam Bateman, "Coastal state regulation of navigation in adjacent waters: The example of the Torres Strait and Great Barrier Reef," Proceedings of the Advisory Board on the Law of the Sea (ABLOS) conference, *Contentious Issues in UNCLOS: Surely Not?* (Monaco, 2010), 4.

88 Michael White, "Navigational rights in sensitive marine environments: The Great Barrier Reef," in Rothwell and Bateman, supra note 83, 230–262, 251. In 1983 the International Maritime Organization (IMO) acceded to Australia's request for it to adopt a resolution to recommend that all vessels carry a pilot when transiting the route. See Roberts, supra note 84, 281.

89 *Great Barrier Reef Marine Park Amendment Act 1991* (Cth), Sch.

internal waters, territorial sea or EEZ.[90] In 2001, the compulsory pilotage regime in the Great Barrier Reef was extended to the Whitsunday Island group (adjacent to Airlie Beach) and the entirety of Hydrographers Passage (a route through the reef from the Pacific Ocean adjacent to Mackay considered the most difficult shipping route within the Great Barrier Reef),[91] both areas being within or landward of Australia's territorial sea.[92] In 2006, the compulsory pilotage regime was extended to the Great North East Channel (reaching from the southern area of the Torres Strait to the north-eastern limit)[93] in order to address the risk posed by the approximately 500 ships, including large container vessels, tankers and other vessels carrying hazardous cargo, which transited the Channel each year without engaging a pilot.[94] The creation of the compulsory pilotage scheme in the Torres Strait was controversial because it applies to waters that comprise the Australian EEZ in which foreign vessels enjoy the high seas freedom of navigation[95] and a strait used for international navigation in which foreign vessels enjoy the right of transit passage.[96] Under Australian legislation vessels that are 70 metres or longer or are carrying oil, chemicals or liquefied gas[97] are required to have a pilot on board when passing through any of the four prescribed areas. The master or owner of such a vessel that navigates without a pilot licensed by the AMSA in a compulsory pilotage area commits an offence, exposing them to a penalty of up to AU$85,000.[98] The compulsory pilotage regime does not apply to naval or government vessels. Ships that are required to take on a licensed pilot may apply for an exemption.[99]

90 *Navigation Act 2012*, supra note 15, ss. 162(2), 163(1) and Marine Order 54 (Coastal Pilotage) 2014 (Cth), cl 7.

91 Great Barrier Reef Marine Park Amendment Regulations 2001 (No 3), sch.

92 See *Mogilyuk and Australian Maritime Safety Authority* [2014] AATA 409 regarding the detention by AMSA of a large international trading vessel for, in part, being "substandard" under the *Navigation Act 2012*, supra note 15, s 248(1)(a) for failure to adequately take into account pilot boarding requirements for the Hydrographers Passage compulsory pilotage regime.

93 Great Barrier Reef Marine Park Regulations 1983, supra note 91, cl 118.

94 Roberts, supra note 84, 286. See also Kaye, supra note 83, 126. More attention was focused on these concerns following the 2002 grounding of the bulk carrier *Agean Falcon* while transiting the Great North East Channel without a pilot. See Anton, supra note 86, 60.

95 LOSC, supra note 33, art 58.

96 *Ibid.*, art 38.

97 *Navigation Act 2012*, supra note 15, s. 162(1).

98 *Great Barrier Reef Marine Park Act 1975* (Cth), s. 59B. A higher penalty may be awarded where a body corporate is convicted of an offence. See also *Navigation Act 2012*, supra note 15, s. 166.

99 Wide discretion can be applied when determining applications for exemptions. Matters that are considered relevant include the qualifications of the vessel's master and details of his or her recent navigational experience in the compulsory pilotage area, the vessel's

Australia's approach to compulsory pilotage has been to work closely with Papua New Guinea as its adjacent State in the Torres Strait and with the support of measures adopted by the International Maritime Organization (IMO). The Marine Environment Protection Committee (MEPC) of the IMO is empowered to adopt non-binding resolutions in which it can designate a marine area to be a Particularly Sensitive Sea Area (PSSA). A PSSA is defined as:

> an area that needs special protection through action by IMO because of its significance for recognized ecological, socio-economic, or scientific attributes where such attributes may be vulnerable to damage by international shipping activities.[100]

PSSAs can cover areas outside national jurisdiction,[101] but must be linked to existing or proposed specific protective measures that would protect a proposed PSSA from an identified risk of environmental damage from international shipping. Associated Protective Measures (APMs) can be used to regulate international shipping in PSSAs, such as specifying routeing requirements, discharge restrictions, no-anchoring areas, vessel reporting and installation of Vessel Traffic Services (VTS).

In 1990, the Great Barrier Reef became the first PSSA.[102] Its designation was accompanied by a resolution of the MEPC that States "inform ships flying their flags to comply with the system of pilotage introduced by Australia."[103] There are currently 16 designated PSSAs, with Australia and Papua New Guinea also achieving PSSA status for the Torres Strait in 2005. This PSSA was extended to

---

draught and cargo and whether it will be stationary in the area or will be there for a short duration. *Navigation Act 2012*, supra note 15, s. 172; Marine Order 54 (Coastal Pilotage) 2014, supra note 90, cl 82; and *Great Barrier Reef Marine Park Act 1975*, supra note 98, s. 59F(3)(4).

100 IMO Assembly, "Revised guidelines for the identification and designation of Particularly Sensitive Sea Areas," Resolution A.982(24) (1 Dec 2005).

101 This conclusion is reached based on the authorizing instrument (IMO Resolution A.982(24), above) not prescribing any jurisdictional requirement for the designation of a PSSA. However, thus far, none of the PSSAs cover high seas. See David Freestone and Viva Harris, "Particularly Sensitive Sea Areas beyond national jurisdiction: Time to chart a new course?", in Myron H Nordquist, John Norton Moore and Ronán Long (eds) *International Marine Economy: Law and Policy* (Brill, 2017) 322–361.

102 Markus J Kachel, *Particularly Sensitive Sea Areas: The IMO's Role in Protecting Vulnerable Marine Areas* (Springer, 2008) 217.

103 IMO Doc. MEPC Resolution 45(30), *Protection of the Great Barrier Reef Region* (16 November 1990).

Australian jurisdiction to the southwest part of the Coral Sea in 2015.[104] The APMs for this region included the designation of a 25,250 square nautical mile "Area to be Avoided" (ATBA) due to the navigational challenges posed by numerous reefs, cays, islets, sandbars and shoal patches, and two two-way shipping routes of five miles breadth adjacent to the ATBA which are intended to reduce the risks of collision and grounding of ships by separating opposing streams of traffic and enabling ships to follow well-defined lanes in order to enhance safety and efficiency of navigation through effective passage planning.[105] Avoidance of the ATBA and use of the shipping routes is recommended, but not mandatory. The AMSA has advised that "ships that demonstrate an operational need to visit a location within the ATBA (e.g. cruise ships) and which have adequate risk mitigation measures in place, may enter the ATBA."[106]

Considerable international controversy was generated when Australia and Papua New Guinea proposed in 2004 to extend Australia's compulsory pilotage regime in the Great Barrier Reef to the Torres Strait and to create a two-way route through the Great North East Channel. This was because the Torres Strait is an international shipping route and, as such, falls under the law of the sea transit passage regime for straits used for international navigation,[107] which supersedes Australia's rights as a coastal State to regulate vessel traffic, including through relevant portions of the territorial sea.[108] The regime of transit passage affords to all vessels the right of continuous and expeditious passage which "shall not be impeded."[109] Vessels while in transit passage are expected to comply with IMO regulations.[110]

The Torres Strait PSSA proposal was debated for two years within the MEPC with opinion divided regarding the international legal basis for requiring

---

104 See IMO, Marine Environment, Particularly Sensitive Sea Areas, <www.imo.org/en/OurWork/Environment/PSSAs/Pages/Default.aspx> [Accessed 13 April 2017].

105 IMO Doc. MEPC Resolution 268(68), *Designation of the south-west Coral Sea as an extension of the Great Barrier Reef and Torres Strait Particularly Sensitive Sea Area* (15 May 2015).

106 AMSA, *IMO-adopted ships' routeing systems to be introduced in the Coral Sea*, Marine Notice 16/2015.

107 The regime applies to straits which are used for international navigation between one part of the high seas or an EEZ and another part of the high seas or an EEZ. See LOSC, supra note 33, art 37. See also Stuart Kaye, *The Torres Strait* (Martinus Nijhoff, 1997) 84.

108 Roberts, supra note 84, 283.

109 LOSC, supra note 33, art. 38.

110 See *ibid.*, art. 39(2). Articles 41 and 42 authorise States bordering straits to designate sea lanes and traffic separation schemes and adopt measures for safety of navigation and pollution prevention.

vessels in transit passage to take on a licensed pilot.[111] States which objected to the measures proposed for the PSSA argued such measures would contravene the rights in the transit passage regime, especially considering that a failure to engage a pilot would presumably lead to State sanctions. The United States and Singapore issued diplomatic notes of protest to Australia.[112] Other States considered that it was legitimate for coastal States to implement pilotage schemes with the support of the IMO to protect sensitive environments and that the proposed measure did not impede or interfere with navigational freedom.[113] The position of Australia and Papua New Guinea was that neither the wording of the LOSC nor its *travaux préparatoires* indicated that a compulsory pilotage scheme could not be introduced in the Torres Strait, there was a "compelling need" for a scheme considering the characteristics of the marine environment and the reliance on its resources by traditional inhabitants of the area, and the considerable navigational challenges in the Strait meant that compulsory pilotage would provide safer navigation and not impede or hamper transit passage.[114] The compromise solution reached was for the MEPC to recommend, rather than require, foreign vessels to comply with Australia's system of pilotage in routes in the Great Barrier Reef and the Torres Strait, including the Great North East Channel.[115]

The United States endorsed environmental protection for the Torres Strait but opposed any attempt to make pilotage compulsory for vessels engaged in transit passage. It has operated on the basis that the MEPC Resolution simply

111 Julian Roberts, *Marine Environment Protection and Biodiversity Conservation: The Application and Future Development of the IMO's Particularly Sensitive Sea Area Concept* (Springer, 2007) 150–159.

112 Robert C Beckman, "PSSAs and transit passage: Australia's pilotage system in the Torres Strait challenges the IMO and UNCLOS," (2007) *Ocean Development and International Law* 38: 325–357, 337.

113 Roberts, supra note 84, 287.

114 See Anton, supra note 86, 62. For criticism of this argument, see Beckman, supra note 112, 343–346.

115 The MEPC Resolution was expressed so that it "recommends" that "Governments recognise the need for effective protection of the Great Barrier Reef and Torres Strait region and inform ships flying their flag that they should act in accordance with Australia's system of pilotage for merchant ships 70 m in length and over or oil tankers, chemical tankers and gas carriers, irrespective of size." MEPC Resolution 133(53), *Designation of the Torres Strait as an extension of the Great Barrier Reef Particularly Sensitive Sea Area* (22 July 2005), Annex 1.

The Resolution also noted the critical habitat the Torres Strait provides for many vulnerable or endangered species, the vulnerability of the area to damage by international shipping activities and potential impact to the several thousands of Indigenous people of the Torres Strait, and the significant navigational hazards for large ships.

recommended ships to engage licensed pilots. The United States has committed to urging its vessels to act in accordance with the recommendatory Australian system to the extent that doing so does not deny, impair, hamper, or impede transit passage.[116]

In 2006, the AMSA issued Marine Notices to notify international mariners of the imminent new legal requirements. It reported that the MEPC had "adopted" Australia's compulsory pilotage regime.[117] This prompted criticism from other States, leading the AMSA to clarify the legal operation of the regime. Rather than identifying specific provisions of the LOSC which authorised the scheme, the AMSA stated that the requirement to carry a licensed pilot was a condition of entry to Australian ports. Arguably, this is a matter that can be regulated by coastal States under the law of the sea.[118] Australia indicated it would not stop or board a vessel while in transit without a pilot but it would notify its flag State and the vessel's master or operator would be liable to prosecution in the event that it entered an Australian port.[119] The Marine Notice also mentioned the availability of a legislative defence where the failure to carry a licensed pilot was due to stress of weather, saving life at sea or other unavoidable cause.[120]

It is clear that the compulsory pilotage regime in the Torres Strait has been successful despite States being at an impasse regarding whether the law of the sea permits vessel passage to be regulated in this manner. There is reportedly 100 per cent compliance of vessels engaging pilots and Australia has not taken any punitive actions, such as commencing prosecutions against a master or denying a vessel entry into port.[121] For vessels of States which oppose the compulsory nature of the pilotage scheme but nevertheless wish to engage a pilot to provide safer navigation through the Torres Strait, a practical compromise is easily reached: the master of the vessel may "request" a pilot notwithstanding Australia's position that the use of a pilot is mandatory.

---

116 J. Ashley Roach and Robert W. Smith, *Excessive Maritime Claims* (3rd ed) (Martinus Nijhoff, 2012) 337–338.

117 AMSA, *Revised pilotage requirements for Torres Strait*, Marine Notice 8/2006 (16 May 2006).

118 This right is based on a coastal State's sovereignty over its internal waters and is implicit in LOSC, supra note 33, provisions such as art 211. See also Lindy S. Johnson, *Coastal State Regulation of International Shipping* (Oceana, 2004) 42.

119 AMSA, *Further information on revised pilotage requirements for Torres Strait*, Marine Notice 16/2006 (3 October 2006). See also AMSA, *Bridge resource management* (BRM) *and Torres Strait pilotage*, Marine Notice 7/2009 (17 April 2009).

120 *Navigation Act 2012*, supra note 15, s. 166(3), (4).

121 Roberts, supra note 84, 289.

8 *Ship Management*

Australia has adopted other measures to manage international shipping, in addition to the compulsory pilotage regime discussed above and other measures within PSSAs. These include areas in which shipping is monitored and traffic is separated. Navigational safety can be improved where coastal States monitor movements and alert ships to possible dangers to avoid collisions and groundings where vessels move beyond defined limits. While recognizing the freedom of navigation in the EEZ and the right of innocent passage in the territorial sea, it can be beneficial for masters of foreign ships to comply with systems in place, even in circumstances where their use is recommended rather than required. Australia's most sophisticated monitoring occurs in heavily-traffic nearshore areas.

The Navigation Act 2012 (Cth) contains broad powers to prescribe requirements for reports by foreign vessels that are entering or leaving Australian ports or are otherwise within Australia's territorial sea or EEZ.[122] The general reporting requirements for foreign vessels extend well beyond Australia's EEZ to the much larger area for which Australia has international responsibility for search and rescue. Operators of specified foreign vessels in this area, including oil and chemical tankers, vessels over 50 metres, and those towing or pushing other vessels, and those not voyaging to Australia, must report information to Australia via automatic identification system (AIS). Reports must include information about the vessel's identity, type, position, course, speed, navigational status any safety related information.[123]

Australia has established vessel traffic services (VTSs) under the *Navigation Act 2012* (Cth).[124] In designated areas, further information must be reported by foreign vessels.[125] A VTS is defined by the IMO as:

> a service…designed to improve the safety and efficiency of vessel traffic and to protect the environment. The service should have the capability to interact with the traffic and to respond to traffic situations developing in the VTS area.[126]

---

122 *Navigation Act 2012*, supra note 15, s. 222.

123 Marine Order 63 (Vessel Reporting Systems) 2015 (Cth), sch 3.

124 *Navigation Act 2012*, supra note 15, ss. 221, 340, 341, 339, 342. See also Marine Order 64 (Vessel Traffic Services) 2013 (Cth).

125 Such as last port of call, draught and cargo. See AMSA, *Great Barrier Reef and Torres Strait Vessel Traffic Service (Reef VTS): User Guide 2016*, 10 and *Navigation Act 2012* (Cth), s. 215.

126 IMO Doc. Assembly Resolution A.857(2), *Guidelines for vessel traffic services* (3 December 1997), annex 1.

Australia's VTS regimes can apply to foreign vessels, including recreational vessels, within Australia's ports, internal waters, territorial sea and EEZ.[127] They enable detailed monitoring of ships transiting VTS areas and communication with them about potential hazards, including other ships and weather conditions.

In 1997, Australia commenced operation of one of the world's earliest mandatory ship reporting systems. The Great Barrier Reef and Torres Strait Ship Reporting System (REEFREP) was established under the International Convention for the Safety of Life at Sea (SOLAS).[128] Further measures known as REEFVTS were introduced with IMO approval in 2004 following maritime incidents such as the 2000 grounding near Cairns of the Malaysian-flagged container ship *Bunga Teratai Satu*. REEFVTS operates 24 hours a day from the VTS Centre in Townsville in northern Queensland. The VTS system collects and analyses shipping information from ships' AIS, radar, automated position reports via Inmarsat C, and route plans provided by ship operators. The system was extended to the southern boundary of the Great Barrier Reef Marine Park following the 2010 grounding of *Shen Neng 1* (above). The REEFVTS monitors about 11,000 ship voyages annually in the Great Barrier Reef and Torres Strait and has been successful in reducing shipping incidents in the region.[129]

Various other measures have been adopted to enhance navigational safety. For example, under the Navigation Act 2012 (Cth) vessels are required to have appropriate nautical charts.[130] Further, "shipping areas," in which international shipping is confined, have been designated for much of the Great Barrier Reef region that lies outside compulsory pilotage areas.[131] Ship operators need a permit from the Great Barrier Reef Marine Park Authority to navigate outside the designated shipping area. A recommended traffic separation scheme has

127 *Navigation Act 2012*, supra note 15, s. 217.

128 Adopted on 1 November 1974, entered into force on 25 May 1980. REEFREP was formally adopted by the IMO's Maritime Safety Committee: IMO Doc. MSC Resolution 52(66), *Mandatory ship reporting systems* (30 May 1996); IMO Doc. MSC Resolution 161(78), *Amendments to the existing mandatory ship reporting system: The Torres Strait and Inner Route of the Great Barrier Reef* (17 May 2004); IMO Doc. MSC Resolution 315(88), *Amendments to the existing mandatory ship reporting system: In the Torres Strait region and the Inner Route of the Great Barrier Reef* (29 November 2010). See *Navigation Act 2012*, supra note 15, s. 218.

129 AMSA, *North-east shipping management plan* (2014) 55–56, available at <www.amsa.gov.au/navigation>.

130 *Navigation Act 2012*, supra note 15, s. 225.

131 *Great Barrier Reef Marine Park Act 1975*, supra note 98, s. 32A and *Great Barrier Reef Zoning Plan 2003* (Cth) 33.

been established in waters off south-west Australia,[132] following the adoption of traffic separation schemes in Bass Strait in south-east Australia.[133]

9 *Ballast Water*

Australia has faced numerous problems from foreign marine invasive species. One well known vector for such arrivals is ballast water exchange. The discharge of ballast water is the subject of the 2004 Ballast Water Convention.[134] Australia regulates ballast water management under the Biosecurity Act 2015 (Cth), which is intended to fulfil Australia's obligations under the Convention. Internationally sourced ballast water must be exchanged in deep waters outside the territorial sea prior to arrival in Australian ports or waters. There are various other legislative requirements for foreign vessels, such as having approved ballast water management methods and ballast water records.[135]

V Conclusion

Australia's challenges for regulating foreign vessel navigation are significant due to the vast size of its maritime jurisdiction, the large amount of international shipping in its waters, the existence of navigationally hazard and environmentally sensitive waters, and the existence of many offshore activities. It has sought to balance domestic concerns about marine incidents with respect for the rights foreign vessels enjoy under the international law of the sea. In some cases its measures have facilitated new interpretations of what may be permissible under the law of the sea, most notably with respect to compulsory pilotage in a strait used for international navigation, and how foreign vessel navigation can be regulated in EEZs under PSSAs for important environmental protection purposes. While contrary views remain about the international lawfulness of the Torres Strait compulsory pilotage regime, there appears to be universal acceptance of the benefits of pilotage in the area and successful use of it by international shipping. Australia's approach can be seen to have contributed to safer shipping in the region and it has been a pioneer in the development of new standards under the IMO regime.

---

132 AMSA, *New IMO-adopted Traffic Separation Schemes off the south-west coast of Australia*, Marine Notice 16/2016.

133 Commonwealth of Australia, *Annual Australian Notice to Mariners* (2015), 81.

134 International Convention for the Control and Management of Ships' Ballast Water and Sediments, IMO Doc BWM/Conf/36 (2004). Australia signed the Convention in 2005.

135 *Biosecurity Act 2015* (Cth), Ch 5. The Act entered into force on 16 June 2016.

CHAPTER 13

Regulating the Navigation of Foreign Vessels: New Zealand Practice

Karen N. Scott

1 Introduction

New Zealand's maritime zone, including its continental shelf beyond 200 nautical miles, comprises more than 5.7 million km^2 or 21 times the area of terrestrial New Zealand.[1] Geographically, New Zealand's maritime jurisdiction extends from the sub-Antarctic waters surrounding Campbell Island 640 km south of Bluff to the sub-tropical waters north of Raoul Island, 1000 km north of Cape Reinga.[2] Eighty percent of New Zealand's biodiversity is located within its marine environment.[3] Despite its relative isolation, New Zealand's marine environment is far from pristine. According to the Global Ocean Health Index,[4] in 2018, New Zealand ranked 23 out of 221 exclusive economic zones (EEZs)[5] with an overall score of 79 out of 100 above of the global average of 70.[6]

New Zealand is highly dependent on shipping for international trade although the 6200 vessels that commercially trade in New Zealand waters on an annual basis represent a fraction of those that ply the waters of the Northern Hemisphere,[7] and is significantly lower than the 28,000 ships that visit Australia every year.[8] Around 880 foreign flagged vessels visit New Zealand's ports

1 Source: Land Information New Zealand at <www.linz.govt.nz/about-linz/what-were-doing/projects/new-zealand-continental-shelf-project/map-continental-shelf>.

2 Dennis P. Gordon et al, "Marine Biodiversity of Aotearoa New Zealand" 5(8) *PLoS ONE* e10905, 1 (2010).

3 Ministry for the Environment, *Environment New Zealand 2007* (Ministry for the Environment, Wellington 2007), 316.

4 See <www.oceanhealthindex.org>. For the background to this project see B.S. Halpern, C. Longo, D. Hardy et al, "An index to assess the health and benefits of the global ocean," 488 *Nature* 615 (2012).

5 <www.oceanhealthindex.org/region-scores/scores/new-zealand>.

6 *Ibid.*

7 Maritime New Zealand, *New Zealand Coastal Navigation Safety Review* (2015), 42, at: <www.safety4sea.com/nz-coastal-navigation-safety-review/>.

8 *Ibid.*, at 44.

DOI:10.1163/9789004396272_014

TABLE 13.1 Principal Regulatory Instruments Managing Navigation and Activities of Foreign Vessels in New Zealand

Principal Regulatory Instruments Managing Navigation and Activities of Foreign Vessels in New Zealand		
1964	Continental Shelf Act	
1971	Marine Reserves Act	
1977	Territorial Sea, Contiguous Zone and Exclusive Economic Zone Act	
1987	New Zealand Nuclear Free Zone, Disarmament and Control Act	
1991	Resource Management Act	New Zealand Coastal Policy Statement 2010 Regional Coastal Plans
1991	Crown Minerals Act	
1991	Maritime Crimes Act	
1992	Ship Registration Act	
1993	Biosecurity Act	
1994	Maritime Transport Act	Maritime and Marine Protection Rules available at: http://www.maritimenz.govt.nz/rules/
1996	Customs and Excise Act	
1996	Fisheries Act	
1996	Submarine Cables and Pipelines Act	
1999	Maritime Crimes Act	
2004	Maritime Security Act	
2012	Exclusive Economic Zone and Continental Shelf (Environmental Effects) Act	

annually.[9] New Zealand's most significant modern maritime disaster occurred on 5 October 2011 when the *Rena*, a 236 tonne container ship registered in Liberia, struck the Astrolabe reef off the coast of Tauranga.[10] The *Rena* was

9 *Maritime New Zealand Annual Report 2015–2016*, 10.

10 Maritime New Zealand, *New Zealand Coastal Navigation Safety Review* (2015), supra note 7, at 37. See also Robert Makgill, Joanna Mossop and Karen N. Scott, "Liability and limits for the Rena pollution incident," *NZ Lawyer* 4 November 2011.

carrying 1733 tonnes of heavy fuel oil and 1368 containers.[11] Despite New Zealand's robust response to the casualty, 350 tonnes of oil and 86 containers were lost.[12] Less dramatically, between 1 July 2010 and 1 July 2015, 3,280 maritime incidents were notified to Maritime New Zealand although only 21 percent of these related to ocean-going foreign and New Zealand registered vessels.[13] Incidents ranged from minor oil spills, equipment failures, crew injuries, fires, collisions, groundings and, more recently, welfare issues.[14] It should be noted that recreational vessels represent the most significant collision hazard in New Zealand waters.[15] The risk factors for vessels operating in New Zealand's waters do not differ from those present elsewhere, comprising economic, financial and human factors.[16]

In light of these factors, it is unsurprising that the priorities for New Zealand's regulation of foreign (and national) vessels comprise: measures for the protection of the environment; measures designed to protect the commercial exploitation of living and, more recently, non-living resources; and measures to protect seafarers working in New Zealand waters. This chapter will outline the broad regulatory context for managing foreign vessels in New Zealand waters including the rules relating to the registration of vessels in New Zealand. The application of safety and environmental standards to foreign vessels, including requirements relating to the provision of information from vessels seeking to enter New Zealand ports or undertake activities within New Zealand's EEZ, is explored in Sections 4 and 5. Port state control, as the primary means of enforcing standards relating to the safety of navigation in New Zealand waters is addressed in Section 6. Rules relating to the passage of foreign vessels within New Zealand's maritime zones as well as their enforcement within these zones are examined in Sections 7 to 9, with concluding remarks in Section 10.

---

11 Maritime New Zealand, *New Zealand Coastal Navigation Safety Review* (2015), *ibid*, at 37.

12 *Ibid.* See further, Maritime Transport Investigation Commission, Inquiry 11–204: Container ship MV *Rena* grounding, on Astrolabe Reef, 5 October 2011 at: <www.taic.org.nz/ReportsandSafetyRecs/MarineReports/tabid/87/ctl/Detail/mid/484/InvNumber/2011-204/language/en-US/Default.aspx?SkinSrc=%5BG%5Dskins%2FtaicMarine%2Fskin_marine>.

13 Maritime New Zealand, *New Zealand Coastal Navigation Safety Review* (2015) supra note 10, at 68.

14 *Ibid.*, at 68 and 27.

15 *Ibid.*, at p. 47.

16 *Ibid.*, at pp. 21–36.

II The Regulatory Context for Managing Foreign Vessels in New Zealand Waters

New Zealand does not have a written constitution and while the 1840 Treaty of Waitangi is not formally part of New Zealand law, its principles must be given effect within the New Zealand legal system.[17] New Zealand ratified the 1982 United Nations Convention on the Law of the Sea (LOSC)[18] in 1996 and is a party to most of the major International Maritime Organisation (IMO) conventions. Most recently, New Zealand ratified the 2006 Maritime Labour Convention,[19] which entered into force for New Zealand on 9 March 2017.

The domestic regulatory framework for managing vessel navigation in New Zealand waters (and beyond, in respect of vessels registered in New Zealand) is comprised of at least 16 Acts of Parliament, subsidiary regulation (primarily under the 1994 Maritime Transport Act) as well as national and regional coastal plans. These legislative instruments are set out in Table 13.1. Maritime New Zealand has the principal role in managing navigation in New Zealand waters and in monitoring maritime safety through systems of inspection and audit.[20] In 2013 the 1994 Maritime Transport Act was amended to explicitly create powers for the Director of Maritime New Zealand to take action or control of foreign vessels in the event of a maritime emergency.[21] Other actors with responsibility for, or mandates associated with, the navigation of all vessels include regional and local councils, port operators and harbourmasters. The Ministry of Transport has overall responsibility for maritime policy and the Ministry of Primary Industries exercises responsibilities in respect of fishing vessels. The New Zealand Hydrographic Authority (based within Land Information New Zealand (LINZ)) provides charting and navigational services and the MetService provides national meteorological services including marine forecasts.

III Registration of Vessels in New Zealand

In contrast to many states New Zealand does not operate an open shipping registry. All New Zealand owned ships of more than 24 metres in length must

17 Derek Nolan (ed.), *Environmental & Resource Management Law* 59 (4th ed. 2011).
18 United Nations Convention on the Law of the Sea (1982 LOSC), art. 2, in force 16 November 1994, 1833 *U.N.T.S.* 397.
19 Maritime Labour Convention, in force 20 August 2013, 46 *I.L.M.* 792 (2006).
20 This role was confirmed in the 2013 amendments to the 2004 Maritime Transport Act.
21 1994 Maritime Transport Act, Section 248.

be registered in Part A of the New Zealand Register of Ships[22] with the exception of pleasure vessels, vessels operating solely on inland waters and barges that do not proceed beyond New Zealand coastal waters.[23] Those vessels not subject to compulsory registration by virtue of Section 6(1) of the 1992 Ship Registration Act may voluntarily register using Part B of the Register under Section 8 of the 1992 Act. Similarly, foreign vessels (other than pleasure vessels) on demise charter to New Zealand based operators (and not registered in a foreign jurisdiction) may also be registered under Section 8 of the 1992 Act.[24] A New Zealand owned ship operated by a foreign national under a demise charter and registered in a foreign register is exempt from registration in the New Zealand Register if approved by the Director of Maritime New Zealand.[25] For the purposes of the 1992 Act a "New Zealand vessel" is owned or majority owned by New Zealand nationals.[26] Ships jointly owned in equal proportions by New Zealand nationals and New Zealand permanent residents or majority owned by New Zealand permanent residents may be registered in Part B of the New Zealand Register of Ships.[27] Foreign registered ships may not be registered under the 1992 Ship Registration Act.[28] New Zealand exercises flag state jurisdiction over New Zealand registered vessels irrespective of where they are operating.[29] The extra-territorial effect of New Zealand domestic law in respect of New Zealand registered vessels, in particular, the 1994 Maritime Transport Act, has been recently confirmed in the New Zealand courts[30] and by subsequent legislative amendment.[31]

In an important recent initiative New Zealand has sought to extend control over health and safety and broader welfare issues of seafarers operating on fishing vessels within New Zealand's EEZ through its system of vessel registration. A series of high profile incidents involving allegations of inadequate living conditions, non-payment of wages, insufficient rest days, assault and sexual abuse on foreign flagged fishing vessels authorised to fish in New

22 Established under Section 65 of the 1992 Ship Registration Act.
23 1992 Ship Registration Act, Section 6.
24 *Ibid.*, Section 8(1)(b).
25 *Ibid.*, Section 6(3).
26 *Ibid.*, Section 3.
27 *Ibid.*, Section 8(2)(ba) and (c).
28 *Ibid.*, Section 9.
29 LOSC, supra note 18, art. 94.
30 *Maritime New Zealand v. Page* [2013] D.C.R. 102 and *Teddy v. Police* [2014] N.Z.C.A. 422.
31 1994 Maritime Transport Act, Section 4(4) (inserted by Section 5 of the Maritime Transport Amendment Act 2013).

Zealand's EEZ over the last decade has caused significant public concern.[32] Commonly involving South Korean operated vessels and Indonesian seafarers, the most notorious incident occurred in October 2010 when the *Oyang 70* sank with the loss of six lives. Surviving crew-members reported conditions on board amounting to modern day-slavery.[33] The ability to exercise national control over working conditions on foreign flagged vessels through port state jurisdiction is limited[34] and was particularly challenging for New Zealand prior to its decision to ratify the 2006 Maritime Labour Convention.[35] Although coastal states may impose licence conditions on foreign nationals fishing in their EEZs under Article 62(4) of the 1982 LOSC, the conditions listed in the Convention do not specify working conditions on board the vessel. Whilst the list is clearly intended to be non-exhaustive,[36] it is equivocal as to whether a licence to fish can impose standards relating to working conditions on foreign vessels in respect of foreign nationals. New Zealand amended the 1996 Fisheries Act in 2014 so that licences to fish in its EEZ can be awarded only to New Zealand registered ships.[37] This rule came into effect in May 2016 and requires New Zealand standards with respect to health, safety and welfare to be applied to all fishing vessels operating in its EEZ by virtue of flag state jurisdiction. The consequence of this amendment is that subject to one very limited exception, in respect of research fishing vessels, after May 2016 no foreign vessel can be licenced to fish in New Zealand waters.

---

32 For an overview of these incidents see Thomas Harré, "Confronting the Challenge of Human Trafficking for Forced Labour in the Pacific: Some Thoughts from New Zealand," 10 *New Zealand Yearbook of International Law* 173, 174–175 (2012) and Christina Stringer, Glenn Simmons and Daren Coulston, "Not in New Zealand's waters, surely? Labour and human rights abuses aboard foreign fishing vessels," (New Zealand Asia Institute Working Paper Series No. 11-01 (2011).

33 See Michael Field, "Every Man for Himself as Ship Sank" 8 March 2013 at: <www.stuff.co.nz/national/8399987/Every-man-for-himself-as-ship-sank>.

34 See generally, Laura Carballo Piñeiro, "Port State Jurisdiction over Labour Conditions: A Private International Law Perspective on Extra-territoriality," 31 *International Journal of Marine and Coastal Law* 531 (2016).

35 2006 Maritime Labour Convention, supra note 19. New Zealand amended relevant Maritime Rules in 2015 to permit the full implementation of the Convention in New Zealand. See Maritime Rules Part 51: Crew Accommodation <www.maritimenz.govt.nz/rules/part-51/Part51-maritime-rule.pdf>; and Maritime Rules Part 52: Maritime Labour Convention, at <www.maritimenz.govt.nz/rules/part-52/Part52-maritime-rule.pdf>.

36 LOSC, supra note 18, art. 62(4) states that "[t]hese laws and regulations shall be consistent with this Convention and may relate, *inter alia*, to the following:"

37 1996 Fisheries Act, Section 103. A very narrow exception to this requirement is permitted with respect to fisheries research vessels (Section 103A).

IV Regulating Foreign Vessels in New Zealand Waters

New Zealand exercises its right under Articles 21 and 211(5) of the 1982 LOSC to apply internationally accepted standards to foreign vessels exercising rights of passage within its territorial sea and navigation within its EEZ. The Minister is granted a wide discretion to prescribe maritime standards under the 1994 Maritime Transport Act,[38] but the Act stipulates that "maritime rules and emergency maritime rules shall not be inconsistent with international standards relating to maritime safety, and the health and welfare of seafarers, to the extent adopted by New Zealand."[39] This rule was confirmed by the New Zealand Court of Appeal in 1998 in *Sellers v. Maritime Safety Inspector*[40] where the imposition of a domestic requirement on a foreign pleasure craft leaving a New Zealand port was characterised as having extra-territorial effect and compromised the vessel's freedom of navigation.[41] Thus foreign vessels (as well as New Zealand registered vessels) must meet construction, equipment, manning and operational standards as set out in the major IMO conventions including (but not limited to): the 1973/78 International Convention for the Prevention of Pollution from Ships as Modified by the Protocol of 1978 relating thereto (MARPOL);[42] the 1974 International Convention for the Safety of Life at Sea (SOLAS);[43] the 1978 International Convention on Standards of Training, Certification and Watchkeeping for Seafarers (as revised) (STCW);[44] and the 2004 International Convention for the Control and Management of Ships' Ballast Water and Sediments.[45] These international standards (and provisions for their enforcement) are implemented domestically in New Zealand through a number of statutes including the 1994 Maritime Transport Act (and the Maritime and Marine Protection Rules), the 1993 Biosecurity Act and the 2004 Maritime Security Act. Foreign vessels operating in New Zealand waters must carry international or equivalent maritime documents as set out in the

38 1994 Maritime Transport Act, Section 36.

39 *Ibid.*, Section 39(1).

40 *Sellers v. Maritime Safety Inspector* [1999] 2 *N.Z.L.R.* 44 (CA).

41 The application of *Sellers v. Maritime Safety Inspector* to port state jurisdiction and control is discussed below.

42 International Convention for the Prevention of Pollution from Ships as Modified by the Protocol of 1978 relating thereto, in force 2 October 1983, 1340 *U.N.T.S.* 62.

43 International Convention for the Safety of Life at Sea, in force 25 May 1980, 1184 *U.N.T.S.* 278.

44 International Convention on Standards of Training, Certification and Watchkeeping for Seafarers, in force 28 April 1984, 1361 *U.N.T.S.* 190 (as revised).

45 International Convention for the Control and Management of Ships' Ballast Water and Sediments (due to enter into force on 8 September 2017) IMO Doc BWM/Conf/36 (2004).

Maritime and Marine Protection Rules adopted pursuant to the 1994 Maritime Transport Act.[46]

The 1994 Maritime Transport Act prohibits the discharge of harmful substances from vessels within New Zealand's EEZ[47] and implements the detail of the regulation through the Marine Protection Rules.[48] The transfer of oil or noxious substances are also prohibited in New Zealand waters unless notice is given by the Master or ship owner to the Director of Maritime New Zealand or the relevant regional council that the transfer accords with relevant maritime rules.[49] The Act imposes rules on foreign vessels relating to reporting or responding to discharges[50] and provides for measures to be taken by Maritime New Zealand in the event of an incident,[51] including taking control of a foreign vessel where it is deemed "hazardous."[52] These powers are consistent with New Zealand's rights under international law to take measures to respond to actual or threatened damage to its coastline or related interest as set out in Article 221 of the 1982 LOSC. Unsurprisingly, in light of New Zealand's strict approach to biosecurity with respect to its terrestrial territory, ballast water may only be discharged into New Zealand's waters where it has been exchanged with mid-ocean seawater en route to New Zealand at least 200 nautical miles from land or where it is fresh water or where it has been treated.[53] Moreover, from 2018, vessels arriving in New Zealand (defined as anchoring, berthing or entering a port) must have a "clean hull" as defined in the Craft Risk Management Standard: Biofouling on Vessels Arriving to New Zealand.[54]

V Information Requirements Relating to Foreign Vessels Arriving at New Zealand Ports or Entering New Zealand Waters

Globally, over the last decade vessels are required to provide increasing amounts of information to coastal and port states en route to a port or even

46 1994 Maritime Transport Act, Section 34.

47 *Ibid.*, Section 226.

48 These are set out at: <www.maritimenz.govt.nz/rules/>.

49 1994 Maritime Transport Act, Section 230.

50 *Ibid.*, Sections 227–228.

51 *Ibid.*, Sections 233–236.

52 *Ibid.*, Section 248.

53 Import Health Standard, *Ballast Water from all Countries* (issued 17 May 2016) at: <www.mpi.govt.nz/law-and-policy/requirements/import-health-standards/>. The Import Health Standard was issued pursuant to Section 24 of the 1993 Biosecurity Act.

54 Issued on 15 May 2014 at: <www.mpi.govt.nz/importing/border-clearance/vessels/biofouling-management/>.

when traversing a coastal state's maritime zones.[55] All vessels en route to New Zealand ports must provide information relating to their intended port of entry, crew and passengers, cargo and ballast water designation form 48 hours prior to arrival under Section 21 of the 1996 Customs and Excise Act. Pursuant to its international obligations with respect to maritime security, New Zealand also requires vessels to provide information on whether they are carrying an approved international ship security certificate, confirm the security level at which the vessel is operating and the security level at which the vessel operated at during its last port of call.[56] Vessels must also provide information on whether they are carrying oil or hazardous and noxious cargo.[57] A more unusual requirement is set out in Sections 17, 162AF and 162AG of the 1993 Biosecurity Act whereby vessels "arriving" into New Zealand's EEZ must give notice prior to arrival and information on their approximate intended location. "Arrival" for the purposes of this part of the Act means "to anchor in, berth in, or operate in the EEZ for the purpose of exploring or exploiting resources in the EEZ, or in preparation or support for such a purpose, after a voyage originating beyond the outer limits of the EEZ."[58] Nonetheless, the Biosecurity Act stipulates that powers and requirements under the Act must be interpreted in a manner that is consistent with the right of innocent passage within the territorial sea[59] and the freedom of navigation within New Zealand's EEZ.[60]

VI Port State Jurisdiction and Control

The exercise of port state jurisdiction and control over foreign vessels has emerged as the principal tool to support the exercise of flag state jurisdiction in enforcing international rules relating to safety of navigation, marine pollution and, increasingly, fisheries.[61] New Zealand exercises its jurisdiction – both prescriptive and enforcement – as a port state over foreign vessels in relation

55 See generally, Bevan Marten, *Port State Jurisdiction over Vessel Information: Territoriality, Extra-territoriality and the Future of Shipping Regulation* 31 *International Journal of Marine and Coastal Law* 470 (2016).

56 2004 Maritime Security Act, Section 30.

57 1994 Maritime Transport Act, Section 229.

58 1993 Biosecurity Act, Section 162AA.

59 *Ibid.*, Section 4.

60 *Ibid.*, Section 162AB.

61 See generally, Sophia Kopela, "Port-State Jurisdiction, Extraterritoriality, and the Protection of the Global Commons," 47 *Ocean Development and International Law* 89 (2016); Erik J. Molenaar, "Port and Coastal States," 280 in *The Oxford Handbook of The Law of the Sea* (Donald R. Rothwell, Alex G Oude Elferink, Karen N. Scott and Tim Stephens eds., 2015);

to: safety of navigation and prevention of pollution under the 1994 Maritime Transport Act and 1993 Biosecurity Act; maritime security under the 2004 Maritime Security Act and the 1991 Maritime Crimes Act; and fisheries under the 1996 Fisheries Act. All Acts provide New Zealand with rights of inspection, detention, expulsion from port and the initiation of enforcement proceedings. Under the 2004 Maritime Security Act an exclusion zone around a vessel may be declared, which may include restrictions on access or exit.[62] New Zealand participates in the 1993 Memoranda of Understanding on Port State Control in the Asia Pacific Region (Tokyo MOU)[63] and contributes data from its inspections to the Asia Pacific Computerized Information System (APCIS) database.[64] New Zealand also collaborates closely with Australia with respect to port state control inspections and the training of inspectors.[65]

As noted above, New Zealand has taken a conservative approach to prescribing domestic standards for foreign vessels as a port state where those standards may have an extra-territorial effect. In *Sellers v. Maritime Safety Inspector*[66] Mr Sellers, the owner and operator of a foreign registered pleasure craft left New Zealand without a radio and emergency locator beacon as prescribed by the (then) Director of Maritime Safety under domestic law. Mr Sellers argued that as there was no requirement under international law for pleasure craft to carry a radio and emergency locator beacon that New Zealand's action against the vessel compromised the principle of the freedom of navigation on the high seas. The Court of Appeal agreed:

> Our conclusion on the relevant rules of international law is, accordingly, that a port state has no general power to unilaterally impose its own requirements on foreign ships relating to their construction, their safety and other equipment and their crewing if the requirements are to have effect on the high seas. Any requirements cannot go beyond those generally accepted, especially in the maritime conventions and regulations; we were referred to no generally accepted requirements relating to the equipment particularly in issue in this case so far as pleasure craft were concerned.[67]

Judith Swan, "Port State Measures – from Residual Port State Jurisdiction to Global Standards," 31 *International Journal of Marine and Coastal Law* 395 (2016).

62 2004 Maritime Security Act, Sections 59 and 61.

63 The text of the Tokyo MOU is available at: <www.tokyo-mou.org>.

64 Maritime New Zealand, *New Zealand Coastal Navigation Safety Review* (2015), supra note 7, at 55.

65 *Ibid.*, at 57.

66 *Sellers v. Maritime Safety Inspector*, supra note 40.

67 *Ibid.*, at 57.

Although the decision in *Sellers* has been confirmed by the New Zealand courts,[68] it has been subject to trenchant academic criticism. In particular, Molenaar writes:

> It is submitted that the New Zealand decision is flawed. The Court appears to have: misinterpreted Article 211(3) of the LOS Convention, failed to discuss the absence of a right of access to ports under general international law and Article 25(2) of the LOS Convention, incorrectly linking the notion of "generally accepted" to port state jurisdiction, misinterpreted the function of regional merchant shipping PSC regimes, and failed to refer to the savings clauses therein.[69]

Similarly, Marten argues that New Zealand could have applied its domestic requirements to Seller's foreign registered boat on the basis that the "vessel was within New Zealand's territory, and subject to New Zealand laws."[70] Churchill reaches a similar conclusion suggesting that the New Zealand Court of Appeal:

> was wrong to suggest that a State cannot legislate in respect of CDEM [construction, design, equipment and management] standards for foreign ships calling at its ports, even though such requirements will also unavoidably have to be complied with on the high seas before and after visiting the port, in other words, that there is an exercise of extraterritorial jurisdiction.[71]

These criticisms of the *Sellers* case arguably go too far and overlook a key feature of the domestic requirement as set out in the (then) Section 21 of the 1994 Maritime Transport Act. Namely, that the requirement was applied only to pleasure craft departing New Zealand ports. It was not framed as being a

---

68 *Teddy v. Police* [2014] N.Z.C.A. 422 and *Maritime New Zealand v. Page* [2013] DC 102. It has also been welcomed by academic commentators. See J.S. Davidson, "Freedom of Navigation on the High Seas: Sellers v. Maritime Safety Inspector," 14 *International Journal of Marine and Coastal Law* 435 (1999) and D. Devine, "Port State Jurisdiction: A Judicial Contribution from New Zealand," 24 *Marine Policy* 215 (2000).

69 Erik Jaap Molenaar, "Port State Jurisdiction: Toward Comprehensive, Mandatory and Global Coverage," 38 *Ocean Development & International Law* 225, 322 (footnotes omitted) (2007).

70 Bevan Marten, "Port State Jurisdiction in New Zealand: The Problem with Sellers," 44 *Victoria University of Wellington Law Review* 559, 566 (2013).

71 Robin Churchill, "Port State Jurisdiction Relating to the Safety of Shipping and Pollution from Ships – What Degree of Extra-territoriality?," 31 *International Journal of Marine and Coastal Law* 442, 454 (2016).

condition of entry into port.[72] Articles 211(3) and 25(2) of the LOSC cited by Molenaar both permit states to stipulate conditions relating to entry into port, and this is consistent with and supports the absence of a customary right of entry of vessels into ports. The distinction between entry into and exit from a port is important. A state can legitimately prevent a vessel from entering a port where that vessel fails to meet domestic conditions of entry and such action is consistent with its rights and obligations as a port state under international law.[73] Preventing a vessel from exiting a port on the basis of domestic (as opposed to international rules) on the other hand, risks breaching that vessel's right to innocent passage and freedom of navigation and potentially puts the port state in breach of international law. The Court of Appeal in *Sellers* expressly did not deal with whether New Zealand had a right to impose conditions of entry to port and confined its analysis to the legality of setting conditions relating to exiting a port and the extra-territorial implications of exercising such a right. The decision in *Sellers*, therefore, does not support the position that New Zealand cannot impose standards and requirements that differ from international standards and requirements as a condition of entry into its ports. The right of port states to set entry requirements for their port, and to apply and enforce those standards as a consequence of port state jurisdiction is consistent with the prevailing interpretation of both the 1982 LOSC and customary international law.[74] This is the case even where setting such requirements may in practice have an extra-territorial effect on the high seas in circumstances where requirements (such as double hull) cannot be easily abandoned on leaving a port.

VII Regulating Passage of Foreign Vessels in New Zealand Internal Waters: Nuclear Ships

In 1987 the New Zealand Nuclear Free Zone was established, encompassing all land, internal waters, territorial sea and sovereign airspace within New Zealand.[75] Nuclear powered ships are not permitted to enter New Zealand's

72 *Sellers v. Maritime Safety Inspector*, supra note 40, at p. 49.

73 Preventing a vessel entering a port may nevertheless be a potential breach of bilateral treaties of friendship between states or possibly even trade rules under the World Trade Organization (WTO) although the latter is unlikely unless the condition of entry is applied on a discriminatory basis between states.

74 As supported by Molenaar, supra note 69; Marten, supra note 70; and Churchill, supra note 71.

75 1987 New Zealand Nuclear Free Zone, Disarmament and Arms Control Act, Section 4.

internal waters (including ports)[76] and warships may only be granted entry into internal waters if the Prime Minister of New Zealand is satisfied that it is not carrying any nuclear explosive device upon entry into internal waters.[77] In making such a decision the Prime Minister "shall have regard to all relevant information and advice that may be available… including information and advice concerning the strategic and security interests of New Zealand."[78] Section 12 of the 1987 Act confirms that its provisions are not to be interpreted to limit the freedom of innocent passage through New Zealand's territorial sea or transit passage through or over any strait or to limit rights relating to ships or aircraft in distress provided those rights are exercised in accordance with international law.[79] The provisions of the 1987 Act accord with New Zealand's right to manage vessel movements within its internal waters. Foreign vessels have no right of innocent passage within internal waters under customary international law. Nevertheless, New Zealand's robust anti-nuclear stance has, until recently, strained relations with the United States, particularly in respect of military cooperation. For over three decades no U.S. warship has visited a New Zealand port owing to the U.S. refusal to confirm or deny whether its naval vessels carry nuclear explosive devices.[80] However, in November 2016, in commemoration of the 75th anniversary of the New Zealand Navy, the USS *Sampson* entered Port Auckland, following due diligence carried out by the Prime Minister's Office establishing that the vessel was neither nuclear propelled nor carrying nuclear explosive devices.[81]

---

76 *Ibid.*, Section 11. Internal waters are defined as "any areas of the sea that are on the landward side of the baseline of the territorial sea of New Zealand" by Section 4 of the Territorial Sea, Contiguous Zone and Exclusive Economic Zone Act 1977.

77 *Ibid.*, Section 9(2).

78 *Ibid.*, Section 9(1).

79 In 2002 the New Zealand Nuclear Free Zone Extension Bill was put forward to amend the 1987 Act to prohibit the passage of nuclear powered vessels through New Zealand's territorial sea. It was defeated on the basis that such a restriction would be contrary to the rights of innocent passage of all vessels under the law of the sea. See the Parliamentary Debate on the issue from 29 May 2002 archived on New Zealand Hansard at: <www.vdig.net/hansard/archive.jsp?y=2002&m=05&d=29&o=4&p=4>.

80 See Vernon Small, "US-New Zealand relations shipshape again," *The Press*, July 23, 2016, at A11.

81 See "US Navy destroyer cleared to visit New Zealand" 18 October 2016 available at: <www.radionz.co.nz/news/political/315935/us-navy-destroyer-cleared-to-visit-nz>. In the event the USS *Sampson* was diverted from Port Auckland to Kaikoura in order to assist in providing relief following the 7.8 Kaikoura earthquake on 14 November 2016.

VIII Regulating Passage of Foreign Vessels in New Zealand's Territorial Sea and EEZ

Owing to the low volume of traffic operating in and around New Zealand there are relatively few restrictions in the New Zealand laws on the navigation of foreign vessels within its territorial sea and EEZ. In 1993 New Zealand adopted the Voluntary Code for Vessels Carrying Oil and Other Harmful Liquid Substances[82] recommending that oil and chemical tankers navigate at least five nautical miles from land, islands and hazards except when entering port. A 2015 review into the safety of navigation in New Zealand found that, notwithstanding its voluntary status, the Code is generally well complied with by both foreign and New Zealand registered vessels.[83] Although there is no formal system of ship routing in New Zealand, Admiralty Sailing Directions provide information on routing directions for entry into ports[84] and, under the 1991 Resource Management Act, regional authorities can require sensitive areas to be avoided or provide for compulsory pilotage. Such measures may not, however, impede the right of innocent passage through the territorial sea. Vessel passage is not restricted through New Zealand's marine reserves[85] although specific activities such as fishing or recreational activities may be prohibited.[86] Some restrictions on anchoring are provided for under the 1996 Submarine Cables and Pipelines Act.[87]

New Zealand has designated two areas to be avoided and one precautionary area within its maritime zone. Three Kings Island was designated an Area to be Avoided by vessels over 500gt in 1995 in conjunction with the IMO.[88]

82 The Code was revised in 1996 and 2001. See: <www.maritimenz.govt.nz/commercial/environment/operators/ship-routeing.asp#ship_routeing>.

83 Maritime New Zealand, *New Zealand Coastal Navigation Safety Review* (2015) supra note 7, at 58.

84 Information on the New Zealand Nautical Almanac can be found at: <www.linz.govt.nz/sea/nautical-information/new-zealand-nautical-almanac-nz-204>.

85 1971 Marine Reserves Act, Section 23.

86 The 1971 Marine Reserves Act and marine protected areas more generally are slated for reform in New Zealand. The proposed reforms however, are unlikely to impact significantly on the right of innocent passage of foreign vessels. See Ministry for the Environment, *A New Marine Protected Areas Act: Consultation Document* (2016) available at <www.mfe.govt.nz> and Karen N. Scott, "Evolving MPA Management in New Zealand: Between Principle and Pragmatism," 47(3) *Ocean Development and International Law* 289 (2016).

87 1996 Submarine Cables and Pipelines Act, Sections 12 and 13.

88 Marine Protection Rules Part 190: Mandatory Ship Routing available at: <www.maritimenz.govt.nz/rules/part-190/Part190-marine-protection-rule.pdf>.

However, the area is not actively monitored by Maritime New Zealand.[89] The Poor Knights Islands were designated an Area to be Avoided by the IMO and New Zealand in 2004 and restrictions apply to vessels of more than 45 metres in length.[90] In contrast to Three Kings Island the Poor Knights Islands Area to be Avoided is actively monitored and it is estimated that about three vessels a month are required to leave the area.[91] Finally, the Taranaki Precautionary Area was declared in 2007 in order to protect oil production activities taking place therein. Vessels are required to navigate with particular caution in the Area[92] although this Area is also not actively monitored.[93] The 2015 Coastal Navigation Safety Review concluded that notwithstanding the lack of monitoring in two of the three areas specially designated the measures are all largely complied with by foreign and New Zealand registered vessels.[94] The Review recommended however, that three other areas in New Zealand would benefit from more active management.[95] First, the Hauraki Gulf, which is the location of New Zealand's busiest port (and city), Auckland, in addition to a large number of recreational vessels. The Gulf is environmentally vulnerable and provides ecosystem support for a number of important species including a population of Brydes whales.[96] Second, Cook Strait, which has the highest volume of vessel traffic in New Zealand including passenger vessels and is particularly vulnerable to unpredictable weather conditions.[97] Finally, Foveaux Strait, which separates the South Island from Stewart Island, and is a complex maritime environment owing to challenging weather and Sea conditions.[98]

Consistent with its rights under international law,[99] New Zealand reserves the right to establish safety zones of up to 500 metres around installations or devices on its continental shelf.[100] The term "device" is defined in Section 7(5) of the 1964 Continental Shelf Act as "any ship or floating platform or aircraft

89 Maritime New Zealand, *New Zealand Coastal Navigation Safety Review* (2015) supra note 7, at 51.
90 Marine Protection Rules Part 190, supra note 88.
91 Maritime New Zealand, *New Zealand Coastal Navigation Safety Review* (2015) supra note 7, at 50.
92 Marine Protection Rules Part 190, supra note 88.
93 Maritime New Zealand, *New Zealand Coastal Navigation Safety Review* (2015) supra note 7, at 50.
94 *Ibid.*, at 42.
95 *Ibid.*, at 52–54.
96 *Ibid.*, at 52.
97 *Ibid.*, at 53.
98 *Ibid.*, at 54.
99 LOSC, supra note 18, arts. 60(4)-(6) and 80.
100 1964 Continental Shelf Act, Section 8.

that is used in connection with any installation or device." Ships may be prevented from entering established safety zones[101] and New Zealand has established six such safety zones to date.[102]

In response to public disquiet over oil exploration activities and protest action interfering with survey activities at sea,[103] New Zealand adopted amendments to the 1991 Crown Minerals Act in 2013 creating new offences of intentionally damaging or interfering with a structure or a vessel involved in minerals operations[104] or entering, without reasonable excuse, a non-interference zone surrounding a structure or a vessel involved in mining operations.[105] Notably, in prosecuting for the offence of entering without reasonable cause a non-interference zone, it is not necessary to prove that the person intended to commit the offence.[106] It is therefore possible that a person may be prosecuted for inadvertently entering an interference zone unless it is determined that the lack of knowledge of the existence of the zone amounts to "reasonable cause." Powers to enforce these rules are provided for under Section 101C of the 1991 Crown Minerals Act and permit an authorised enforcement officer to stop a vessel from entering a zone, board a vessel, give directions to a Master of a vessel and make an arrest. These offences and powers of enforcement apply to foreign vessels as well as New Zealand registered vessels within New Zealand's territorial sea and EEZ but proceedings may only be brought against persons on foreign registered ships with the consent of the New Zealand Attorney General.[107]

To the extent that the 2013 amendments provide for the creation of exclusion zones and associated offences around vessels (as opposed to structures) they arguably represent an expansion of coastal state rights as traditionally

101 *Ibid.*, Section 8(1)(e).

102 Continental Shelf (Maui A Safety Zone) Regulations 1975; Continental Shelf (Maui B Safety Zone) Regulations 1991; Continental Shelf (Pohokura B Safety Zone) Regulations 2006; Continental Shelf (Kupe Safety Zone) Regulations 2006; Continental Shelf (Umuroa Installation Safety Zone) Regulations 2008; and Continental Shelf (Maari Development Safety Zones) Regulations 2008.

103 One protest at sea resulted in legal action taken against protestors under the 1994 Maritime Transport Act, where the New Zealand Court of Appeal confirmed that the 1994 Act had extraterritorial effect and was applicable to activities beyond 12 nautical miles. See *Teddy v. Police* [2014] N.Z.C.A. 422. The 1994 Maritime Transport Act was subsequently amended to clearly reflect its extraterritorial impact with respect to New Zealand registered vessels.

104 1991 Crown Minerals Act, Section 101B(1).

105 *Ibid.*, Section 101B(2).

106 *Ibid.*, Section 101B(3).

107 *Ibid.*, Section 101B(9).

recognised in international law. Article 60 of the 1982 LOSC, which permits the establishment of safety zones, relates to artificial islands, installations and structures but is silent on the whether such zones may be established around vessels associated with the exploitation of the non-living resources of the EEZ and continental shelf. However, there appears to be no rule expressly prohibiting the creation of safety zones around survey and other vessels and, applying the so-called *Lotus* principle,[108] the absence of such a prohibition may in fact create a permission under international law.[109] Support for this conclusion was arguably provided by the LOSC Annex VII Tribunal in the 2014 *Arctic Sunrise Arbitration* between The Netherlands and the Russian Federation in relation to a dispute over protest activities on and around Russian oil installations.[110] Although the dispute in the case focused on safety zones and offences associated with an installation rather than a vessel, the Tribunal nevertheless confirmed that coastal states have a more general right to take measures to prevent interference with, and enforcement action relating to, the protection of its sovereign rights to exploit the non-living resources of its EEZ and continental Shelf.[111] Although the Tribunal refused to be drawn on the scope of this right[112] – which appears to flow from the existence of a coastal state's sovereign rights rather than any specific provision of the law of the sea[113] – it would arguably extend to measures associated with and enforcement action against vessels interfering with the activities of survey or other vessels exploring for or exploiting non-living resources.[114] Moreover, this conclusion concurs with emerging state practice. Safety or non-interference zones have been declared

108 *Lotus*, Judgment No. 9, 1927 *P.C.I.J.* Ser. A. No. 10.

109 This controversial proposition was effectively relied upon to justify the lawfulness of a unilateral declaration of independence by the International Court of Justice in *Accordance with International Law of the Unilateral Declaration of Independence in Respect of Kosovo, Advisory Opinion, I.C.J. Reports 2010*, p. 403 and to suggest (obiter) that an arrest warrant could be issued in respect of a crime subject to universal jurisdiction under customary law in circumstances where the subject of the warrant is outside of the jurisdiction of the authorities issuing the warrant in *Arrest Warrant of 11 April 2000 (Democratic Republic of the Congo v. Belgium), Judgment, I.C.J. Reports 2002*, p. 3.

110 In the Matter of the *Arctic Sunrise* Arbitration before An Arbitral Tribunal Constituted under Annex VII to the 1982 United Nations Convention on the Law of the Sea between *The Kingdom of the Netherlands and the Russian Federation* (Merits) (14 August 2015) (hereinafter referred to as the *Arctic Sunrise Arbitration* (Merits) PCA Case No 2014-02. See Joanna Mossop, "Protests Against Oil Exploration at Sea: Lessons from the Arctic Sunrise Arbitration," 31 *International Journal of Marine and Coastal Law* 60 (2016).

111 *Arctic Sunrise Arbitration* (Merits), supra note 110, paras. 284 and 324.

112 *Ibid.*, at para. 284.

113 Mossop, supra note 110, at 80.

114 *Ibid.*, at 85.

around survey and other vessels associated with minerals exploitation by the United States, Canada and South Africa in addition to New Zealand.[115]

Nevertheless, the Tribunal in the *Arctic Sunrise Arbitration* also acknowledged the right to reasonable protest at sea related to the freedom of navigation.[116] This suggests that the interest of protestors and the interests of coastal states need to be balanced and, as Mossop concludes, "some level of interference may need to be tolerated."[117] Moreover, the Tribunal adopted a relatively conservative approach to the rights of the coastal state to enforce breaches of safety zones, noting that there is no general right to board a vessel for such breach within the EEZ unless the coastal state is exercising the right of hot pursuit or has the permission of the flag state.[118] Therefore, while the expansion of non-interference zones and associated offences would appear to be a legitimate extension of New Zealand's rights as a coastal state under the law of the sea, care will need to be taken when enforcing those rights against foreign vessels. In particular, it would appear that the enforcement rights set out in Section 101C of the 1991 Crown Minerals Act are limited to those being taken against vessels in actual breach of the non-interference zone or against vessels subject to a legitimate hot pursuit according to the terms of Article 111 of the 1982 LOSC. In practice, this may limit the practical enforcement of these new offences against foreign vessels protesting in New Zealand waters.

Finally, the 1994 Maritime Transport Act and the 2004 Maritime Security Act do not apply to foreign warships or foreign government owned ships on non-commercial service.[119] New Zealand does not impose special conditions or requirements on the innocent passage of foreign military vessels through its territorial sea or EEZ. The relaxed New Zealand approach to foreign naval vessels was illustrated in February 2016 when the Australian frigate *HMS Warramunga* was identified as speeding in breach of regional regulations in the Marlborough Sounds. Despite twelve complaints and damage to a wharf, the Harbour Master confirmed that the *HMAS Warramunga* was not obliged to abide by the local speed limit on the basis of its sovereign immunity.[120]

115 See *ibid.*, at 77 and 79.

116 *Arctic Sunrise Arbitration* (Merits), supra note 110, para. 227.

117 Mossop, supra note 110, at 80.

118 *Arctic Sunrise Arbitration* (Merits), supra note 110, para. 244.

119 1994 Maritime Transport Act, Section 4 and 2004 Maritime Security Act, Section 4.

120 Jennifer Eder and Oliver Lewis, "Australian Frigate HMAS Warramunga reported speeding in Marlborough Sounds," February 24 2016 at: <www.stuff.co.nz/national/77229322/Australian-frigate-HMAS-Warramunga-reported-speeding-in-Marlborough-Sounds>. A state can nevertheless demand that a warship leave its territorial sea immediately pursuant to its rights under LOSC, supra note 18, art. 30.

IX The Ross Dependency

In order to ensure consistency with its legal and diplomatic commitments under the 1959 Antarctic Treaty,[121] New Zealand does not in practice exercise port or coastal state jurisdiction over foreign vessels operating in the Ross Sea region. It does support the efforts of the Commission established under the 1980 Convention for the Conservation of Antarctic Marine Living Resources (CCAMLR)[122] to ensure compliance with the Convention through the scheme of national and international inspection established under the Convention and through metropolitan port state control. As a gateway Antarctic state New Zealand will also have an important role to play ensuring that vessels leaving its ports for the Antarctic comply with the International Code for Ships Operating in Polar Waters (Polar Code).[123]

X Concluding Remarks

In contrast to other regions, New Zealand benefits from relative geographic isolation and a low level of vessel traffic operating in its waters. This has permitted a relatively "light touch" regulatory approach with respect to managing the navigation of foreign vessels within its maritime zones. By and large New Zealand has implemented the key IMO and International Labour Organization international standards at the domestic level and provided for effective means of enforcement through port state control. It has, with some limited exceptions, such as in relation to notification requirements for vessels operating within its EEZ for example, refrained from developing comprehensive domestic standards that depart from international rules. Similarly, domestic controls on navigation in vulnerable areas are relatively sparse, with only three special protection zones identified, although there is potential to increase this, particularly in the area of the Hauraki Gulf, Cook Strait and the Foveaux Strait. Nevertheless, New Zealand has taken bold action from time to time in order to implement political priorities. Examples include the banning of nuclear

121 Antarctic Treaty, in force 23 June 1961, 402 *U.N.T.S.* 71.

122 Convention for the Conservation of Antarctic Marine Living Resources, in force 7 April 1982, 1329 *U.N.T.S.* 47.

123 The Polar Code was incorporated into the 1974 SOLAS Convention, supra note 43, at the 94th Session of the Maritime Safety Committee in 2014 and into 1973/78 MARPOL Convention, supra note 42, at the 68th Session of the Marine Environment Protection Committee in 2015. The full text of the Polar Code is available at IMO, MEPC 68/21/Add.1 (Annex 10).

powered vessels and vessels carrying nuclear explosive devices from New Zealand internal waters and the more recent requirement that only New Zealand registered vessels be licensed to fish in New Zealand waters in order to address health and welfare issues of seafarers working on board foreign licensed fishing vessels. The creation and enforcement of non-interference zones around survey and other vessels provides a clear example of an expansionist approach to coastal state jurisdiction – in this case, apparently cautiously endorsed by the LOSC Arbitral Tribunal in the *Arctic Sunrise Arbitration*, and New Zealand is at the forefront to contributing to state practice in this area. In conclusion, New Zealand's approach to regulating foreign vessels within its waters is to rely largely on the domestic implementation of international standards and to actively work at the international level to influence and shape those standards to maximize navigational safety and minimize marine environmental pollution in order to protect New Zealand's maritime environment.

Index